No More Enemies

Deb Reich

Kindle eBook published April 2011 by Joshua Joshua & Reich
ISBN 978-965-91713-0-9

This print edition published June 2011 by Joshua Joshua & Reich
ISBN 978-965-91713-1-6

www.NoMoreEnemies.net

Cataloging data

Reich, Deb.
    No more enemies / Deb Reich.
    399 pp.
    Includes bibliographical references.
    ISBN 978-965-91713-1-6
                1. Arab-Israeli conflict – Peace. 2. Enemies.
                3. Reconciliation. 4. Peace movements--Israel. 5. Women and
                Peace. I. Title.
    DS119.76 .R444 2011
    956.04

Printed in the United States of America

For Maya and Amos, who always believed

Contents

Introduction

There is a pattern... Nothing goes right
but as part of the pattern. Only in it is freedom.

---*Ursula K. Le Guin,* **Tales from Earthsea**

Over the last 30 years, I have been privileged to develop friendships with some very wonderful people who, by popular consensus, are supposed to be among my enemies—because I am a Jewish-American-Israeli and they are Palestinian Arabs.

That was my first reason for writing this book.

I wanted to share, as widely as possible, the simple fact that a great many such friendships do happen. Letting more people know that such friendships actually exist can help reshape the popular consensus about *them* and *us*—and maybe, finally, take away this painful burden of dissonance.

"Enemies" is an idea whose time is past. This I believe, passionately—based on my own experience and what I see, and hear, and read. My adventures as a Jew living and working in harmony with Muslim and Christian Arabs have given me a laboratory demonstration of just how obsolete the idea of enemies really is. If telling stories like mine helps to shift the consensus away from the old notion of enemies, we could all live a freer and more equal life. We could finally direct our energies to building a better shared world instead of spending so much effort on throwing off the yoke of suffering: our own, but not only our own.

This new orientation would help liberate people whose lives as someone's designated enemies have been grossly stunted, while other people are privileged at their expense. The new orientation could also liberate many of the unfairly or accidentally privileged

1

from the spiritual wilderness of unearned advantage in which they pass their days. Less grandly, but perhaps no less vitally, all of us whose friendships cross closed borders could finally see each other more often—whenever we wish!—and could enjoy ourselves together as friends do, in a more normal fashion. If only the enemies paradigm and its elaborate entourage of death and destruction would get out of our way!

To help humanity survive and flourish, imagine us updating our mental maps to align better with the evolving globally internetworked experience of everyday reality—especially among young people, and especially in cyberspace. Imagine us outgrowing this now-destructive idea of enemies and leaving it behind us—and the sooner, the better. Like many other basic ideas that we unconsciously think *with* rather than consciously think *about*, the idea of enemies may take some time to be thoroughly left behind. But one day soon, and sooner than we may think, it will have become a historical curiosity: something for anthropologists to ponder.

The right to refuse to be enemies is the next big thing for human rights. It will take the current understanding of human rights a giant step forward into a new, interactive dimension. Many of the most difficult dilemmas we face will lend themselves to solutions in a different mode than has been possible until now.

Meantime, the notion of *enemies* is to humanity what HIV is to the immune system: big trouble. In the body, this sort of trouble can lead to AIDS; in the human community, it can lead to war. AIDS and war lead in similar directions, to needless suffering and death—often on a massive scale.

Indeed, the paradigm of reality that features the concept of enemies is like an autoimmune disease of the human collective: dysfunctional, and killing us[1]. The entire paradigm of adversarial, confrontational, aggressive, competitive taking-of-sides, featuring

[1] At the 2nd Annual International Conference on Youth & Interfaith Communication at Jos, Nigeria, Oct. 2010, Emmanuel Ande Ivorgba, Director of New Era Educational and Charitable Support Initiative, gave a name to this disease: HRV (Human Relationship-Deficiency Virus). http://www.ammado.com/member/106946

the notion of enemies at its conceptual apex, is overdue for retirement. The paradigm emerging to take its place offers a very different orientation, featuring networking, interdependence, mediated conflict transformation, constructive cooperation, co-development and partnership.

Like many other people, I cherish a strong desire to leave the world a better place than I found it. I intend to do that by helping to create a vibrant public conversation around the idea that the very notion of enemies is obsolete. Then I will do what I can to help translate the idea into action.

That's the second reason I have written this book.

Some readers may wonder, at least initially, if possibly I'm completely off my rocker. I mean, look around at all the wars and mayhem in this world. Where I live, in Israel/Palestine, we are like a poster child for the idea of enemies. And we are not alone. Everywhere in the world, in almost every country, whether the people there are currently at war with the neighbors or not, the *enemies* paradigm is part of the existing reality; that is undeniable.

At the same time, however, we can look around and behold the very different orientation of the emergent new reality of tomorrow. Consider the tremendous initiatives toward interconnectedness, social and technical networking, manifold forms of interactivity, open source technology (freely and collegially developed, accessed, and shared), and myriad models of partnership all around us: Not only are they novel and amazing, but they are growing exponentially. As soon as we bring this same interactive orientation to our ideas of human rights and social justice, many things will improve. In fact, things will "co-improve."

In this emergent new world, there will certainly be obstacles, but there will be less and less room for enemies. Obstacles will be depersonalized. That means that we will think less in terms of bad guys, and more in terms of bad problems. So-called adversaries will increasingly be viewed as partners, or at least potential partners, in our shared project. The opponents will all be part of the project team: yin and yang, in one circle.

3

The project we will all be sharing is the building of a better, healthier, and more compassionate future for all beings, for all of creation.

And finally, a special word to all the hard-working and dedicated young (and formerly young) people engaged in activism for social, economic, political, and environmental justice. You already know, or have sensed, that there is a way of being in the world that does not require enemies. Practicing that way, walking that path, will lead us toward the better society you envision. Hold onto your faith that you can be part of getting us there. This book should help! Enjoy.

Deb Reich
Jerusalem, Israel / Al Quds, Palestine
Spring 2011

Part I – No More Enemies
(the idea is explained, globally)

Archetypes turn into millstones, large simplicities get complicated, chaos becomes elegant, and what everybody knows is true turns out to be what some people used to think.

--*Ursula K. Le Guin,* **Tales from Earthsea**

If you are afraid of "them"–read this book!

If there is a "them" you are afraid of, read this book.

If you are a Jew afraid of Arabs, or an Arab afraid of Jews; if you are a Muslim afraid of Hindus, or a Hindu afraid of Muslims; if you are an American afraid of Iranians, or an Iranian afraid of Americans–if you are afraid of anyone from some national, religious, ethnic, or political group that you see as a threat–read this book.

I write this book in my many voices–and one very central voice is my inner "I used to be afraid of them until I made them my friends" voice. If I can do it, anyone can do it. You can, too.

All my life I've been a seeker. I think most people are–but then the business of life gets in our way and all kinds of things distract us, and we abandon the quest to understand, beyond what is necessary to survive and, if possible, to thrive.

Even if we've lost the quest for a while, though, we can get back to it.

Do you remember, as a youngster, seeing that the world-as-it-is wanted you to choose: Be the boss or the slave. Be the one who gives orders or the one who takes orders. Be the dominator or the oppressed. And do you remember saying to yourself: There has to be a third way…?

Well, guess what? There is. The third way–partnership–today has many eloquent spokespersons. One good place to begin is online, at the Center for Partnership Studies[2].

Partnership is an idea whose time has come. *Enemies* is an idea whose time is past.

Let's get with the new program, folks.

Listen to your inner reaction to what you just read. If it sounds good to you, read on. You may find yourself moving through these pages with the feeling that I've articulated things you have

---

[2] The home page for the Center is at: http://www.partnershipway.org/

long agreed with, but maybe never thought to formulate in quite this way. Read and enjoy, because we're on the same wavelength.

And if your response so far is: "But…"–I implore you: read this book! It may change your life.

We (you and I and others) are going to transform our old enemies into new partners, because that's the best–maybe the only–road to a sustainable future on this planet for our children and grandchildren.

In the process, we will go a long way toward solving the "energy crisis" (among various other crises we will help to solve), because an unimaginably huge reservoir of constructive latent energy is waiting out there to be tapped. It is literally embodied in the flesh and bones, the minds and souls of all of the world's oppressed people. Oppressed people are not only constrained from fully exercising their basic human rights. They also have been prevented from making the unique and important contribution that only they can make–each and every one of them–to the world's wellbeing.

Moreover, the more privileged folks also stand to benefit from the paradigm shift that is coming–even if, at first, they may see only the price they will pay in privileges lost. Meantime, however, their preoccupation with protecting their privileged status does not leave them free to make their own fullest contribution to the broader human welfare.

Think of all that energy just waiting to be tapped. It's beyond huge!

So, are you ready?

Better than winning

"No More Enemies" and all that the phrase implies is our new, vibrant alternative to fear, war, scarcity, decline, and eventual system collapse.

We are failing to see this very vibrant alternative that is right before our eyes because we are blinded by the prior success of the old method. (The old method can be summed up as: Whatever you feel entitled to, go ahead and take it by force plus spin, and then keep it by force plus spin.) Nearly every country on the planet was originally created through the use of force or is governed by a regime that seized power violently, or both. The old-style economics is based on naked power and the commodification of all resources, including human resources. Corporations are very powerful, more powerful than governments—and that situation feels like success to the leadership elites involved, if not to the peons doing the work... although, actually, a surprising percentage of the downtrodden and exploited identify with the values that, at their expense, serve mainly or exclusively the elites.

Paradigms based on force are hard to jettison when they have so often delivered what the decision-makers wanted.

The challenge is that the paradigms of force can no longer deliver, because what is wanted has changed. Even the powerful are beginning to sense that this shift is underway. "Winning" is no longer enough and we must wean ourselves from seeing "winning" as something positive. In fact, "winning" has finally shown itself in its true colors: winning is really losing! Why? Because the entire win-lose paradigm has proven itself unsustainable. It creates only short-term "gains" at the cost of guaranteeing long-term havoc—eventually generating the inevitable renewal of the struggle over resources or land or prestige or whatever was at stake in the first place, with all the attendant downsides. Following a win-lose paradigm channels priceless energy away from constructively networked partnerships into long-term "loser enterprises" characterized by short-sightedness, cruelty and greed: weapons manufacture and distribution, military expansion, corporate cartels, exploitation of the other, warehousing of "undesirable" or "surplus" populations who refuse to comply, the "war on drugs," the "war on terrorism," and so on and so forth.

Wars, in the long term, are always unwinnable. We know this already, but we are having a hard time assimilating the ramifications because the requisite shift in perspective is so drastic.

No More Enemies is better than winning.

The next big thing in human rights

The next big thing in human rights is going to be the right not to be enemies.

What is inadequate about the concept of "human rights," as we now understand it, is that it is essentially static, mono-dimensional and self-oriented. It focuses on rights that accrue to me or my group; and in the same way, to you and your group; but without any connection between us. This is no longer enough. In the emergent global reality, our shared pursuit of sustainable egalitarian societies will have to be more synchronously coordinated and more dynamic.

Consider the right to the most basic necessities of survival—food, clothing, shelter—and to freedom of speech and assembly, freedom of mobility, of religion and of the press, freedom of conscience, freedom to earn a living, etc. These are about me and us (my group, or me and my family, etc.) and you and your group. Every person has the right to.... Every group has the right to… And so forth.

Of course, hundreds of millions of people around the world do not enjoy even the minimum of human rights today. There is still a long way to go to assure everyone the same minimum. So what am I talking about?

I'm talking about the fact that there is little or no dimension of interactivity in the way we have understood the notion of "human rights" thus far. In the way we have understood human rights until now, there is no connectedness; no inbuilt network; no co-evolving or co-being, in the Buddhist sense. The absence of that conceptual aspect may have been a factor in delaying us for so long in attaining the minimum spectrum of rights for so many millions on this planet. Maybe what we have traditionally understood as human rights can't be more widely attained with-

13

out introducing more interactivity into the transformative process of attaining them.

Maybe it is not only about what I or we or you are entitled to, but what we are entitled to in relation to each other.

The right not to be enemies is an interactive human right; it opens up a whole new dimension for us. It's not just MY right to this or that, or even OUR right to this or that. It's my right AND your right interactively not to be enemies. It's our right not to hurt or abuse or make war on and slaughter one another; not to be forced into playing, each vis-à-vis the other, a zero-sum game, a win-lose game, where one side can live free and prosper–but only at the other's expense. It's our right to reject the idea that one must dominate and the other be dominated; that one must play the boot on the neck and the other must play the neck under the boot, with no other roles to choose from!

No more! Time to reject that!

I knew by the age of sixteen that the world into which I was born was going to be unbearable because, no matter which way I looked at my choices, the world seemed to insist that I choose between two standard and polarized roles: bully or victim; oppressor or oppressed; advantaged or disadvantaged; privileged or disenfranchised. I have a vivid memory connected to this. One very hot summer day when everyone in the family was elsewhere, I retreated to my mother's bedroom–the one room in our house with an air conditioner. I lay on the floor and cried because I did not want to live in that kind of world, though I wasn't quite ready to check out of it, either. I spent the next four decades looking, more or less consciously, for some way out of that trap. I spent most of that time in Israel, where I had gone in search of my "ethnic roots."

When the "We refuse to be enemies" campaign was created by a mixed Jewish and Palestinian group of mostly women activists in Israel in the autumn of 2000, I was enthusiastic; but the deeper import of the campaign slogan did not sink in right away. My old quest–wasn't there a third way?–had finally found its resolution, but the realization required another few years until it finally broke through into my active awareness.

Suddenly, I understood. This refusal–the refusal to be enemies–this has to become the new floor under our notion of human rights. As articulated so brilliantly by Dr. Riane Eisler (founder of the Center for Partnership Studies) and others, we are meant to build partnerships on this earth, evolving and progressing toward greater cooperation and coordination and sharing. For me, one implication is that anyone and anything that tries to force us backward, into brutality and dominance, is violating our fundamental human right to refuse to be enemies. We cannot realize this right in isolation, but only together.

How unsurprising that, in Israel at least, the articulation of this newly evolving understanding came from a feminist campaign, borne forward by both women and men but led, mainly, by women.

Physicist Fritjof Capra (in *The Turning Point*, 1982) and many other visionary social commentators over the last half century have been suggesting that we have entered an era when women's influence is going to come into its own. Apparently the world really needs women's voices to speak out now for healing and reconciliation, for a new awareness, for our continued survival and a new shared prosperity. Many recent studies and policy initiatives have buttressed this idea, by demonstrating that peacemaking and development outcomes around the world have improved with broad participation by women, and by insisting that even greater participation by women will improve outcomes even further.[3]

The Palestinian Arab and Jewish women of the Israel-based peace movement in October 2000 went one giant step beyond the existing modality of human rights and broke through into a

---

[3]There is now extensive literature on this subject. See an online bibliography at www.peacedocs.com under Women and Peace. Or enter "women + peacemaking" in any search engine and explore for yourself.

new awareness, a new dimension: declaring their inalienable right to partnership by refusing to be enemies at the behest of their respective societies' leaderships or anyone else.

They said: We will not be enemies. We refuse. No more! No more enemies.

Here at last is the brilliant breakthrough this sorry world has been waiting for: ordinary people–mostly women, yes, but ordinary women, not politicians or generals or princesses or queens, not divas or any kind of celebrities–saying: This far and no farther!

Years, decades, centuries of conflict–for what?!

No more! We refuse! We refuse to be enemies.

Meanwhile, this iconic refusal has begun appearing elsewhere in Israel/Palestine and far beyond our borders here. Women's determined peacemaking across religious and ethnic boundaries is spreading.[4] And the refusal to be enemies is being heard also in contexts where the leadership is not necessarily female–like Bil'in and Al-Walaja[5].

The images of partnership from October 2000 in Israel remain vivid to me, alongside images of the needless bloodshed, the rage and despair and fear that dominated the media images at that time and finally evoked that amazing partnership response. The tableau that I see in my mind's eye today, as emblematic of this shifting paradigm, is the one from the autumn of 2000, with these women and men standing vigil along the highway through Wadi Ara.

The demonstrators, many of them neighbors from nearby towns, were standing at the roadside along a few hundred meters of Route 65. This is the southernmost end of the ancient caravan

---

[4] For example: An amazing film, *Pray the Devil Back to Hell,* winner of multiple awards worldwide, was made about the Liberian women's peace movement, which has embraced both Muslim and Christian Liberian women; the film has a web site at http://www.praythedevilbacktohell.com/

[5] Bil'in and Walaja are two of the Palestinian villages on the West Bank with very strong grassroots movements for nonviolent protest at the continuing loss of their lands and freedom to Israel's Separation Wall. Search online using the village names.

route that leads inland from the port of Caesarea on the Mediterranean coast. The road itself winds northeast through the hills, past Megiddo and the plains it overlooks, which the Bible calls the Plains of Armageddon. It continues past Mount Tabor and reaches Tiberias on the Sea of Galilee. Finally, it leads you up into the mountains and, if you follow it long enough, on to Damascus.

On the day of the vigil, the usual automobile traffic streamed by while the men and women stood together at the roadside, holding hands, Jews and Arabs united in solidarity, from Kufr Qar'e to Arara to the Wadi Ara police station and on toward Umm al Fahm, the largest Muslim town in the area. They were holding hands, they were holding signs, and they were holding a vision of a different future for humanity in their hearts.

In Hebrew, Arabic, and English, the signs said: WE REFUSE TO BE ENEMIES.

See the pattern

Harold R. Isaacs, an intrepid journalist and political scientist who taught at MIT in the last half of the 20th century, listed all the known tribal conflicts—dozens, hundreds of them—then raging around the globe, in his book *Idols of the Tribe* (1975).

Do you see a familiar pattern here? We are all supposedly the enemies of someone. It's not that we are bad people. It's the paradigm.

This is an axiom you will read repeatedly in these pages: It's not the people; it's the paradigm.

Collectively, thanks to research and experience and the accumulated wisdom of many practitioners in many fields, from yoga and meditation and mysticism to neurobiology and advanced medical imaging, we now have the skill and knowledge to map the impact on ourselves of our own ideas and thoughts. Using those maps, we can work to alter the pattern of our behavior—by working together to reshape our assumptions, expectations, visualizations, affirmations, and finally our actions.

It's up to us!

Time to redesign! [6]

---

[6] The valuable idea that social problems can be recast more productively as design challenges, I adapted from the approach to environmental issues presented by William McDonough and Michael Braungart in their book, *Cradle to Cradle: Remaking the Way We Make Things* (New York: North Point Press, 2002). There is more on their ideas in Part II of this book; see the heading "Towards Intelligent Redesign."

Beyond accusation to inclusion

If a vision is exclusionary, its success typically will generate violence and destruction. If two exclusionary visions are active side by side (as in Palestine and Israel this last century or so), then you cannot fix the mess by bashing the visions, but only by creating an expanded, shared frame into which both of them can fit. Then you can midwife a more inclusive shared vision, capable of embracing both of the more particularist visions together.

The problem is not the two visions themselves, but the paradigm that we use to try to contain their energy in close proximity. It is like the poles of a magnet: two negative poles will repel each other, and even two positive poles will repel each other. But there is a way to juxtapose the two that enables you to combine their energy fields, and then they bond.

Moreover, in general, the paradigm of pluralism can contain various paradigms of particularism, but a particularistic paradigm cannot contain pluralism. You could say that "live and let live" can contain "my way or the highway" (in its assigned space), but not the other way around.

When you are trying to resolve a conflict between two exclusionary visions, you can easily ruin your chances of a transformative outcome by slipping into the view that one or the other of them is a problem, or even *the* problem. This only pushes people away. Better to see both of the original visions for what they can *become*: components of a creative, inclusionary, shared new paradigm.

Before a "problem" can serve as part of a solution, we have to see it that way.

When failing to see it that way, partners to a conflict often mirror each other. To each, the other is the problem. To the aware observer, meanwhile, both partners to the conflict are also partners to the as-yet-unborn transformative solution.

19

Accusatory analysis (name-calling; assigning blame) is rarely beneficial; it is almost always counterproductive.

Pejorative labels are destructive unless they become tools to help someone journey from unconsciousness of their role in the problem, to awareness of their role, to a sense of guilt over their role, to responsibility for helping create change, to partnership in transformation coming from love. It is a progression: a process. Labeling people pejoratively ("racist," e.g.) and leaving it at that, can easily derail efforts toward partnership.

Exclusionary passions are resistant to change because they are self-justifying closed systems. Attacking the believers only intensifies the resistance. You can intervene positively by wooing the players to a field of inclusion that credits their passion as worthwhile, insofar as possible, and then by encouraging them to go further. Arrange for them to discover for themselves that the horizons of their passion are expandable. Help create for them new opportunities for transformative shared experience (like the programs for volunteers to rebuild homes after a hurricane or an earthquake).

Given new opportunities and some encouragement to broaden their horizon of inclusion, many people respond enthusiastically, like thirsty flowers in a spring rain.

The emergent paradigm: partnership as the new "enemies"

For some decades now, we have been learning–from science, from history, from ancient mystic traditions in both East and West–that we can re-envision the world and thereby co-create and re-create it.

Why, then, isn't the world getting repaired? Well, perhaps it *is* getting repaired and it's just too soon to tell. Maybe it's like turning in a new direction when you are at the helm of a giant container ship traveling at full speed: The change does not happen quickly; the ship travels several more miles before the course change takes effect.

On the other hand, perhaps we haven't been able to arrange an effective course correction because we haven't been entirely sure where we want to go. We can see that our world is in trouble, but we can't set a new course for a new destination unless we know what it is.

Now, at last, we are getting a clearer picture. The entire enemies paradigm has to be retired, in favor of the emergent paradigm of partnership. The very idea of *enemies* must become taboo. No More Enemies!

If we want to counter the preexisting momentum and change course quicker, now that we know where we are going, we need more people who can affirmatively and powerfully envision a world of cooperation and partnership and shared prosperity and safety for all. It won't do to be deflected from this important work just because someone ridicules us as naïve dreamers or Pollyannas. We need to share the theory and practice of this new approach with all the people who are still accustomed to imagining a future that lives up to all their worst fears, and who are thus unconsciously projecting THAT out into the shared reality-in-the-making.

Negative vision and negative enterprise have hardened, in modern times, into a kind of global "death industry." Aggressive *battles*, even ostensibly *good battles* by well-intentioned reformers, cannot put the death industries out of business—because "battle" mode is *part of the problem* and hence can lead only to temporary solutions which, in their turn, will duly be reversed. Only love trumps hate and fear; dark visions are harder to actualize in an environment deeply suffused with trust, partnership, and positive affirmation.

How can we act to promote less and less negativity-boosting and more and more partnership-oriented envisioning among increasing numbers of people? How can we find our way to that new environment we wish to enjoy?

There is this one simple way to begin, that I know of: Each of us who is already aware of her power to absorb fear and hate and then transmute it into hope and love, can promote the broader shift we wish to aid, by doing what we do, more and more; by becoming ever more adept at it; by modeling the behavior and inspiring others to emulate it; by taking joy in the exercise of this ability, moment to moment. In other words: Be like trees! Breathe in, breathe out, and whoever passes by with their eyes open will see the beauty in what you are doing.

There is a kind of *chemistry of mutual co-evolution* that we are creating—and you can add your efforts to the wave. Just as this earth evidently evolved from an environment toxic to oxygen-breathers into the majority oxygen-breathers' habitat it is today, so too can the moral climate morph into one wherein affirmative partnership will flourish as the enemies era fades away.

Some big problems don't get fixed; we just evolve beyond them

When there does not appear to be much reason for hope, that does not mean that there is, in fact, no hope.

People look around here in Palestine/Israel, at the ground zero of so-called "intractable conflicts," and wonder how we can ever climb out of the mess we have made of things here, even if everyone were to join together and really try.

The despair people feel is real, and quite understandable, and even warranted. But there really is good reason to remain hopeful.

If you look back in history, you can find lots of seemingly unsalvageable situations that were repaired in the end, not because the core problem was *resolved*, but because we evolved past it. Events, life, reality, or the spirit of the times simply moved past the problem, like a stream flowing around a very large rock. Downstream from what had been the problem, life became livable again.

Consider, for example, the emergence of modern Western science and the struggle for ascendancy between it and the established European religious authorities of a few centuries ago. Galileo was brought up on charges by the Church hierarchy for insisting that the earth revolved around the sun instead of vice versa. If you were a budding scientist back then, you were flirting with a very dangerous vocation. It was heretical for anyone to hold, on whatever evidence, opinions that ran counter to established religious doctrine. At some point this "intractable problem" about astronomy simply disappeared, when the proof became overwhelming with regard to what revolved around what. Few people today would insist that the earth is flat or that the sun revolves around the earth.

When the very idea of "enemies" is finally understood to be obsolete, the madness in Palestine/Israel and other such conflict hot spots will be seen as the last gasp of an unjust and sadistic exercise in bad governance. In this exercise, old-school leaders with outdated mental maps are cheered on by extremists and the super-rich to delude the masses of clueless citizens who have detached from the painful reality all around them, while suppressing the disenfranchised and downtrodden who cannot detach and who continue struggling to try to make change.

Spending time with Palestinian Arab friends and colleagues as well as with Israeli Jewish friends and colleagues has persuaded me of one thing: There is a huge reservoir of constructive energy here, waiting to be utilized. If you just took all the energy that is now actively used in negative, destructive, and violent ways here, and redirected it to constructive projects and tasks, that would be great. But there is a lot more energy sitting on the sidelines—especially on the Palestinian side, where it has been accumulating through sixty years of dispossession and dispersion and forty years of military occupation. As I write this, today, Palestinians under occupation are still not being permitted to fulfill even a fraction of their potential and make their rightful contribution to the human community, but instead are warehoused and neutralized.

Once we opt for deep change and flow with the stream past that rock, manifold possibilities will open up for us, in Palestine/Israel as in many other places. There is enough untapped positive human potential here to power the planet for another millennium.

Inspired synthesizers, unite!

Peace and Conflict Studies is a major academic field today. Is it helping those of us who live in war zones? That is hard to measure. Could academia be doing more to help? I think so.

Academic research in general tends to go deeper and deeper into one thing, continually illuminating crucial new aspects of it. Only rarely–and even then, often by accident–does research explore the significance of something in relation to all the other subjects of study in other, related fields, and even more rarely in relation to very distant or seemingly unrelated fields. In addition, academia has been organized for some time in such a way that its best people must spend a lot of their energy producing very highly structured outputs that are incomprehensible to anyone outside their subspecialty, so that, from a practical standpoint, their best work is largely hidden from public view. Every academic knows about the problem, but the solution is yet to appear.

On the plus side, interdisciplinary study is gaining ground in myriad academic centers. Occasionally there are bright flashes of inspired synthesis to light up the landscape of our thinking with generous interdisciplinary insights, broadly conceived and accessibly articulated. Riane Eisler's work, for example, advocates persuasively for a comprehensive cross-disciplinary *partnership orientation*, the antidote to eons of destruction driven by its obverse, which she terms the *dominator* or *dominance orientation.*

The theme elaborated on in these pages–that the concept of enemies is obsolete–is a sister to the idea of a partnership orientation. Dr. Eisler has argued persuasively that a partnership orientation, when widely adopted, can and will reduce conflict, diminish economic and social injustice, aid in the eradication of domestic violence, and improve by several orders of magnitude the way we educate our children. In her books, she makes a good case for all of those benefits, and more.

The idea of *no more enemies* will, I hope, call attention to the fact that our unconscious, deep-seated, lingering fidelity to *enemies* scenarios, to the very notion of *enemies* itself, is a serious roadblock on the path to a partnership-oriented world. Being open to partnerships with neutral parties is not enough. We need to open ourselves to the somewhat more radical idea that even so-called enemies are really potential partners waiting for a transformative scenario to come along that unites them and us as co-actors in a more positive script. NME can help us create such scenarios.

A broad adoption of the NME worldview should be a big help in resolving many different and longstanding problems that worry us now. Regional conflicts will be fewer and fewer, as today's enemies become tomorrow's partners. The world's youth will be recruited together as partners in addressing the challenges facing us all, instead of as violent revolutionaries with a narrow sectarian agenda obliging them to destroy one another. Women's lives will be better because the mess generated by war and conflict always disproportionately falls on women and children. NME advocates can also help build bridges to the deep wisdom of aboriginal cultures and spiritual traditions in which the idea of all creatures as partners is already acknowledged. The global energy crisis will abate as former enemies "work smarter" by working together toward environmentally sustainable energy technologies. We will all work smarter on a lot of problems when we begin utilizing the positive potential contributions of all those people who were formerly excluded from the game altogether because we labeled them "enemies."

The NME paradigm will do all that because, like its sister idea, the idea of partnership, the NME approach bridges and encompasses many different fields, specialties, and perspectives. The idea of NME is broadly synthesizing, and its time has come.

No enemies: no exceptions!

The decision, the intention, to move toward No More Enemies does not mean that every person walking the earth is suddenly benign, compassionate, and looking to promote the greatest good for everyone. But by labeling them enemies, we only intensify and prolong the lack of harmony and synergy. What other paths might be open to us?

Picture in your mind the president of a company that makes missiles, say. Call him Mike. He gets up in the morning and while he is standing over the sink, shaving, Mike does not look at his reflection in the mirror and think, "I am a hideous warmongering weapons maker." He has a responsible job, he has shareholders to satisfy, he has investment analysts to please, he has two kids in college and one in graduate school, he is a responsible member of his community. He is a deacon at his church, he gives generously to charity. Antiwar activists think of this man as their enemy, but how is that advancing their agenda?

Byron Katie, the therapist, and various Eastern religions talk about things being the way they are because that is how they are supposed to be at this moment; what is the point of raging against things as they are? Change begins by fully accepting things as they are, and moving on from there. When Byron Katie was in Israel, someone asked her (I saw this on a video clip on YouTube) about Palestinian militants who might target her and try to kill her, and what did she think about that? She said something like: *If I had been through, in my life, all the things that they have been through, I might well have reached the conclusion they reached, and be prepared to kill someone.* She would not be baited.

People do what they do for what seem to them to be very good reasons. Demonizing them is not going to get us anywhere useful. Holding them accountable for their actions and their choices is necessary; demonizing them is a waste of energy. We

27

would do well, at the same time, to be holding accountable the folks on the other side against whom the militants' rage is directed. Maybe there's some work to be done there.

We can also talk about political parties, football teams, etc., when people passionately line up on opposite sides to the point of homicidal impulses. We could even create a scale of competitive and aggressive leisure pursuits. Chess (or rummy, or solitaire): the game involves no violence and the "kill" is 100 percent intellectual. Sports like football: the game is rough, even violent, and the "kill" often involves injuries. War: the game is mostly about killing and there is typically a lot of it, including of bystanders, notably women, children, and old people, and there is conquest and occupation, slavery, etc.

If we have strong inbuilt tendencies toward competition and aggression, what creative things do we plan to do so as to de-fang this programming of ours? Why passively go along with it, now that we understand it better? Some newer research, incidentally, supports the opposite conclusion: that we have inbuilt tendencies toward cooperation and positive emotions.[7]

Finally, we can talk about sociopaths and psychopaths, i.e., people whose neurochemistry, or some cause we don't know yet, makes them behave as if they lack any human instinct to decency. Theoretically, a psychopath could behead his own mother and feel nothing. This makes such people a serious problem to themselves and others. We can acknowledge as much without labeling them "the enemy." Moreover, there may be far fewer such folks than we imagine. A psychologist I know who has worked a lot with prisoners labeled psychopathic or sociopathic, says that they are mostly mislabeled. If you arrange to give them a real opportunity to behave like ordinary folks, he says, they do. That, at least, has been his experience.

---

[7] Dacher Keltner, *Born To Be Good: The science of a meaningful life* (New York: W.W. Norton & Co., 2009). Thanks to Len and Libby Traubman for the heads up on this one.

Ordinary people in many cultures, driven by hormones or culture or evolution or whatever, seem to love competition and get a thrill from violence. The most creative vision of how to channel this constructively that I have seen, thus far, is the notion of the "holodeck" on the old Star Trek series. The holodeck was a virtual environment for entertainment purposes. Someone wishing to engage in high-adrenaline social games could book themselves a session on the holodeck and engage with a cast of holographic figures programmed to perform as requested. A person wishing to feel the thrill of danger could do it without endangering any other humans. Arguably, we could actually achieve, in the not so distant future, the technical sophistication to create something similar ourselves.

A No More Enemies ethos with no exceptions will not be easy to achieve. That doesn't mean we should not attempt it.

Conquest and context

The boundary between an act or event and its context is actually quite fuzzy.

When we narrate, we like to draw the boundary between fact and context so as to maintain our "absolute facts" in a clean zone of certainty, untainted by what is deemed context and hence open to debate.

When someone else narrates, they may want to redraw the boundary–likewise trying to increase their credibility by keeping their "absolute facts" in a clean zone of certainty, untainted by the amorphous nature of context.

The real story is not a continuum with "facts" at one end and context at the other. Context is more like a hub. An amorphous blob of context is concentrated at the center but is also distributed outward around, under and over, and beyond the discrete "facts" or events. As we try to separate between our narrative account and this amorphous field of context, we distort the field… everywhere. The context slips and shifts around our own story and everyone else's, too.

Maybe that is partly why collective histories as told by adversaries like Israel and Palestine seem so mutually contradictory. The context of conquests has especially fuzzy boundaries.

Many good people spend entire careers debating the conflicting historical accounts, draining away vital energy that could be much better utilized in building new partnerships. The missing piece of the puzzle that could bring new clarity amid all the confusion is the insight that the underlying paradigm of enemies is obsolete.

Ideas we think with

There are ideas we think *about*, and there are ideas we think *with*. This distinction has been made by linguists, philosophers, and others for decades; it is not new but it is often overlooked.

An idea we think *with* is so embedded in our worldview that we are not conscious of how it serves, like a lens, to modify everything else we look at, think about, debate. Social Darwinism (the theory of "survival of the fittest" as applied to the human community) is one such idea. Social Darwinism is what underlies the belief that the underclass must have something wrong with it or it wouldn't *be* the underclass, and that the elite must be especially fit to rule or it wouldn't *be* the elite; whereas people who do not view society through the Social Darwinist lens call this "blaming the victim."

The idea that it is *necessary* to view some people or groups as our enemies is so firmly embedded in our worldview that we find it difficult to imagine a world in which there are no enemies. I am not obliged to see someone who disagrees with me, who discriminates against me, who steals from me, or even who wants to kill me, as my enemy.

This is, of course, an extreme position to take, given the acrimonious, conflict-centered, and violent culture that has developed in many human societies thus far. The omnipresence of the notion of enemies does not oblige me to accept it as valid. I much prefer to see someone who disagrees with me as a teacher from whom I have much to learn; and to see someone with a weapon who wants to kill me as a potential partner in the grip of a wrongheaded notion that eliminating me will contribute to his wellbeing or that of his family and community.

I will do what I can to avoid dying needlessly, but I will not agree to think of that guy as my enemy. When this new orientation has become an idea we think with, rather than an idea we think about, the NME paradigm will be well established.

On labeling people "racist"

If I label some person or group "racist," I am simply reducing to near zero the likelihood that they will want to work in partnership with me. So what does this labeling get me, other than the fleeting satisfaction of feeling more virtuous than they are? Some of this counterproductive labeling takes place in sports stadiums; some, in university lecture halls.

In the quest for a better world, the rhetoric of accusatory "ists" (even when, technically, it may be accurate) often causes more trouble than it is worth.

On sustainability

Progressives today love the notion of sustainability: a vision of something that can go on, and on, and on, because it is well designed in the first place and does not contain the seed of its own eventual downfall, overthrow, repeal, or collapse.

Yet we know that nothing lasts forever. Everything contains the germ of its own eventual end. The life cycle of various phenomena can be extended, however, even if not indefinitely: with excellent planning; complete integration into natural cycles of energy, material, and process; and the flexibility and wherewithal to self-correct.

The bottom line seems to be that for a phenomenon to go on and on, it has to incorporate change as a key constant.

Maybe that's why most "isms"–even when originally invented to make positive change (communism, e.g.)–can end up being trouble: their definitions are too rigid to permit meaningful change. Reality rolls on past most "isms."

That rigidity, set against the ever-changing flow of people's lives as they are really lived, can create enemies needlessly. People tend to develop passionate feelings for or against an "ism" and may forget to do reality checks from time to time.

Food for thought.

Death

Attachment to life at all costs, and the fear of death (they go together), plus the unremitting attachment to material things, are two of the most difficult obstacles in the path of the great shift we are moving toward.

So long as we accept modern Western culture's stated or unstated dictum that death is to be avoided at any price for as long as possible, we cannot truly come to see death as part of the cycle of life–perhaps not something to be sought out, but to be welcomed when it comes as the next step in the dance.

I accept that I find it a lot easier to contemplate my own death with equanimity than the death of a child. And yet, loss is part of the tapestry. I can see how the doctrine of reincarnation can be comforting to people: one could perhaps let go more easily because death is not seen as final. We all come back, however, whether we believe in reincarnation or not. No energy is lost from the system, and when I stop breathing, the breath will be breathed somewhere else, somehow, if not as a new baby, then as grass or starlight.

As for attachment to things, well, they are just things. They flow in and they flow out. In our attachment to things, we are like children who see a beautiful butterfly or a ladybug and want to keep it in a jar. Children do it–but the decision to stop and hold this bit of loveliness will kill it. This in its simplest terms is the outcome of our attachment to stuff. We clutch it to us and it dies or, at the very least, clogs up the flow of energy, of life, of the river.

Imagine life as a great shouting leap from a high cliff toward a cold clear dark lake. The joy of the leap and the grace of sailing through the air are immense, and the splash at the end is inevitable–but it is not the end of the story. It is only the end of one particular arc.

Sometimes I imagine that birth is like that—like being launched from a very, very high cliff—miles and miles high. The trip down is our life—in free fall. We don't experience it as falling, though. We experience it as a journey. We don't think much about the day when we will inevitably hit bottom and disintegrate. The trick is not to spend the entire time worrying about the final crash, but to enjoy the ride: not to think of it as falling but rather as sailing, or floating, or dancing, or flying.

If you prefer a gentler image, think of yourself as a rich note that is sounded by your favorite instrument—a cello, maybe, or a brass gong, or a sublime tenor, or a splendid soprano. The note sounds, and lingers, and finally ends (we die)—but is heard in memory forever by those who were there to hear.

What does this have to do with the idea of NME? Well, I'm not sure. Unless perhaps it is that even death, the ultimate adversary, is not, after all, our enemy.

Things can be both simple and complicated

Things can be simple and complicated at the same time.

Take an illness like, say, bronchitis. Wikipedia explains it in several hundred words: acute, chronic, bacterial, etc. But basically, it's a congested chest.

We could try looking at the paradigms of inter-group conflict between "enemies" in the simplest and most straightforward way–just as an exercise. Let's look at the dynamics of a generic international conflict at the simplest possible level.

When some people in another country organize themselves into a group that wants to hurt our country, we decide that their country is our enemy. Some of our politicians, looking to their own domestic polling data, are always eager to take us down that road. But sometimes that antagonistic group is actually a very small percentage of the citizens over there. Many radical groups make a lot of noise but actually have only a relatively small following. In a country of 25 million people, a violent radical fringe movement that is wildly successful at recruiting and attracts 25,000 people is still only being driven by one-tenth of one percent of the population (and many violent fringe groups have far fewer adherents). Is it accurate to say that Country X hates us because of the ideology of that one-tenth of one percent?

Meanwhile, the other 99.9 percent of the country's people may have nothing very major against us, or anyhow may not be antagonistic toward us to the point of violence. They might be open to allying with us to prevent their lunatic fringe from hurting us. Once we declare their entire country to be our enemy, however, all those 25 million people have a serious gripe against us: We told them that their country is our country's enemy! At that point, of course, the radical fringe group's recruitment may get nice and brisk all of a sudden, and a terrible self-fulfilling dynamic gets into motion and begins to spiral towards war.

37

Why do we do this dance, over and over? I think it's a neural anomaly: a strange brain dysfunction that makes us vulnerable to this non-logic. "They" are a collectivity we don't visualize clearly to begin with; so if some of "them" are nasty to us, it's quite easy to imagine the perceived behavior as coming from *all* of "them"; easy, but inaccurate.

The only ones who win in these scenarios are the arms merchants, the generals, the politicians, and the savvy investors in the ensuing war economy. All the rest of us, in our own country and in theirs, are the losers.

If I'd been born Iraqi or Palestinian or Pakistani or… (you fill in the country), I'd see the world from that perspective, and the perspective I was actually born with in this life here and now would seem peculiar to me. We are all interchangeable, in that sense. Inter-group conflict has to be about the paradigm, not the people.

So the question is: Now what? When will we stop beating up on each other and fully embrace the new possibilities?

How about today?

NME and terrorism

Many well-qualified analysts spend a lot of time and energy looking at the phenomenon of modern terrorism. Their analyses are often very sophisticated. I want to say something simple about it here. I believe that the ascendance of the NME worldview cannot fail to have a positive effect on this phenomenon.

Note that terrorism is typically defined as organized non-state violence, whether centralized or decentralized–as opposed to state-sponsored violence. State-sponsored violence, even when illegal under the laws of the country perpetrating it, is generally not labeled "terrorism," although sometimes it is called "state terror."

From a NME standpoint, organized violence that is directed against other living beings and their environment is a byproduct of the *enemies* paradigm. Whether it is state-sponsored or independently organized, whether we call it war or terror or terrorism, in a No More Enemies world there is no hierarchy of acceptability to accord state terror a higher standing than non-state terror (or the other way around). Call it "war" or "resistance" or "targeted assassination" or "retaliation" or whatever you wish: all of it "terrorizes" people. All of it destroys. When there are no "enemies," there is no justification for any of it. Violence is retired as an instrument of communication, persuasion, or adjudication.

As we increasingly turn toward a No More Enemies paradigm, we will witness a dramatic diminishing of all forms of violent destruction, including what we call "terrorism." In fact, the *enemies* worldview itself is a form of conceptual terrorism that we have inadvertently aimed at ourselves, collectively.

Even during the transition time, the movement toward a No More Enemies worldview can have a constructive impact on the frequency of both kinds of violence–state-sponsored, and independent: When we abandon the notion of "enemies" and invite everyone into the circle of shared humanity and shared prosperity, with dignity and respect for all, the ostensible rationale for violent combat of every kind will begin to collapse at its foundations.

Bear in mind that many of today's mainstream politicians and diplomats were, once upon a time, terrorists. When they were welcomed into the game and given a seat at the table, they become official players rather than spoilers. But so long as the game being played was based on an enemies worldview, they often simply exchanged the use of non-state violence for state-sponsored violence. This is a non-solution.

Not every terrorist group or philosophy will magically disappear the day the world begins tilting decisively toward an NME philosophy, of course. Nor will every formally constituted government declare an end to war that very day. Most likely we will not even be able to identify the actual turning point, when it comes, with any precision. But the trend will make itself felt, unmistakably.

And as the trend gathers momentum, potential new recruits to terrorism will instead be busy helping the rest of us figure out how to deal with the holdouts, like teenage computer hackers who go to work for Interppol. The circle of cooperating partners who have renounced violence will grow much larger, one day at a time.

In the meantime, we need to stop being afraid of the very idea of *terrorism*. The dreaded thing we have named *terrorism* is like a painful side effect of a medication (official, state-sponsored violence) that we have been prescribed, for a preventable disease (enemies-driven thinking) that has made us ill due to our own bad decisions. As we begin making better decisions, the illness will fade away over time, the medication will become superfluous, and the painful side effect will be, finally, just a bad memory.

On testosterone

Research done on male American voters in the November 2008 elections revealed that their testosterone levels dropped when their favored candidates lost, as was widely reported in the media when the results came out about a year later.[8] We already knew that testosterone levels change when men win or lose a contest personally; now science has found this hormonal response (via saliva samples) occurring when men lose only vicariously–by proxy, so to speak.

But of course the testosterone thing is interactive, and the path is two-way: when a guy or his candidate is defeated in life, his testosterone level goes down; but when his testosterone level goes up (at puberty, in particular), his lust for combat balloons. This is a no-brainer: just look around.

The idea of No More Enemies cannot change biology in one fell swoop. Arguably, a few thousand or hundred thousand years of cultural redesign might alter the biology eventually. But in the meantime, we need productive and constructive and collaborative projects for guys to excel at, when the urge to strut strikes them. We don't want to curtail all that raw male energy heralded by the teen upsurge in hormones. The energy, as such, is great. The goal is to redirect it away from killing and mayhem, and put it to work for humanity.

Isn't that what education is all about, anyway?

Testosterone is not the enemy. It's just a hormone. It can be put to work for death or for life. We have some redesigning to do.

---

[8] For example: Charles Q. Choi (October 23, 2009). "Jock the Vote: Election Outcomes Affect Testosterone Levels in Men," *Scientific American*. Retrieved from http://www.scientificamerican.com/article.cfm?id=vote-election-testosterone

NME and the status of women

How could a fundamental shift in consciousness to a No More Enemies worldview fail to improve the lot of women in this world?

Millions of women around the world are treated, in their own homes and in the public sphere, in wartime and in peace, in rich countries and in poor, as the enemy—to be used and abused, owned, sold, traded, exploited, undervalued and disenfranchised.

To segue into a No More Enemies worldview is to shift all those behaviors beyond the pale—to a marginal, barely human fringe, no longer acceptable. Of course the definition of equal status is elusive and culturally diverse. (When you cover your body with a traditional mode of dress, is that protection, modesty, dignity, or subjugation? etc.) But, as Alice was instructed by the unicorn on the other side of the Looking Glass: *First you pass the cake around, and then you cut it up.*[9]

The NME paradigm assumes that everyone is first brought into the circle; then we figure out the details.

No one is left out and no one goes hungry. No one is abused, either.

---

[9] The Unicorn's original words were: `Hand it round first, and cut it afterwards.' Retrieved from http://www.literature.org/authors/carroll-lewis/through-the-looking-glass/chapter-07.html
The paraphrase is from John Briggs and F. David Peat, *Looking-Glass Universe: The Emerging Science of Wholeness* (New York: Simon & Schuster, 1986).

NME and aboriginal cultures

What does NME have to do with aboriginal cultures? Didn't aboriginal people also have enemies?

Well, yes. But consider: The wisdom of "first peoples" typically includes a deep understanding that each creature is a partner in a complex, shared puzzle and that while there may be adversaries, they, too, are a part of the puzzle. No one is "outside."

Certainly the history of some aboriginal cultures also includes warfare and bloodshed. There is no idyllic aboriginal past to return to, even if we could. Still, in contrast to the modern Western human-centered orientation, the conceptual paradigm of a partnership embracing all of creation is one that could help us get closer to a broad No More Enemies orientation.

In this worldview, no human is so privileged as to exploit another living creature unthinkingly or without proper humility and gratitude, for pleasure or gain or even survival. And a living being who is understood to be sacrificing itself (as food, for instance) so that another may live is conceived not as a lesser creature, but as a respected partner in a sacred transaction.

If I had to guess, I would guess that we humans will eliminate the notion of *enemies* before we eliminate all killing. But one has to start somewhere.

NME and the energy crisis

We talk a lot about an energy crisis, but do we stop to consider what we really mean? Fuel (to power machines, production, transportation, appliances, etc.) is only one form of energy. The idea of energy overall is much bigger than just fuel.

We have all experienced something we would call "positive energy" and something else we would call "negative energy." One builds, the other destroys; one gives, the other grabs. We might have a hard time agreeing on a precise definition of positive versus negative energy or the difference between them—but we have all experienced it.

I am amazed that so few people seem to stop and think about this one basic fact: whereas positive energy compounds itself, negative energy depletes itself.

The most magical positive energy on the planet is that of motivated human beings. If one group has energy and another group has energy, and if they are synchronized to harmonize somehow, their collaborative efforts multiply geometrically the available energy, even allowing for the hard work of achieving mutual understanding across cultural and other differences. In a relationship of domination by force, on the other hand, much of the stronger group's energy is wasted on holding the other group down. Then the squelched and thwarted group's energies are wasted on resistance to humiliation and to indignity instead of being channeled for the general good.

Reclaiming all that wasted energy should not be too difficult. First, we can embrace a very different understanding of the governing dynamic. A system relying on notions of *enemies* is like a village full of leaky plumbing: a precious and valuable resource is flowing away to no purpose, while the people get thirstier and thirstier. In the NME world, the leaking energies are identified and reclaimed very promptly: If there's no able NME technician in my neighborhood, there's sure to be one down the road or across that fence.

Sound bites and patterns

Communication is increasingly dominated by sound bites. The era of the 30-second, or 15-second, advertisement has evolved, via new digital technologies, into the era of texting, Twitter, and so forth.

No More Enemies is a good sound bite. It carries a powerful message in three words. We can use it like a mantra to remind ourselves of what game we are playing and what the goal is. A sound bite, however, is but the tip of the iceberg of deep social change. The rest of the iceberg is about patterns–deep patterns– of thought, of behavior, of institutional and communal and individual processes, directions, means and ends.

In this context, too, we humans are patterning beings in a patterning universe. Our tools of communication are all about patterning: language, music and dance, the arts and the sciences.

When issues come up for discussion that we think of in negative or discouraging terms, terms that almost automatically suggest that the odds are overwhelmingly against us–terms like *addiction* or *the privatization of prisons* or *the crash of the global economy*, we can immediately hit a mental Reset button and switch to a realm called "repatterning."

Western science is learning more every day about how old, bad patterns can be mended (repatterned) with various focused interventions, from bone marrow transplants to biofeedback. Eastern schools of thought have long stressed patterning (context; interrelationship), not only in health and medicine (energy flows and meridians) and philosophy (yin and yang), but in general: Recent perceptual studies have shown that Asians tend to look first at a scene in its entirety, to see the whole composition in its context, while Westerners tend to look first and longest at the largest single individual item in the foreground of the scene.[10]

It is my conviction that, if you find yourself behaving humanely in a No More Enemies mode, and the society around you deems that to be a radical or extreme stance–then it is the society around you that needs repatterning!

If a huge silent majority is complicit in the face of oppression of the neighbors or of a domestic minority of some kind (gays, Africans, the disabled, Jews, Muslims, whatever), then that distribution of opinion needs to be prodded and pushed and dragged over to a place where the oppression is understood to be marginal behavior. If the mainstream is in a bad place, there is a bad pattern at work. To alter the mainstream perspective, to reawaken ordinary people's compassion for the suffering of others, we have to alter the underlying pattern.

As an NME enthusiast, remember that you are not crazy. You are just a little ahead of your time.

Don't despair and don't give up. Be persistent. Be patient. Laugh a lot. Your hour will come.

---

[10] Retrieved from: Associated Press, "In Asia, the Eyes Have It" 8.23.05 reporting on research by Hannah-Faye Chua, Richard Nisbett and others in PNAS, August 2005; http://www.wired.com/news/culture/0,1284,68626,00.html

The enemy is us

You probably have heard of that famous quote from the late Walt Kelly, the American cartoonist who created the character of Pogo in the USA half a century ago: "We have met the enemy and he is us."

Kelly first used the wording, "we have met the enemy and he is us" on a poster for Earth Day in 1970, and in 1972 it was the title of a Kelly book: *Pogo: We have met the enemy and he is us*. The fuller and original quote on which this famous snippet draws was actually from Kelly's introduction to a book called *The Pogo Papers*, published in the 1950s, which reads in part:

> ...*Traces of nobility, gentleness and courage persist in all people, do what we will to stamp out the trend. So, too, do those characteristics which are ugly. It is just unfortunate that in the clumsy hands of a cartoonist all traits become ridiculous, leading to a certain amount of self-conscious expostulation and the desire to join battle.*
> *There is no need to sally forth, for it remains true that those things which make us human are, curiously enough, always close at hand. Resolve then, that on this very ground, with small flags waving and tinny blast on tiny trumpets, we shall meet the enemy, and not only may he be ours, he may be us.*
> *Forward!*[11]

I've always thought of this quote as meaning that, when there is trouble and grief, we needn't place the blame on people in some other place, some other group, some other country, because we ourselves are just as responsible as anyone.

---

[11] For all the quotes and background, see online at, e.g.:
http://www.igopogo.com/we_have_met.htm or enter "Pogo" in any search engine.

Lately I've been thinking about a deeper layer of meaning there. Not just that we are "the enemy" in the sense of having our share of responsibility for bad stuff that has happened; but also that "the enemy" over there are people just like us. On some fundamental level, they are us… and we are them.

As the Sufi sage said: I am you and you are me.

The point is not to replace blaming others with blaming oneself. Why make it about blame? Blame is a waste of energy. We can take responsibility, share responsibility, instead.

A strange immunity

Who can distance themselves from the prevailing paradigms in their culture, even if those paradigms are toxic, so long as they remain overwhelmingly accepted as natural and proper by nearly everyone?

A very small percentage of people, I think, have a strange natural immunity that predisposes them to recognize and reject a toxic paradigm. They are immunized perhaps by personality, inclination, training, education, or some combination of these.

A bad paradigm will usually disorient and corrupt the behavior of all but a few such hardy souls who are, somehow, immune.

On the other hand, a transformational paradigm can reorient and redeem the behavior of all but a few, irreparably confused or oblivious souls.

It's not the people; it's the paradigm. And we can redesign it.

No More Enemies.

Shortcuts and identities

They say there are no shortcuts, but it's not true. There are. This book is your shortcut to No More Enemies. If you can't believe in shortcuts, think of it as a wormhole (like in deep space). Some of the greatest scientific minds of our generation are persuaded that wormholes exist–and what is a wormhole if not a shortcut, a kind of express subway line, from one neighborhood in the universe to another? At least until we find out they don't exist, they make a great metaphor for inspired shortcuts.

Certainly a lot of the things scholars and experts say turn out not to be true; or they turn out to be true but to embody only part of the whole truth; or to be true in certain circumstances, but not in others.

Take the idea so popular today that our *identities* are deeply rooted and resistant to change, for example. I first began to worry about this idea in the context of inter-group encounter work with Israeli Jews and Palestinians. Even the encounter facilitators, based on their own and others' careful research, had come to accept that people's identities are bonded to the psyche as if with super-glue. This has made for a lot of pessimism about bringing change to the Israeli-Palestinian-Jewish-Arab sphere of relationships. The identities-oriented encounter model requires that each side adjust its identity to accommodate the equal humanity and equal rights of the other group. In other words, we are not alone here and the other people here are neither less human nor more human than we are, with all that that implies for equal opportunity, equal access to resources, and so forth.

This model was revolutionary when it emerged and is still used productively to do good inter-group encounter work. My problem with the model is that every time one of its practitioners writes, or says aloud, that identities are deeply rooted and resistant to change, he or she is making that idea more powerful and spreading it around a bit more. Every time.

And if identities are so powerful and so resistant to change, and we believe we have to adjust them to bring a better future to this or any other region, then the prospects for change can appear discouragingly weak.

So I began to question this axiom about identities, because it does not advance my purpose, which is to help people create a better future in this region or anywhere else. To do that, we first have to envision a way that it is *possible*. Envisioning how *im*possible it is does not help! The existing literature about identities (and there is a lot of it) is of interest to me, in our present context, only insofar as it can help us make progress toward a No More Enemies ethos. Otherwise, we need new theories!

I thought about my own experience in life, and my own identity, or identities. I am a human being, a woman, a New Yorker, a Jew, a freethinker, an American, an Israeli, a writer, an editor, a translator, and so forth. I also sometimes feel like a Buddhist, or a Mennonite, or a Quaker... In fact, we all have many identities and the ones to which we are especially attached are almost impossible to detach us from. I will always be a New Yorker. But the good news is that, to grow and change, we need not abandon any of our identity(ies). Rather, we can add on new ones. We do it all the time.

Suppose I am an alcoholic. I discover AA. Bingo! Now I am a *recovering* alcoholic. Or: You are a Hindu and you earn a Ph.D.: Bingo! A new layer of identity. Now when you go to conferences, people may address you as "Doctor"; you are still a Hindu, but at conferences it may well be the academic title that is stronger in your felt identity. And so forth.

The crucial point is that we can always be growing, and our identity can be growing and evolving with us, and may feel different in different contexts. I can become an environmental activist without giving up "New Yorker," right? And you can become a believer in No More Enemies without having to renounce any of your own existing identity, in the same way.

If the house of worship you currently attend has a clergyperson who preaches that you must struggle to defeat some particular enemy—I would not presume to argue. What I am doing is changing the game for you, so that that advice will no longer be relevant. Once you convert your enemy into a partner or at least a potential partner, you no longer have an enemy to struggle against. You don't need to stage any bitter confrontations with your community's spiritual leadership. Just buy them a copy of this book, and go on walking your path. You may be surprised, down the road, to see your clergyperson walking alongside you.

There is a tale in Jewish lore of a man who goes to talk to the rabbi and tells him, Rabbi, I don't know what to do. I can't seem to believe in God. The rabbi tells him to pray to God and he will learn to believe. But I don't know how to pray, confides the man, deeply troubled. Then pray that you learn how to pray, counsels the rabbi.

If you feel that you can't really get your mind around the idea of No More Enemies—if something in you resists, and you just can't believe that the idea is sound—I suggest that you not worry. Assume that the idea of No More Enemies is absolutely true, authentic, and valid. Assume that you already believe this, deep down. Assume that you will believe this consciously and with all your heart one day, when you have grown past whatever is standing in your way right now.

That's a shortcut, my friend. You can decide to believe that you believe, or that you will believe, that we have entered an era of No More Enemies, and that you can let go of all your own enemies and begin exploring how to make them into partners. If you don't *feel* the belief yet—that's okay. You will. Eventually.

Meantime, people often say to me: But the enemy you are telling me I don't have any more, might murder me in the meantime, with a bomb or whatever, while I am walking my new path of converting him to a partner. You know what? You're right. Life is a gamble. We have good evidence from many fields (psychology, diplomacy, peace studies, history, drama therapy, etc.) that the guy or group you fear is less likely to do you harm if you make a commitment to ratchet down your hatred (even if you are afraid) and reorient your rhetoric toward partnership. But in truth there are no guarantees. It only takes one fanatic, speaking in the name of some group or other, or a small group of fanatics, to blow a lot of people away.

Personally, however, even if I find myself being blown away by someone or some group like that, as I breathe my last I would prefer to think of them as potential partners who did not reach their fullest potential, rather than as "enemies." I'll be just as dead, but I'll be happier.

Frame-shifting

When reality is framed in a certain way, that frame will tend to orient people in certain identifiable directions in terms of how they use their energies and spend their time. To make a big change in that behavior, you need to reframe reality. You can change people's perspective, and literally shift their views, by shifting the frame so that you overhaul the definition of what people view as mainstream and what they view as marginal.

On a computer, the Google Maps function is a good illustration of the dynamics of frame-shifting. You enter an address or the name of an institution and it shows you a map with that address at the center: say, the Red Fort in Delhi, in India. You can move the up, down, right and left arrows in the corner of the screen to travel in any direction on the map (which extends on and on beyond the edges of the window on your computer screen). A different area of the map will shift along into your viewing window so that you are looking at quite another picture, with something else at its center: the Oberoi Maidens Hotel in Delhi or even the Taj Mahal, in the distant city of Agra. Or let's say you look at the New York Public Library in Manhattan, New York, USA; and then shift around to see a different frame, centered on Washington Square Park, or the Brooklyn Bridge, or farther away until you're at Philadelphia, a city hundreds of miles away.

In each case as you shift your map around, or shift your view of the map, you end up with a newly framed map which has something quite different as its center. You can click your computer mouse in the new center, and what you now see becomes the virtual landscape in this present moment. The earlier one is, for the present, gone.

This is how I envision NME shifting our general worldview. I see cooperation with anyone labeled "them" as a natural thing, as our birthright, as our salvation. I see that perception moving into the center of the popular mental map for earthlings. And I see the old way of dividing the world into *us-versus-our-enemies* moving way off to the fringe, where it will become an artifact of history and nothing more. We can all make this shift, as each of us makes it individually and together. It's up to us.

No More Enemies: The Rant

The NME rant is a holistic one–beyond multidisciplinary. It's about rehabilitating the way we see others and our shared world. You can create your own NME rant when you are ready.

My NME rant says, Let's reorient the public discussion away from an exclusive focus on struggles revolving primarily around rights (especially competing rights), to embrace the idea of *potentiating* people. Why this shift?

When the discussion and our activism are oriented mainly toward rights, our canvas is vivid and high-energy, featuring people denied their rights, and people denying them their rights. Some of the people denying others their rights actually live in countries that are signatories to international agreements that forbid such behavior.

An orientation geared more toward potentiating, on the other hand, could help to focus on insuring that everyone will have the opportunity to contribute their maximum to the general good. Clearly they can do that only in an atmosphere in which the free exercise of basic rights is universal. That is the nurturing, nutrient-rich environment in which all the potential, of everyone, can grow and flourish. Wherever that free exercise is blocked, it has to be unblocked, and the process has to include accountability, restitution, reconciliation and healing.

The NME world is full of excitement and adventure. Building something with ex-enemies is hot! Shooting or humiliating them is not!

The NME world is full of mutual co-empowerment. The NME generation knows that power only works well if it's shared around. Hoard your power for yourself and it slowly destroys you (and "them"). Share the power you have and it introduces a wave of energy that lifts everyone to greater accomplishments.

The NME dynamic encourages people to orient toward, to be preoccupied with, what the experts call "best practices" for evoking the optimal contribution from each and all. This enlarges the shared pie instead of focusing on blame, guilt, defensiveness, scarcity, restrictions, and constraints.

The conduct of *caring and caregiving*, in Riane Eisler's telling phrase, actually changes the caregivers in important and positive ways not experienced by people not engaged in that kind of effort, that kind of work. Caring and caregiving work, for all we know now, may even alter the biochemistry of the caregivers in ways that will be passed on as cultural memes, if not genetically, to the next generation, and the next. We know that pollution can damage chromosomes in teratogenic ways. Maybe involvement in caring and caregiving gradually creates transformational neurobiological alterations that the caring person benefits from, and (who knows?) passes on. Maybe NME activism does that, too. I hope someone is researching this.

Icing on the cake

Sometimes, research is like the icing on the cake of an idea.

Research can dress up the idea and make it tastier, but the basic idea transcends the research used to elaborate and explore it.

First comes the idea; then the research. We need good research, even inspired research; the idea comes first, though.

Ask any good scientist.

Sometimes research may seem to disprove an idea, but not really disprove it exactly; that is, the researcher is not persuaded to junk the idea altogether. The scientist says to herself: Well, it was a great idea but somehow maybe I had it backwards. I need to go through the looking glass, and consider this idea from the other side, or anyhow from a different angle, and run the experiments again.

If the idea of NME were to be shot down by research next week, I would bet that we would then find that the researcher was looking at the idea from the wrong angle entirely, through the crosshairs of a warlike orientation.

Please don't wait for the research to prove that the *enemies* paradigm is killing us. We don't have that kind of time.

Alien viewpoint (not)

If a visitor from some other, more advanced civilization dropped in on our planet, she would have trouble understanding why all these people are fighting.

I have no trouble imagining myself as a member of an alien civilization. It's imagining myself as a member of this one that I have trouble with!

I'll bet that's a more common feeling than we realize.

Team Earth!

Much of humanity still acts like a baby sitting on a playground for grownups, sucking its thumb, and surrounded with high-tech toys, which we call weapons. These toys are dangerous. Indeed they are lethal, and getting more lethal all the time. Giant robot warriors; long-distance drone aircraft; untraceable chemical poisons.

An activist's typical response is to get mad at the baby and lecture it about the military-industrial complex, colonialism, corporatism, and so on. This accomplishes very little. A more constructive response might be for creative thinkers to design better, more life-affirming, more ecologically appropriate and sustainable toys: toys that are more useful and more fun than weapons; games that are really tools to build communities and relationships and explore the far reaches of science and of the spirit, crafted lovingly in service to All Our Relations (as the first Americans would say). If the new toys are really hot items, promising a fine profit to whoever constructs them and distributes them, then the makers of today's lethal and useless weapon-toys will retool to make the new kind. Helping the process along with government regulation and appropriate tax policy won't hurt, but it can't replace a really good retooling strategy.

A recent YouTube video documents an experiment in Stockholm to test the theory that, rather than using punishment, making something fun can effectively change behavior: The steps of a staircase connecting street level with an underground mass transit platform were decorated to look like a piano keyboard, so that stepping on the "keys" activated hidden sensors to produce musical notes. The object was to see whether more people would use the stairs, a healthier alternative to the escalator, if the stairs were "fun." Lo and behold, the percentage of people using the stairs spiked sharply—as adults and children jumped around on the "keys" for fun–and escalator use correspondingly dropped, at least initially.[12]

We may indeed be at a crucial turning point in the eternal struggle between Team Carrot and Team Stick: The prize is the world's loyalty and imagination, indeed the very future of humanity and its habitat and of the other creatures living in that habitat. If you are trying to put the Stick out of the game (and let's be clear here: I don't mean all discipline or disincentives, but rather violence, coercion, domination), then what you have left to send onto the field is the Carrot… and superb strategy.

Go, Team Earth!

---

[12] See this and other such ideas online at http://www.thefuntheory.com/ - a Volkswagen initiative; retrieved at
http://www.youtube.com/watch?v=2lXh2n0aPyw on YouTube, where I first viewed the Stockholm Piano Staircase experiment.

Where's my oxygen?!

The magnitude of the cultural, and possibly biological, paradigm shift that we are witnessing now, from enemies to cooperation and partnership, is probably equivalent in magnitude to the paradigm shift that took place on planet Earth when an atmosphere congenial to creatures breathing oxygen replaced the prior atmosphere that was toxic to oxygen-breathers.

This is the magnitude of the shift. The great magnitude probably helps explain why everything seems so confused and why so many people feel so bewildered and enraged. If they cannot yet see beyond the old way, not even a little bit, then they must be feeling that the reality they live and breathe is literally disappearing–their reality is vanishing before their very eyes.

Brute force used to work well as a tool for the elites, and could be sustained for long periods. People and organizations and regimes that have achieved much and thrived impressively under the old system have been very powerfully rewarded; they will not find it easy to give up what has proven so useful. Like it or not, however, we are now straining against the limits of sustainability for brute force, because of global environmental constraints. The playground for brute force has, it turns out, finite limits.

Even those whom the old system has plowed under are strongly conditioned to see it as eternal, and they can have difficulty imagining anything different, much less stronger. Consider: A constructively networked world of partnerships will be stronger than the old (brute force) way, because less energy will be wasted on null activities that do not enhance the overall functioning of the whole. Activities like killing and oppressing and incarcerating do not utilize the energies of the killers very well; killing is not a productive occupation. Nor do those activities utilize the energies of the oppressed effectively; instead, they constrain or even eliminate those energies. Aside from being immoral, that is terribly wasteful.

Meantime, those of us who are busy trying to envision and to midwife the shift to a new paradigm get discouraged because, from our tiny human scale, the grand movement is almost undetectable... but it is happening.

Many people worry that the holdouts—the Dr. Strangeloves, the maniacal corporatists, the psychotechno fanatics—can torpedo the shift simply by becoming the last ones to maintain tools of brute force. That is a scary thought, yes—but consider this: In the schoolyard, when the big bad bully is beating someone up, a bunch of determined but unarmed children, however scrawny they may be individually, can face down the bully and send him packing. There is an energy at work in such scenarios that is greater than the sum of the individual players. We are learning more about that energy all the time now; we will become more sophisticated in its use. It will be there when we need it.

The evolving human condition

We know today that "we are what we eat," in the sense that the kinds of food we consume (along with exercise and a healthy lifestyle) can, gradually, over a long period, make us very healthy... or not. The basic principle is that engaging in a pattern of certain behaviors can slowly reshape who we are, who we become.

The same principle is at work for humanity as a whole, and today we are more aware of how it functions. Our greater awareness could be very advantageous.

Until now, groups of people who are engaged in some familiar pattern of behavior have tended to become pawns of the pattern, without seeing where it is taking them. For example, people flee from persecution by migrating to some distant place, yet in the place where they land, they create an unfree society that oppresses the people who were already there, or the people who come there next, or both. They run away from the force being used to embitter their lives but they take with them the principle of social organization by force and then recreate the patterns they were running away from. Of the original 13 American colonies (of mainly white Europeans, plus African slaves) on the East coast of what is now the USA, for example, nearly all of them severely restricted freedom of religion, despite the fact that the quest for religious freedom was what had brought many of those colonists to leave their countries of origin in the first place. (Not to mention the freedoms of the people whose lands they colonized.)

This pattern is part of the human condition—so far. But suppose humans collectively and consciously aspire to change that, to learn a less cruel pattern and pursue it? The state of the human condition could improve: after all, humanity is always evolving, continually evolving.

Once we recognize that the human condition in general is universal and that the patterns of behavior we observe in others are part of the human condition, then even if the behavior is hateful, we have organized our worldview in such a way that we can reject the current status of the human condition rather than the actual humans who are doing hateful things. This distinction is basic.

If we want to improve the human condition, we can begin by modeling the human behavior we hope will become the norm. We can stop condemning and hating others. That shift actually feels good to us because condemning and hating are unhealthy for us and ineffective in making constructive change. Instead, we can decide to use our energies to help to set up opportunities for others to join us in modeling more aware, compassionate, and generous norms of behavior.

When we approach life this way, we emanate a compassionate energy that draws others to work with us and to behave that way, themselves. We transform "hate energy" into "love energy." The net energy in the world may not be greater or less, but it is transformed. The patterns underlying the human condition as-it-has-been are shifted a little, in small increments, in a more sacred direction. Thanks to us and our transformational energy!

Quantitative reasoning

Energy crisis, economic crisis, global warming, wars between civilizations, terrorism: all these things are related, not just qualitatively, but also quantitatively–but not in the way the conventional wisdom portrays them.

The energy of individual human beings and of people in groups is vast, provided they have a minimum of physical and spiritual sustenance. What's interesting is that, while this minimum physical need for food, clothing, and shelter, and even for basic dignity and respect, is quite modest–the metaphysical energy that people can contribute is almost infinite.

This simple quantitative truth about human energy is not taught in most schools.

Another equally simple, and significant, quantitative axiom that too few people seem conscious of, as yet: If we tie up a lot of energy oppressing people–denying them their minimal needs, treating them as less than human, warehousing them in ghettoes and prisons, labeling them negatively as worthless or terrorists or backward or any of the other fashionable pejoratives–we are burning off the tremendous amount of energy used by everyone concerned, to little constructive effect. All the energy used to put people down and constrain and control and belittle them, energy that could have gone to building a beautiful world filled with shared natural abundance for all, all that energy is wasted. And all the energy from the enslaved and embittered people who are never permitted a reasonable opportunity to make their unique contribution to humanity, all that energy turns to less worthwhile ends: to bare survival both physical and psychic and often, of course, to rebellion, escape, and revenge. Who can blame them? Who is to say we would behave any differently, if that had been our fate?

What is less easy to fathom is precisely where and how anyone can usefully break into this habitual cycle of global energy drain. The downtrodden will claim, with justice, that they must throw off their oppressors—and they will claim a right to act with violence, if necessary (since they are violently suppressed); and the privileged will claim, and will even believe, that they are merely defending themselves against the raging hordes at the gates.

After thirty or so years observing, from up close, the dysfunctional social tapestry of Israel/Palestine and reading about its sorry history (more of the same), I am persuaded of this, at least: Only in the human will to break free of this vicious cycle are the oppressor and the oppressed, as individual human beings, more or less equal. The will to break free comes from the deepest soul sources of energy, from a profound understanding that "this is not the way" and that a really different way will require cooperation across the boundaries of hatred, fear and distrust: cooperation with the other side.

Some of the damage already inflicted is irreversible. The dead will not be brought back to life, the wounded and traumatized will not be as they were, the inward and outward landscape has been forever altered. This is where the idea of reparations comes in. And so long as we persist on traveling that same road, the damage continues. This is where a sense of urgency comes in.

Several of the foremost, most spiritually aware proponents of a different way have come, in our time, from the ranks of the disenfranchised: Gandhi; King; Mandela; Aung San Suu Kyi. Clearly they have striven not to simply perpetuate the same old dynamic of dominance with only the major roles switched between the players. Clearly they have looked toward a different dimension of human cooperation for the future.

Note that I said equality in the "will to break free" of the dysfunctional dynamic. There is no parity in the ability to act on that conviction, because the group in control is way ahead in access to power, resources, media, wealth, etc. So there is no equality on the instrumental level, perhaps, but only on the soul level. Nonetheless, when a person of strong conviction decides to work for constructive change, whether that person comes from the ranks of the elite or of the downtrodden, the impact can be considerable, even given all the constraints. There is a mysterious power, almost a force field, wielded by a determined advocate for compassion, conscience and justice. This power is not well understood or even widely admitted to exist, and is hard to quantify with any precision, but we know it is big. Its impressive effect is quite transparent when it ushers out a tyrannical regime and brings new freedom to the populace. When ordinary people join their efforts together, they can feel this power collectively.

We would do well to wake up and recognize our allies, many of whom are on the other side of the fence, of the border, of the discourse. With that recognition, comes a new spirit of joyfulness; we call it "solidarity."

Constructive solidarity–synergy, if you prefer–is the ultimate energy source, virtually unlimited. It is right there in front of us. To know its value, just do the math.

Bridging the disconnect

NME–the No More Enemies paradigm–can help bridge the disconnect that so many people seem to experience between their actions and their values. For example: you are a committed Christian and you don't believe in killing, but you work in a factory and make weapons that kill people, most of them civilians, perhaps.

What smothers the deep dissonance you would otherwise feel under such circumstances is the notion that those whom the missiles will kill are "the enemy." Without the *enemies* paradigm, *all* war and war-related industry is a "war crime."

To what unworthy battles may you be lending, right now, your valuable energy and the labor of your unique gifts?

NME tells you to think again about how you are living what poet Mary Oliver termed "your one wild and precious life."

Possibilities

In her book *World as Lover, World as Self*, noted scholar of Buddhism Joanna Macy talks at length about working with people who are losing or have lost hope. The vast suffering in the world and humanity's role in creating it often push people into despair, which has to be acknowledged and addressed. Joanna Macy recounts that she asked Christian theologian Hal Douglass, a longtime anti-nuclear activist who went to prison more than once for his beliefs, how he deals with despair:

"What do you substitute for hope?" she asks. He smiles.

"Possibilities," he says. "You can't predict [them]. Just make space for them." [13]

Children, unless they are brutally discouraged or exploited, seriously ill or abused, or attending a school they really loathe, do this automatically. They jump out of bed every morning to engage with all the possibilities that a new day can bring.

As adults, we can nurture this image of possibilities to help us dispel the blues. Despair rests on the assumption that all possibilities have been exhausted.

It's hardly ever true. Maybe it's never true. Think about it.

---

[13] Joanna Macy, *World as Lover, World As Self* (Berkeley, California: Parallax Press, 1991, pp. 27-28).

This may be a long process

Remember: "enemies" is not just an idea.

It is not just an idea we think about.

Enemies is an idea we think with… and now we have to learn to think without it.

That means replacing it with some other, more constructive paradigm: partnership, harmony, compassion. Diversity. The ability to hold two mutually contradictory ideas in our consciousness simultaneously, without the need to disparage either one.

It may happen more quickly than we anticipate, but then again, it may be a long process.

You don't need a Pocahontas-and-John experience

Romantic experiences of passionate love between enemies do happen, but they are not necessary for reconciliation. Sagas like the story of *Pocahontas* (for whom, actually, things ended rather badly) or *Dancing with Wolves*, in which the hero or heroine from the newly arrived culture falls in love with someone from the local "enemy" culture, are most likely not going to happen to everyone. But that's fine.

Romance is fine, as far as it goes, but we don't need romantic love to achieve a deep awareness of the other's humanity. One ordinary cross-border friendship is enough.

Edward T. Hall, a 20th-century pioneer in the study of cultural diversity, insisted that to understand our own embedded, unconscious, cultural assumptions about reality, we need only seek with curiosity to learn about someone else's. The epiphanies are in the contrasts.

This other person need not be a foreigner, Hall said; even someone from our own culture who is much older or younger than we are can give us this gift of perspective.

Ultimately as our perspective expands to embrace the other's full humanity, we come to see that, from the other person's perspective, *we* are the enemy–that is, the bad guy. But of course, we know we're the good guy, and so do the other people know that about themselves. When this insight is intense enough, the *enemies* paradigm implodes.

Pot-luck supper

There are very few fatally toxic people, but a great many fatally toxic cultural paradigms.

When people are trapped in a highly toxic cultural paradigm and are suffering, they will tend to look for someone to blame. This quite natural response is highly ineffective.

The paradigm itself is to blame.

When some creative person or group within such a situation grasps this concept, they get a huge boost toward an eventual resolution–first, because their new understanding automatically enlarges the pool of human talent available to design a solution. Second, they get an added bonus in the hybridization, cross-fertilization, and creative synthesis that can emerge when more than one stakeholder group or neighborhood or culture addresses the situation.

Like a pot-luck supper–everyone contributes something uniquely theirs. To ignore this richness is willfully to stumble around in the dark when light is available for the asking.

Maybe this is another reason that killing is forbidden. Maybe part of the reason that killing is such a sin is that, when we take a life, we have precluded any possibility of transformation: That "enemy" can never become a partner now, because they are gone, and their unique energy and potential contribution are gone along with them. The bountiful pot-luck supper–our shared future–is going to happen, but they won't be there to embellish it.

What a waste!

Think bigger; think transformational

Think bigger! Think several generations down the line. We can consciously help to evolve the species over successive generations from *homo sapiens* into partnership people. Taking a leaf from physicist Rupert Sheldrake's morphic resonance theory[14], the more partnership-oriented people there are, growing together in partnership mode, the easier it should be for others to join them.

This is another answer to a form of "the prisoner's dilemma"– the question of what happens if we all give up violence, and then the last violent group, the last one with weapons and no scruples about using them, takes over and rules in the end. Well, in the meantime, we can help evolve ourselves so that humanity will outgrow that. Why not?

I won't pretend that the evolutionary graph will necessarily be an ascending straight line. Setbacks will happen.

So how badly do we want to be part of this transformation, and how sturdily are we prepared to face the sacrifices demanded of us along the way?

Think transformational. Your enemy is not your enemy, but your ticket to a better future. He or she is waiting for you to "get it"! Then you can get to work together, building the shared future for your great-great-great-grandchildren.

---

[14] For an online summary of Rupert Sheldrake's well-known theory of morphic resonance and morphic fields, see his web site at http://www.sheldrake.org/

Courage

They say that courage is not a lack of fear, nor the opposite of being afraid. In frightening situations, being afraid is normal and not being afraid is foolish. Courage is about pushing on through, even when you are afraid.

In an analogous way, the opposite of being *racist* is not a state of harboring no stereotypes of the other (an ideal impossible to achieve; we all harbor stereotypes and fears about people who are different from us). The aim—what is the positive opposite of "racist" anyway?"—is to push on through to partnership in spite of the stereotypes and fears: to treat the other as "not other," as an act of faith—the way firefighters head into a flaming building, believing they can save the innocent and come out alive themselves, because that is their job on this planet.

Our job on this planet is to be human, and to treat all other creatures as human. Whether we are afraid or not, and even if we sometimes get burned.

Mate, predator, prey—or partner!

Organisms in general have tended to evolve all kinds of mechanisms to help them distinguish whether the stranger approaching them is a potential predator, potential prey (food), or a potential mate. Something like: Ahoy there—are you going to consume me for lunch, am I going to consume you for lunch, or are we going to propagate the species together?

In the post-enemies-paradigm world, we humans will learn to see every other organism "not us" as a potential partner rather than in terms of the category of the transaction we may or may not engage in together. In a post-"might-makes-right" reality, partners will explore, define, and agree on "right" together. The environmentalist's cradle-to-cradle principle not only moves us beyond a "less waste" orientation to the design of positive, self-sufficient energy loops; it also gives us insight into how we can evolve more sustainable relationships between human groups as well as between humans and the planet.

The axiom that there is no such location as "away"—a mythical place where we can safely and legitimately stow the trash generated by poor design—is just as valid for inter-group relations. Even if it were not immoral to do so, no human population can be banished, "warehoused," or otherwise dispensed with securely or legitimately or sustainably. Solutions must include everyone. That is our design challenge in a post-enemies-paradigm world.

Fortunately, the vast untapped pools of talent waiting behind the walls and barbed wire, in the slums and prisons and refugee camps, will amply repay humanity's efforts to make new social design solutions universally inclusive, whether they are local or global in scope.

SET (Serial Endosymbiotic Theory) and NME

MIT professor Lynn Margulis is my hero in the world of biology for insisting (for decades, and despite widespread resistance among most mainstream biologists) that competition as an explanation for how things work in general, and how species evolve in particular, is highly overrated. [15] Beginning in the late 1960s, she also championed the idea that discrete micro-organisms must have joined together symbiotically to create certain more complex organisms at crucial points in biological history, an idea first proposed by Konstantin Mereschkowsky in 1926. Margulis and her students have since demonstrated in the laboratory most of the processes that she predicted would be involved, as described in her *Symbiotic Planet: A New View of Evolution.*[16]

Margulis provides a lucid and rather entertaining account of what she termed SET: serial endosymbiotic theory. Endosymbiosis means mutual cooperation internally, within an organism. Early proto-cells, she hypothesized, may have originally become endosymbionts (interdependent partners with one inside the other) via either failed ingestion or failed sexual congress. This means either that one microscopic critter tried to eat another and, having swallowed it, failed to digest it; or that one such critter tried to mate with a different kind and got in, so to speak, but then got stuck there. Either way, the organisms had to somehow function together in their new joined state, or die. I am not a biologist and there is no point in trying to portray at length here what Margulis describes so much better in her own books. If this interests you, go look at the original. *Symbiotic Planet* has the fur-

---

[15] Retrieved from summary at: http://en.wikipedia.org/wiki/Symbiogenesis
[16] Lynn Margulis, *Symbiotic Planet: A New Look at Evolution* (New York: Basic Books, 1998).

ther attraction of using bits of Emily Dickinson's poems as chapter epigraphs.

Margulis is also the co-developer, along with fellow biologist James Lovelock who first proposed it, of the Gaia theory—suggesting that planet Earth is a self-organizing, sentient entity and hence in some sense, at least, is alive. But that's another story.

For NME purposes what is most crucial about the SET work of Lynn Margulis is her unshakeable orientation to the importance of cooperation alongside, if not instead of, competition. "The tendency of independent life," she says, "is to bind together and re-emerge in a new wholeness at a higher, larger level of organization."[17] And in an article co-authored with her son Dorion Sagan, they say: "Life did not take over the globe by combat, but by networking."[18] How different this is from the old mainstream thinking among biologists and others who are still wedded to the evolution-as-combat approach.

In our time, science has acquired tools to help confirm what mystics have been saying for centuries: To evolve to a higher level, we humans must work together. Insofar as we resist evolving new partnerships, we hold back our own evolution.

The *enemies* paradigm is obsolete.

No More Enemies.

---

[17] *Symbiotic Planet*, p.11 (see note 16).
[18] Lynn Margulis and Dorion Sagan (2001). "Marvellous microbes". *Resurgence* 206: 10–12; retrieved at http://www.answers.com/topic/endosymbiotic-theory

We can choose

The enemies paradigm is a problem for us all: for humanity. We are very accustomed to it; we are, in a sense, comfortable with it. Nevertheless, we can choose to walk away from it; we can choose to leave it behind.

Probably there will always be people who tend toward adversarial responses. Plus, those who find themselves discriminated against, oppressed, or enslaved will nearly always conceive of the ruling power as "the enemy"–failing to realize that the enemies paradigm is what leads or allows an oppressor to behave oppressively in the first place. While unfortunate, this oversight is understandable. Not everyone can be Gandhi.

It therefore falls doubly to those of us fortunate enough not to be living under such threats, to pull and push others toward our paradigm, ceaselessly, patiently, compassionately, but determinedly.

The ultimate goal may be viewed in terms of making the enemies paradigm taboo–universally taboo. The idea of course is to transform, not just the lexicon, but the individual and collective social behavior that is driven by the enemies paradigm and its conceptual foundations.

It's the paradigm, and the paradigm golems—not the people

Look around at the chaos and conflict in the world. Take any one case and examine it closely.

The people are just people—just people like you or me. The people can't be the problem; they're just folks.

So if the problem is not the people, it must be the paradigm.

And in fact, today we have a pandemic of "paradigm golems[19]"—all kinds of cultural paradigms that evolved to solve particular problems but are now killing us.

People get caught up in these paradigms, they point their guns at us, we get angry and rise up against the enemy, but those people are not really our enemies. The paradigm is the problem. The people can all band together (us and them) and choose a new paradigm that lets us all be partners, encourages us to be partners, facilitates our being partners—instead of enemies.

"They" have skills, talents, cultural tools, languages, experiences and other attributes that can hugely enrich the common pool. We need all those gifts. Why throw them away? We can bring those people and all their gifts into the circle of commonality, with all the other humans and the other creatures and the living and inanimate environment—all the rest of creation of which we are all a part.

---

[19] In Jewish folklore, a *golem* is an artificial humanoid life form created to help people resolve some kind of difficulty.

Despair, perspective, hope

One day we will see the production, distribution and sale of weapons as an inherently barbaric and primitive behavior. Perhaps as the bounds of "us" expand to include all of humanity and all creatures on earth, the violent fringe will focus only on what is beyond: other, possibly unfriendly, species from elsewhere. One would hope that we would also leave the door open to *friendly* species from elsewhere, rather than repeat our earth-based patterns endlessly, even in far-flung galaxies.

Meantime, here on earth, violent death for profit will go out of style, permanently. Perhaps in films and video games, too… And what will replace all this, for "thrills"? Who knows?! The creative young designers of planet Earth will eventually give us something like the Star Trek "holodeck" where adventure is programmable and the adrenalin is real, but no one suffers mortal wounds, because it's all illusion.

Someone will figure out a way, soon, to import the New Games paradigm to industry. So-called "New Games," which became popular late in the 20th century, were designed to create fun via cooperation instead of competition, and to build trust instead of mistrust. Could the New Games ethos ever replace profit? If we were to define the "profit motive" more broadly to include all stakeholders, including the environment, etc., would the idea of "profit" still be useful? Why not? We can remix "profit" so that what is gained is not necessarily or primarily financial. Existing social constructs can be transformed, or translated, into NME mode.

Meantime, what about the tyranny of the quarterly earnings report? Or the tyranny of the financial analyst, who can kill a company's future with a bit of bad press? How to restore long-term perspective?

There is a sociocidal aspect to rampant creation of fake wealth by the financial sector: the few enjoy, while the many see their world implode. It's like a pyramid with a bright star on top and the whole foundation turning to sand.

How will the top sustain itself later, when the bottom collapses? You can't buy back the Amazon or the arctic ice once they're gone. You cannot, in the end, eat money.

Doesn't greed have somewhat different outcomes today than in past times? Once, oppression of the many by the few only destroyed the lives of the many in the present time and maybe ravaged the environment for a short time. Now, the greed of the elite sectors is destroying the quality of life for everyone, including the elite, and including the environment for generations to come. Fortunately, there is reason for hope; the future is in our hands. NME mode requires us to understand ourselves as being all in the same boat.

Meantime, all around us, people are worried. The more they pay attention to reality, and the more thoroughly they delve into the problems, the more despair they sometimes feel. Hence it is doubly important to spread the word on NME: There is reason for hope, and the future is up to us.

Patterning, un-patterning, re-patterning

Remember that we are patterning creatures, we humans.

If we have continually tended to cycle back to ugly, destructive patterns, nevertheless we can reinvent our patterns, imagine new patterns, and co-create a new reality using more harmonious patterns. Not easily nor all at once; but we can choose to walk in that direction.

If we see that, until now, we have been oriented in an awkward, even tragic, direction—we can reorient.

We don't have to try to do it alone; we are not required to do it alone. We can help one another.

When we decide that our enemies will no longer be enemies, but partners-in-the-making, we acquire more help for the repatterning and reorienting process. We are acquiring more help for our experiment in becoming more whole.

Old enemies become new partners in transformation.

Leaving Ur

Legend has it that my ancestor Abraham, the "father of monotheism," was driven by an idea so compelling that, in its service, he was prepared to leave behind his home, his family, and his community—a place called Ur.

When a powerful idea takes you over, to deny it is a type of self-destruct. If following that idea where it leads means that you are distanced from friends, family, and community—so be it. As you surrender to the idea, you become more and more who you were meant to be. There's a kind of joy in that, even if it's sometimes bittersweet.

Abraham rejected a pantheon of idols and envisioned the One, all-powerful God. But he lived in a time of tribes: many tribes. God was One but the tribes were not.

Now, in our era, it is time to outgrow the idea of many tribes as our organizing principle. We will keep our tribes, maybe, but at the same time we will reorganize ourselves in a different dimension where we are all more connected.

In this new dimension, we are all one tribe. Nothing makes this clearer than environmental problems: there are no impermeable boundaries in the planetary ecosystem. What harms one tribe (or country, or continent) harms all. You are me, and I am you. We are all one.

In traditional Jewish liturgy, there is an important blessing that says: "Blessed art Thou, O Lord our God, Who has chosen us from among all peoples (*asher bakhar banu mikol ha'amim*) and given us His Torah." This prayer is so central in Jewish religious ritual that abandoning it is not an option.

Too long ago to track, now, I heard about some Jewish scholar's analysis that this idea of having been chosen as a people is not as arrogant as it sounds to our more modern ears. The ancient Hebrews, in this analysis, would not have presumed to think of themselves as "choosing God," i.e., opting for a way of life constructed around certain divinely ordained (in their view) ethical beliefs and practices. To them, in their day, the idea of "We choose God" would have seemed too presumptuous. So they took the idea and inverted it: God has chosen us!

Nonetheless, even if one accepts this analysis, it does not resolve the dilemma of what to do about that prayer.

One day about 15 years ago at the Har El Synagogue in Jerusalem, Rabbi Tuvia Ben-Horin was leading the congregation in prayer. I happened to be there because the daughter of old friends of mine was Bat Mitzvah that day. When it came to the prayer I find so problematical, Rabbi Tuvia surprised me by intoning, "...who has chosen us *together with* all peoples.." (*asher bakhar banu im kol ha'amim*). This, with a change in only one Hebrew syllable.

Wow! I thought: an elegant solution. But in the years since, I've rarely heard this alternate version elsewhere. Evidently it has not caught on widely enough yet.

There is another central prayer in Judaism envisioning God bringing peace "to us and to all Israel"—as if we Jews, a minute fraction of the world's population, could have any meaningful peace in this world all by ourselves! The Tuvia Ben-Horin school of thought has given this prayer a universal riff at the end: "...to us and to all Israel, and to all humanity, amen."

This, too, is elegant. But again, it has not universally entered the liturgy, by any means. At leisurely Shabbat or holiday dinners with old and dear friends in Jerusalem, I listen in vain for these more universalist phrases during the prayers before the meal. My Jerusalem friends are nearly all from Reform (liberal, or progressive, Judaism) backgrounds. But at home with their families, they still chant the time-honored tribal chant in its exact and traditional form, and they appear not to be concerned about it. I sit mutely and keep them company, feeling that I belong and don't belong at the same time: I enjoy listening to the rituals I grew up with, but I can no longer chant those words. Sometimes I will chant the alternative version under my breath, but no one hears me unless I sing obnoxiously loud. I suppose if anyone were interested enough to notice, they would see me as accepting the burden of this tradition, with all the implications–but I do not accept it.

The dissonance makes me sad; I have left my Ur, and sometimes that feels lonely.

The spiritual community where I most naturally fit now is dispersed all over the world, but united by a vision. This vision was elegantly conveyed by some people at a protest demonstration in Toronto whose hand-lettered sign I saw online once. Their sign said: ALL PEOPLE ARE CHOSEN. ALL LAND IS HOLY.

It's time. It's past time. There is only one tribe now, and we all belong. We will all flourish and prosper, all together, or not: it is our choice.

Salvation, when it comes

Salvation, when it seems most distant and out of reach, may approach unheralded from a novel direction and knock quietly at our door. Surprise! The one small step then required of us is to open the door and let it enter.

Or it may be sitting there on the threshold, awaiting discovery at our initiative. Sometimes a little initiative goes a long way!

Today, the idea that the *enemies* paradigm is obsolete is creeping up on us from diverse directions. If you go and explore, with an adventurous and hopeful heart, in your own field of interest–from anthropology to zoology–you will find a budding awareness of this idea there, somewhere.

There is already a readiness among many people around the planet to move beyond the *enemies* paradigm. You who are ready–speak up now. This is your hour.

As others hear your call, they will join us. This is our new day dawning.

A little humor can't hurt either

A 2008 article in the *Journal of Biochemical Technology* reported that yeast cells can distinguish different smells. One day, suggested authors Eugenia Y. Xu, Addison D. Ault, and James R. Broach, "engineered yeast cells incorporated into sensory arrays" could be "used as biosensors or artificial noses."[20]

In other words–anything's possible.

If yeast can follow a trail of scents just like Lassie does, surely the enemies paradigm can be declared obsolete and become, one day, taboo.

---

[20] The article appeared in the *Journal of Biochemical Technology*, ISSN: 09742328, 2008; the quoted summary here is taken from the *Directory of Open Access Journals* at: http://www.doaj.org/doaj?func=abstract&id=512397

Then, there is no more enemy

My enemy completes me.
--Elaine Pagels, **The Gnostic Gospels**

We all came into this world as members of the human race, without enemies. We can go out of this world the same way, when our time comes.

It's up to us.

The mysterious idea of "my enemy completes me" can be understood in many ways. My understanding is this: Once we incorporate the enemy into ourselves, once we complete ourselves and become whole by understanding that the enemy is me and I am the enemy, that I am you and you are me, then we are one. Then, there is no more enemy. The transformation is complete; together, we have transcended "enemies."

It's up to us.

Part II - NME for Israel and Palestine
(the idea is applied, locally)

The ones who hold the guns and shoot at us, the [soldier] who spit at you, they are not the makers of the war. The war makers are in comfortable offices in Beijing, Moscow, and Washington, D.C. It was a wrong policy born of a wrong understanding... A wrong perception was responsible for a wrong policy, and a wrong policy was responsible for the deaths of many thousands of American and Vietnamese soldiers, and several million Vietnamese civilians... If you nourish your hatred and your anger, you burn yourself. Understanding is the only way out.

--Thich Nhat Hanh, **The Heart of the Buddha's Teaching**

Nobody can be free alone. Not even a mage.

--Ursula K. LeGuin, **Tales from Earthsea**

The thrill of it all

When I first got involved in working for peace in Israel in 1981 at the age of 33, I was astounded to encounter the amazing adrenalin rush that came with discovering "the other" and experiencing our deep affinity for each other.

Certainly, games of war and death provide a rush; but that is not the only us/them rush available and, arguably, may not even be the best rush available. The war-and-death rush divides the self into a part that takes pleasure and a part that suppresses shame. In peace work, there is both joy and fear—fear of the unknown, and fear of the stranger—but there is no shame to be suppressed. No energy is wasted on hushing up the persistent inner voice that *knows* it's wrong to kill and maim and destroy.

These days, when I chat with Israeli Jewish young people doing their compulsory army service, they talk about the challenge, the self-discovery, the growth, the learning. My young nephew was inducted in 2009, after a year of community service in Jaffa. He opted for a combat role and was selected for a junior officers' course, which he completed with highest distinction. "Basic training was boring," he confided; "but this course has been great! I'm learning so many useful skills—how to manage people, to motivate my guys, to make sure they accomplish their mission…" Inwardly, as I listened, I flinched—thinking that "their mission" ultimately is killing and destroying. I was also thinking of my daughter Maya, at college in California at the time, talking in much the same terms about her intensive training as a CA (community assistant) in the dorm: learning to be responsible for monitoring the welfare of others, management skills, communication skills, counseling skills.

This put me in mind of an experience I had a few years back, visiting Palestinian Israeli friends on the coastal plain east of Caesarea. I spent one evening with my friend Ramzia, whom I've known for more than 30 years—since my volunteer days doing cooperative community work where she grew up, in Wadi Ara. Now a married woman and mother of six wonderful kids, Ramzia took me out for coffee at a café at the entrance to Umm al Fahm in the Wadi Ara hills. We reminisced unhurriedly for a while, enjoying a mild feminist thrill as two women choosing to sit outdoors together and talk at a café in a public place—of a kind frequented mostly by men and by married couples in a conservative Muslim city. Afterwards, Ramzia offered to drive me up to the highest point in the town, to see the historic tomb of Sheikh Iskander. Up we drove, then parked the car and walked around at the summit, enjoying the view. In one direction were the hills of Wadi Ara, lights twinkling in the houses; opposite, the Separation Barrier and, beyond that, the West Bank.

Palestinian laborers from the other side used to walk through Umm al Fahm (and through the town garbage dump, a daily humiliation) to catch rides or buses to work in Israel. The same route was also used on a few occasions by suicide bombers during more violent years. The barrier had now put a stop to all such foot traffic, innocent or otherwise. Designed to discourage militant infiltrators, it also deprives laborers of an income and families of a way to put food on the table, and keeps ordinary Israelis and Palestinians locked in their terrible isolation from each other.

When Ramzia and I had first met, both of us single, she was in her 20s, I in my 30s, it was the summer of 1981, and we still thought peace might be just around the corner. Now I was nearly 60 and Ramzia nearly 50, with 8 children between the two of us… but no peace in sight yet. Our friendship, however, had endured. We stood there on the windy hilltop by the tomb of Iskander and shared the bittersweet flavor of the moment, companionably, in silence.

I stayed overnight that night with my adopted kibbutz mom at her kibbutz about half an hour's drive from Ramzia's house. The kibbutz sits on the road that goes to Baka al Gharbiyye from the Border Guards junction (named for the rather phallic Border

Guards monument there) on route 65. In the morning as I drove out again on my way to work, I stopped on an impulse for a young woman soldier hitching a ride in the same direction, going to the bus stop on the main road. I like to talk to soldiers from time to time to hear what they have to say, even if it makes me sad or angry, which is often the case. So, too, on this particular morning.

"What do you do in the army, if it's not a secret?" I began, smiling encouragingly at her. She was a slender blonde and my first guess (a Russian immigrant) was verified by her accent when she began to speak.

"Oh, I work at a radar post at the border… next to Umm al Fahm, just inside the Fence," she confided.

Indeed! Probably within a hundred or so meters of where I'd stood the previous night with Ramzia, gazing at the Wall.

"And what do you think of the army?" I prompted her— whereupon I got the usual mantra about meeting all kinds of new people, being off on one's own away from home and family, learning new skills, broadening one's horizons, stretching one's abilities.

"And how is your job—for you?" I asked curiously.

"Oh well… not too bad, really," she confided earnestly. "I have a special night-vision camera attached to my surveillance equipment, and if I see anyone at the fence, I have to push a button and photograph them."

I nodded, visualizing it.

"Most of the time it's rather boring," she assured me. "And when something happens, it's not that bad. The girls who work along the Gaza border have a much tougher time at this job. They don't have a camera attached to their scope, like I do; they have a rifle."

She paused—earnest, thin, young, and painfully (to me) unaware. "Yes, in Gaza it's harder. If the girls on the job there see someone at the fence," she concluded, "they have to shoot them."

97

What's really going on here?

Many people abroad, people who don't have first-hand experience of Israel and Palestine, or who have very little first-hand experience, want very much to understand what is going on here.

When speaking to groups abroad, one has difficulty knowing where to begin, because the preconceptions and misconceptions are so vast, the myths so old and elaborated, the reality so nuanced and complex. Which thread to pull first? Which particular bit of misinformation or prejudice to attempt, in a nonthreatening and respectful way, to tackle? Which untruths, with disarming candor and a generous helping of empathy, to hold aloft for examination in the strong spotlight of today's confusing realities in Palestine and Israel? How to fill in the shades of gray, in twenty minutes or twenty hours, in the black-and-white mural that is most people's idea of what is going on in Israel/Palestine?

I was thinking lately that, for me, maybe the best way to begin is to look my audience straight in the eye and explain that what we have here in the (un)Holy Land is a very serious case of The Human Condition.

Things will change here when we dare to aspire to change the human condition.

In a way, all the rest is commentary.

Hostages to the old paradigm

I am encouraged to read about more and more Israelis and Palestinians who are coming to believe that they can live together amicably and productively. Meantime, too many are still absolutely persuaded of the impossibility of making common cause with the other group. So many Israeli Jews I know do not believe they can ever live as good neighbors with Palestinians. Yet, most of these same pessimists do not base their fearful conclusions on meaningful personal experience of Palestinians–because they have never had any meaningful personal experience with Palestinians as equals.

I have good news for those pessimistic Israeli Jews and for people abroad who think similarly. Not only are most of the Palestinians with whom I have lived and worked, wonderful potential partners in a creative shared future; many–very many–are still able to view Jews in Israel as potential added value in this place–despite the legalized theft that has deprived so many Palestinians of their land, and in spite of the vicious behavior of Israel's government even now (2010) as it continues to confiscate, uproot, evict and humiliate. Many–very many–Palestinians continue to distinguish between the intolerable and arrogant policies of the Israeli government and the basic humanity of ordinary Israelis. They know that the basic humanity of ordinary Israelis is not different, in kind or quality, for better or worse, than their own basic humanity.

Extremists there are, on both sides; but they can be and will be marginalized by the rest of us in a No More Enemies world.

True, there are also Palestinians who are not interested in making common cause with the other side: not because they are "extremist" but because they are fully convinced of the absolute rightness of their cause. Their people were displaced, uprooted, expelled, driven out, and are still being driven out; Israelis are, in their eyes, simply the usurpers. I think that, from the Palestinian standpoint, this view is certainly legitimate, but sticking to it has one insurmountable downside: To try to recreate the status quo ante would probably create more injustice than it redresses. Most Israelis and Palestinians alive today were not yet born in 1948 when Israel declared statehood, and a large plurality if not a majority on both sides was not yet born in 1967 when Israel occupied the West Bank and Gaza. Trying to simply roll the film backwards may turn out to be no answer at all, but rather the start of a whole new host of problems.

The entire population of Israel and Palestine is on some level being held hostage, all together, to the continuing hostilities. Both groups are captives of the *enemies* paradigm, which affords no clear way out of the trap we are in. Normal life is perpetually suspended due to the conflict. The only possible solution would seem to be to step out of that world—where we are enemies—and into a different world where we are not enemies. This step is first of all conceptual, and then can become real.

When enough Palestinians and Israelis step into that new world, declaring that former enemies are now partners, we can leave our nightmares behind. Our counterparts on the "other side"—doctor or ditch digger, textile worker or social worker, athlete or accountant—are there waiting for us, waiting to begin a whole new era wherein we are all major players and no one is dispensable or dehumanized, no one is disenfranchised or displaced. I have lived with "them" and I know it's possible. Many ordinary people here tell me that they can envision such a reality. The leadership, on the other hand—that's something else.

Our current leaders have a huge stake in the system as it is now. What does that suggest?

Comfort from inside the cage

When my young friend Sam in Al Bireh–a Palestinian-American who came to Palestine after Oslo, married and is raising a family here–finally was granted residence (in Palestine!) by the Israeli authorities, he began living with the entire reality of the Wall and the checkpoints from the inside, up close and personal, in a different way than formerly.

Until then, he had gone freely to the Israeli side and back again on his American passport and tourist visa (always assuming Israel would renew the visa every three months, which wasn't automatic and in fact did not always happen, but that's another tale[21]). Now he would be, as he put it with a somewhat strangled laugh at the time, "in the cage" with all the other local residents whose mobility is always at the whim of the occupation regime.

That's when the phrase "in the cage" entered my everyday usage. I found it shocking the first time he said it. On reflection, however, as time passes and the political situation does not improve, "in the cage" seems not only accurate but something of an understatement. How else to describe what it feels like to live behind barricades and continually negotiate checkpoints to go anywhere, with the continual presence of troops and the intermittent appearance of armored patrols, gunfire and tanks as part of the landscape of daily life? Try to imagine martial law on your own Main Street or at your mall, and you might get some small sense of the painful and humiliating texture of this kind of life–not just for yourself but also for your children, for the grandparents, everyone. And of course life on the West Bank these days (2010) is paradise compared to Gaza.

---

[21] Entry to and exit from the West Bank, which is possible only through Israeli-controlled crossings, became so problematical that an entire grassroots campaign was created to deal with it. See: http://www.righttoenter.ps/ In Gaza under Hamas rule, the situation at this writing (late 2010) is much worse.

A friend wrote to me from Germany of her visit to Nablus in 2009. Her hosts, a Palestinian professor and his wife, did a lot to cheer her up, she said. The dismal situation on the West Bank had cast her into despair. Her Palestinian friends, living under occupation every single day of their lives, had enough energy and optimism to help her recapture some optimism herself. How (she wondered) do they do that?

I was not surprised by her story. Sam often provides me with that kind of encouragement (mainly by email, now that popping into Jerusalem for a cup of coffee or a business meeting is a very involved undertaking, what with the permit applications and the humiliation and the delays).

Think how amazing it is that we who are basically free to do as we like, most of the time anyway, in Israel or abroad, are so often rescued from despair by the cheerful resilience and comradeship of Palestinians living under an occupation orchestrated by the government to whom we Israelis pay taxes. I find it almost miraculous that it is so often my Palestinian friends who model for me the way to live fully and joyfully as the best antidote to whatever else may be happening, however grim it may be.

I can anticipate the furious reaction of many of my "pro-Israel" friends here and abroad to these sentiments on my part. Don't Palestinians (they will demand to know) have any share in the responsibility for the situation in which they find themselves? Absolutely, I would say; they do. But, I would add, my concern as an Israeli is with the Israeli share of the responsibility (which most observers would say is the lion's share, but certainly by any measure has to be at least half, since there are two partners in this dysfunctional marriage). Have we, as a society, owned up to our share of the responsibility yet? I think not; although lately there seems to have been some progress, however slow and partial. People are beginning to wake up to the urgent need to find a different path.

Gotta have a vision beyond sanctions

Among the people engaged in the quest for a more humane future, a future vision is crucial–alongside the present struggle.

It is dangerous if people in the "progressive camp" do not have, or have but do not loudly promote, a clear positive future vision–because the Dominator types have a very clear vision and they promote it relentlessly, and they capture more youngsters with it every day.

Case in point: When Palestinian civil society organizations in Israel published a series of constructive "Future Vision" documents in 2006-2007,[22] they were mostly ignored. But the organizations behind this effort should persevere with it, and Israeli Jewish society should engage with it eagerly–immediately! Just taking that one step, and bringing Palestinian Israeli civil society activists into the inner circle of planning for Israel's future, would do more to guarantee Israel's future than any amount of defense spending on armaments.

Much of the world is starting (2010) to view Israel as a bunch of tribal barbarians because that is how the country's policies and behavior toward Palestinians–in Israel and in the occupied territories–have cast it. This new trend is positive in the sense that it emerges from a long overdue reassessment of reality, but it is useful only as an interim phase. What comes next? Do we change-agent types have a lively, vivid vision that beckons us toward constructive change? We must speak it clearly... If we do not, the obtuse official *hasbara* (state propaganda) comes to fill the vacuum we have left in the discourse.

---

[22] The first to appear was "The Future Vision of the Palestinian Arabs in Israel," The National Committee of Arab Mayors, 2006.This was a UNDP\UNOPS IN-TERPEACE Action in Israel. The three others were: "The Haifa Declaration," MA-DA al-Carmel, 2007; "The Democratic Constitution," Adalah, 2007; and "An Equal Constitution for All? On a Constitution and Collective Rights for Arab Citizens in Israel," Mossawa Center, 2007.

Do we or do we not hope that the movement for BDS (boycott, divestment and sanctions) will eventually become unnecessary? We who support it—are we or are we not working to "put ourselves out of business" as soon as possible?

If yes: We can invite all the world's artists and musicians to come later (not now) to celebrate.

Imagine a grand arts festival or peace concert in the year two thousand and something—pick a year. Let's say 2012, the year the Mayans or whoever it is say that the world as we know it now will end. So it's 2012 (or 2013 or 2014) and in Jerusalem where the wall now stands, at Abu Dis or somewhere, finally there is no more wall. The expensive concrete has been recycled into homes for former refugees; complete legal equality has been implemented for all people living in Palestine/Israel; everyone has voted in a plebiscite to learn to live together as equals, no exceptions, including women, and children, and people who profess no religion! The military forces of both sides have joined together into a Salvation Army whose chief function is to supervise and monitor an agreed-on, sane land redistribution program that attempts as fairly as possible to restore people to their original places insofar as practical, while compassionately dealing with those who have wittingly or unwittingly displaced them over the years. Given that uprooting people rarely works, and since stealing land is an unsustainable growth policy for any group, the solution has to be something that's more like sharing and partnership and does not rely on dominating others. And so forth.

When we ask an artist or actor or other cultural/creative person not to come here now, we can simultaneously invite them to this as-yet-unscheduled, future grand celebration and also invite them to work toward bringing it about.

Someone said: People can stand anything if they know it's going to end. The pain of violent abuse and oppression for Palestinians; the parallel pain of what Margaret Atwood called "the shadow" (of guilt and non-sustainability of Israeli actions and policies) for Israelis; the painful message of BDS—we have to know that there will be an end to all this, and a new beginning. Pain should not be the whole picture. What comes afterwards?

Unless we promote one, who else will promote a different vision of a post-sanctions horizon? —a vision that says, if you are brave enough to go through the difficult paradigm change for real justice for ALL the people living here, then there is something better out there awaiting you.

This message not only needs to be said, it needs to be reduced to a simple and unforgettable sound bite. And if we who consider ourselves activists don't believe in it ourselves, why should anyone else?

No More Enemies. A true partnership of equals.

Same idea, different timetable

I have heard, countless times, Jews abroad or in Israel ridiculing Palestinian exiles for remaining in refugee camps instead of getting on with rebuilding their lives elsewhere. Financially secure expat Palestinians who, one surmises, could do more for destitute refugees are also ridiculed for "letting them languish" in poverty and squalor. The countries hosting expatriate Palestinians also come in for their share of criticism for not moving to fully rehabilitate the refugees. The claim is made that "the Arabs" want to keep the Palestinian refugees in squalor as a political weapon against Israel. And so forth.

Considering that Israelis themselves belong to a group that has sanctified the meaning of a return to an ancestral homeland after millennia, this energetic critique is a curious reaction. Why would a Jew, who celebrates Jews' return to the Land of Israel after two thousand years, ridicule an exile from that very land who is unwilling, after only a few decades, to relinquish the dream of return to which generations of Jews have proudly clung for so much longer?

It's almost as if we thought we had the copyright on homesickness.

The ones who love the land that I, too, love—are not my enemies. They are my brothers and sisters.

We need one another. Not a single one of us is dispensable.

Calendars and diversity

Dostoevsky, I read somewhere recently, was born October 30, 1821 according to the Julian Calendar, and November 11, 1821 in the Gregorian calendar. Two birthdays!

In Israel and Palestine we have several different calendars functioning side by side: the Gregorian (essentially, today, a secular Western) calendar; the Hebrew or Jewish calendar; and the Muslim Hijri calendar. But the Druze community, a thousand-year-old offshoot of Islam whose members today number about a million worldwide, also has its own calendar. Moreover, various Christian religious groups celebrate some of the same holidays as others but on a different schedule, so that the Eastern Orthodox Easter, for example, typically does not fall on the same day as the Catholic or Protestant Easter. And there are smaller groups of residents and of migrants from Asia and Africa in Israel today, some of them doubtless following yet other calendars.

In January 2001 of the Gregorian calendar when the West embarked on a new millennium, the Jewish calendar year was 5761 and the Muslim Hijri year, 1421.

To complicate things still further, both the Gregorian and the Hebrew calendars incorporate a mechanism (leap years) to adjust lunar monthly time to solar yearly time. The Muslim calendar, by contrast, does not. Hence, Muslim holidays fall about 11 days earlier on the Gregorian calendar each year, moving back through the seasons from summer to spring to winter to fall in a stately cycle that repeats itself every 30 years. The Hebrew calendar, meantime, adds an extra month seven times in every nineteen years according to a complex formula. So the various Jewish holidays slip back a few days each year, until the start of the next cycle when the process begins again. In the Gregorian calendar, by contrast, there is only a quarter of a day's difference annually between the lunar and the solar cycles. Thus the adjustment of one extra day every four years is hardly significant except perhaps for people born on February 29th.

This diversity makes for a certain amount of confusion in a multicultural society, but also generates a shared richness that can be both instructive and enjoyable.

The Hand in Hand Association for Bilingual Education in Israel, which serves Jewish and Arab students from at least three religions, created a wonderful multicultural calendar-diary a few years after the organization's founding. The grassroots community action and training organization called Interns for Peace (established in 1978 in Israel by the late Rabbi Bruce M. Cohen) published a delightful wall calendar once upon a time, in the same spirit. The Oasis of Peace Primary School at the shared Arab-Jewish village of Wahat al Salam-Neve Shalom has educated generations of bilingual children for over 25 years by making extensive use of the cultural similarities and contrasts between different calendars and holiday traditions—in an approach debated, elaborated, and refined over the years by a dedicated staff.

Perhaps rich new learning, a certain degree of confusion, and the need for patience and understanding are all inherent aspects of culturally diverse contexts.[23]

---

[23] The Internet is full of calendar sites, and Wikipedia has a page just for leap years. For an informative overview of ten different religious calendars, some of which are used in Israel and Palestine, see, e.g.:
http://www.religioustolerance.org/rel_calendar.htm

Things I have done a thousand-and-one times with Arab Muslims

Here are some things I have done a thousand-and-one times with Arabs that you don't do with an enemy:

- Live (reside) upstairs, downstairs, or next door to one another.
- Laugh a lot together.
- Cook for each other.
- Share meals.
- Play with each other's children.
- Work together.
- Hug.
- Cry.
- Tell stories.
- Celebrate and mourn together: birthdays, deaths, accidents, graduations, weddings.
- Loan / borrow money.
- Watch movies on TV / at a cinema together.
- Watch the 2009 Obama inauguration on TV in Arabic with the family next door, while listening to the English broadcast on the Internet via earphones (just one time!).
- Borrow the use of each other's washing machines when ours were broken.
- Prepare traditional holiday sweets together.
- Drive each other to the airport.
- Visit friends and relatives in the hospital together.
- Shop for each other at the supermarket.
- Go walking together.
- Read each other's poetry.

The enemy within

Confusing as this may sound if you are unfamiliar with the demography of Israel and Palestine, some Palestinians are also citizens of Israel. In fact, of a total population of around 7 million Israelis, about 1.3 million Israeli citizens today are Palestinian Arabs (Muslim and Christian), meaning that nearly one in five Israeli citizens is also a Palestinian. (The rest of the Palestinians live either in the occupied Palestinian territory–i.e., in the West Bank and Gaza, or elsewhere in the Middle East or the rest of the world–i.e., in the Palestinian diaspora.)[24]

Speaking as a Jew I can say that, once you get to know some Palestinians really well, you know that they are not our enemy. Meantime, many Israeli Jews, including in the government and civil service, are not yet able to think of the Palestinian citizens of Israel as anything other than a fifth column: the enemy within.

I have a very clear idea of what constitutes "the enemy within" and there are no Palestinians in that picture.

Gandhi preached that the only real enemies we have are inside us, each of us, in our hearts–and that that is where we should be fighting our battles.

This is a crucial perspective, for a few reasons.

First of all, the only person's behavior we can really change, in the long run, is our own.

Secondly, our habit of searching out an enemy with whom to do battle is very strong and at least if we locate this enemy within ourselves, we can avoid the damage that comes from projecting the status of enemy onto others.

And thirdly, in Israel/Palestine as elsewhere, the habits of antagonism are insidious. Given our present mindset, without the

---

[24] For a clear and concise summary of who Palestinians are, written by Palestinians, see "About Palestinians" under "The Palestinian Community" on the Dalia Society web site, at: http://www.dalia.ps/node/13

Palestinian/Israeli struggle, the Jews in Israel would instead be battling each other—secular versus ultra-Orthodox Jews; Jews of European descent versus Jews of Middle Eastern and North African descent; lighter-skinned versus darker-skinned Jews; one rabbi's followers versus another's; and so on. And on the Palestinian side, likewise: Palestinian Muslims versus Palestinian Christians; secular supporters of the Palestine Liberation Organization versus religious supporters of Hamas; and so forth.

Hence, while we are retraining ourselves to think and to operate without the dynamic of enemies, we can at least contain the damage by keeping it inside—in our hearts. That way, the weapons of choice become, not guns and bombs and tanks, but meditation and yoga and study and prayer. This is a bloodless struggle, not easy but without violence. It is the genuine jihad of the devout, the inner quest for truth and justice and peace on this planet.

Our grandchildren will thank us.

On faith and coercion

I have lived with devout Muslims as neighbors and friends for some years and have tried to get a sense of what their religion means to them. They take from their faith, as far as I can tell, pretty much what other people I have known take from other religions, depending on the individual and the family and the community. Muslims who look, find universal concepts of justice and mercy in their Islam; those who prefer to emphasize more aggressive passages in scripture can always find some. Islam in this respect resembles other religions. (All traditional scriptures probably have verses we would rather leave behind.)

Every faith has its sublime truths, if we want to see them. Right now (2010), many non-Muslim people in the West are terribly afraid of Islam—but the many Muslims I know are really not at all scary. I wonder how many of the people who are afraid of Islam or of Muslims actually know any Muslims personally, or know anything about Islam other than the carefully selected bits of combative-sounding scripture that are dished out to us in shock videos about radical Islamic groups.

I wish people would just go back to basics. It seems to me that anyone can easily stay on the safe side of the line separating spiritual guidance from religious coercion. Relax. Surrender to God yourself! Let God organize the rest. Possibly the most authentic way to show others the light is to model an enlightened way. They will see, or not see—but it is not up to you. If you think it is up to you, you may be confusing yourself with God.

So long, thugs!

I dropped out of Barnard College in 1968. When I dropped back in again two years later to finish my degree, radical student activism had become an established part of the campus scene. Certainly at Columbia, SDS (Students for a Democratic Society) was a prominent player. One day there was an SDS-sponsored gathering downtown on the subject of Israel and Palestine. Out of curiosity, I decided to go and listen. As a working student, I hardly went anywhere except to class, to the library, and to work; I almost never had the leisure for time-intensive diversions like politics. But I had lived in Israel in 1966-67 and observed the Six-Day War as an eighteen-year-old working guest on a kibbutz near Israel's border with Jordan and Syria. Once back in New York, I followed the headlines with interest and was curious about what SDS in New York was promoting as a solution to that mess.

I was not then, and in my own view I have never become since, a bona fide "radical activist." Some of my steadfastly moderate civic convictions have increasingly been viewed as radical over the years, especially in Israel, as they have been gradually abandoned by the mainstream: one person, one vote; absolute equality before the law; universal suffrage; "blind" justice that makes no distinction as to color, religion, ethnicity, or national origin. Walking my own path, following that infinite learning curve which is the School of Life, I tried to learn what I could from listening to all kinds of views, radical or otherwise. In that mode, I hopped on the subway and went to this SDS meeting downtown.

Once inside, looking for a seat, I noticed that half a dozen grim-faced, broad-shouldered and thuggish-looking young men were stationed at the front of the hall to protect the security of the speakers. Aside from that, what I remember best about the gathering is the mass chanting of slogans: —"Palestine will win!"

113

and the like. This chorus sounded more like threats than aspirations. I knew nothing at that time about the Palestinian narrative, the Nakba, the view from the other side of the mirror. I had no context to help me make sense of the outrage, but I could feel it. I found the whole scene deeply disturbing, the more so because the audience was full of Jewish students. It seemed to me to border on the nihilistic for Jewish students to be screaming "Palestine will win" when the scenario evoked by such a slogan obviously entailed "Israel will lose." The air in the hall, suffused with deep anger, violent body language, violent rhetoric, and a kind of mob energy, filled me with aversion.

Over the decades since, I have gradually become convinced that the problem was not with the people or with their passionate thirst for justice, but with the old paradigm they had adopted to change things. A win-lose solution is always a non-solution, except in the short term; the winners know in their heart that their good fortune must come at the cost of someone else's loss, and the losers will always feel bad and will always comprise the germ of a reversal–often violent–of today's ostensible solution at some future time.

The ultra-radical critique of reality, featuring negative labels, a tendency to assign blame rather than shoulder responsibility, and theoretical historical analyses in terms of "isms" (racism, colonialism, Zionism), leaves out so much. Notably, in my opinion, the radical critique leaves out the real human motivations of most of the flesh-and-blood players and any indication of a way forward that welcomes everyone, without exception, as a potential participant in the solution.

The radical activism that was popular in my student days in the 1970s featured a lot of unwashed young guys posturing and analyzing and flexing their muscles, while the women mostly ran the mimeograph machines and made coffee. The resemblance to some of today's radical groups–minus the mimeograph machines, of course–is depressing. But the higher profile and arguably greater influence achieved by today's women activists, many of them clearly determined to humanize the political discourse, is encouraging.

As freedom fighters in various places around the world are moved to embrace the philosophy, rhetoric and tactics of non-violence, maybe thuggishness as a political tool of the self-appointed champions of the oppressed will go out of style. That would be a welcome change.

If I were Herzl, I'd be smarter than Herzl

If I were Herzl now, I hope I'd be smarter than Herzl was, back in the day.

There's an old story from the Jewish diaspora in Eastern Europe, maybe a hundred and fifty years ago. Two old Jews, Moishe and Yankel, are drinking a companionable glass of tea ("a glez tea"), and thinking about life and its impenetrable mysteries.

Suddenly Yankel says to Moishe, "You know what? If I were the Baron de Rothschild, merchant banker, I'd be even richer than Rothschild."

Moishe eyes him doubtfully. "What do you mean, richer? How?"

"It's easy," says Yankel, feeling rather clever. "I'd do a little teaching on the side."[25]

From the vantage point of the terrible human relations quagmire that is Israel/Palestine in the early 21st century, I can look back at Theodor Herzl (1860-1905), legendary father of Zionism, and know for a certainty that, visionary though he undoubtedly was, there were some serious holes in his thinking.

Herzl's Zionism was a movement born in relative if not absolute innocence as the national liberation movement of the Jewish people of Eastern Europe and wherever else they might need to be liberated from; a movement designed to give the archetypal "wandering Jew" a home of his own and end his millennia of often bitter exile as a frequently unwelcome guest in other people's countries. It all began in the late 1800s; long before Hitler.

Influenced by the revolutionary nationalist fervor percolating all around him in the Europe of his day, Herzl envisioned a Jewish state in Palestine and was able to promote his vision so suc-

---

[25] I read it in *A Treasury of Jewish Folklore*, ed. Nathan Ausubel (New York: Crown, 1963).

116

cessfully that it eventually came into being—helped along by waves of dedicated volunteers, serious philanthropy, political maneuvering, and world events, including but not limited to the sincere desire of many Europeans to make amends for past anti-Semitism and, more specifically, for complicity in the Nazis' Final Solution for the "Jewish problem."

But I'd bet my last dime that Herzl never foresaw an Israel that would construct "Jews only" roads on the West Bank, steal land and water from Palestinian Arab farm families to build upscale new Jewish towns with green lawns and swimming pools, become infected with rampant xenophobia, and permit religious extremists to gradually take over the country's army. I'm sure Herzl never foresaw the transformation of large Palestinian Arab population centers into open-air prisons where upwards of 3.5 million ordinary men, women and children are warehoused indefinitely in a precarious parody of normal life, while too many of the jailers—ordinary Israeli Jews—carry on experiencing themselves as eternal victims.

Herzl surely never foresaw that the eventual price to be paid, for transforming Jews from downtrodden residents of ghettoes surrounded by hostile gentiles, would include creating ghettoes for gentiles—surrounded by hostile Jews.

If I'd been Herzl, I'd have been smarter than Herzl.

I'd have made sure to do a lot more culturally sensitive, historically timely, creative social engineering on the side.

But anyhow I wasn't and he didn't, and that was then and this is now. Our century is going to be the century of interdependence and co-evolution. Today's young people, linked globally by the cyber networks, know something that Herzl arguably could not have foreseen in 1900: the "Jewish problem" and the "Palestinian situation" are one. United we stand; divided we fall. No more enemies. We have a lot of work to do.

What, the Greeks too?

When I turned 30, I gave up my conventional life as a single professional woman in Manhattan and signed on in the spring of 1981 for a two-year volunteer commitment to work for Jewish-Arab cooperation in Israel, beginning the following September. I wanted some kind of break—an interlude—between the old movie and the new one. My sister in southern Israel arranged for me to spend the summer working on her kibbutz in the desert. Perfect! I decided that instead of flying there, which would lift me out of my old life and deposit me in the new one less than 24 hours later, I would go by boat. That way, I'd have a relaxing break in which to get myself mentally prepared and reoriented.

I bought a ticket on a Greek container ship and was one of only five passengers. The other four were two retired American couples. The crew below decks was all South Asian. The officers were Greek. All five of the passengers dined at the captain's table daily in the homey little officers' mess. Two weeks at sea afforded plenty of time to talk with these men during the day, when they weren't busy, as well as over dinner in the little dining room.

The ship's officers, mostly young, pretended politely to be interested in what I was planning to do on my arrival in Israel: working to help mend some deep flaws in Israeli society, helping to promote greater equality—it was my number one topic, all the time. One day I found myself explaining indignantly to Xavier, the first officer, that a Jew and a non-Jew could not marry in Israel because, unlike the democratic norm in the USA, the country had no civil marriage at all: Jews were married by a rabbi in a Jewish ceremony, Christians in a church, Muslims according to Islamic law, and so forth. I thought of this as highly undemocratic because intermarriage, while not actually forbidden, was technically impossible unless the couple went abroad to be married. What kind of society in this day and age (I expostulated) still tries

118

to dictate to its citizens whom they should marry, and where, and how?! And so forth.

When I was all done and stopped for breath, Xavier had a surprising response. "There is no civil marriage in Greece, either," he said.

"What?" I couldn't believe it.

"No: none. Greek Orthodox people are married in their church; Jews are married in their synagogue; and so on…"

This was a very important turning point for me.

In retrospect, after all these years, I'm amused to recall how amazed I was to be reminded that other countries are also afflicted by imperfect social policies and also suffer from imperfect domestic democracy. Somehow it seems important to be aware of this context; not to struggle any less wholeheartedly to fix what might be broken in Israel, but to stay grounded in a broader context while so engaged.

Nowadays, apologists for various Israeli policies that violate international law like to cry foul because, they say, there are so many other nations doing the same sorts of things to unfortunate populations elsewhere in the world. Why, they demand to know, does the world focus so exclusively (it sometimes seems) on Israel? I find something really repulsive in this strategy of expiation by comparison and contrast. Nonetheless, I do think it is important to understand what goes on elsewhere. When people ask me why I'm not concerned about sins on the Palestinian side, however, I say that, as an Israeli Jew, I am not responsible for their sins, only for ours. But it is helpful to strive for clarity and to reach for the broadest possible perspective.

As activists struggling to repair our own society, we can easily lose sight of the imperfections of other societies. This is risky, not because the faults of others should make us less anxious to correct our own faults (they shouldn't), or because the sins of others somehow render our own sins more palatable (they don't). It is risky because an ignorance of the realities in other societies can, by skewing our judgment, inordinately discourage and depress us regarding our own.

Kill a Turk and rest / Another Jew dead

Legend has it that, once upon a time, a worried Jewish mother in Czarist Russia sending her newly conscripted son off to fight the Turks would admonish him: "Kill a Turk and rest; kill a Turk and rest." The phrase came to Israel with immigrant Jews decades ago and persists to this day in Hebrew, as a commonly used synonym for "Take it easy; what's the hurry?" When people use this phrase in ordinary conversation, they seem unaware of any note of aggression, of any disparagement of Turkish people, or of violence.[26] But it turns out that this phenomenon (like so much else here) crosses borders, too.

My young friend Luis, a Jewish peace activist who is a fluent Arabic speaker, once told me a story in this vein, from the other side of the looking glass, as it were. "I was visiting very old friends in the Galilee," he related. "This was a Christian Arab family. And as we're sitting around in the living room, just being together, from time to time someone would break the silence by saying, 'Another Jew dead.' So we sat there and, every once in a while, someone would say–in Arabic, of course: 'Another Jew dead.' They had obviously forgotten that I am a Jew, or forgotten what the words meant." It was a kind of mantra, like *ahlan wa'sahlan* ("you are welcome here"), uttered automatically as a way of punctuating the silence.

Luis felt a dilemma: to mention this, or not to mention this, to his friends? "On the one hand, it made me uncomfortable that they would say that," he explained to me; "yet at the same time, I realized it was 'just a phrase.' I knew if I brought it up, it might ruin a very pleasant friendship; and yet, if I did not bring it up, I would go on feeling uncomfortable."

---

[26] Journalist Amira Hass wrote about this: "What does the Turk have against us?" *Haaretz*, September 29, 2004. Retrieved at: http://www.haaretz.com/print-Niraion/opinion/what-does-the-turk-have-against-us-1.136059

121

In the end, he raised the issue and, as he had foreseen, after all the apologies and explanations on the part of his horrified hosts, who had intended no insult to him or even to Jews in general—the easy harmony of their old relationship was irrevocably altered. Not ruined; but somehow damaged.

Maybe that's part of the price we all have to pay to stretch our awareness until everyone on earth can come in from the rain and shelter under the same umbrella, together.

Cousins

An Israeli, Tsvi Misinai, a high-tech type, has taken on the mission of spreading the news of the extent to which Israeli Jews and Palestinian Muslims share the same genetic profile. He sees it as a mission to promote mutual acceptance and peace. You can see him on video,[27] very much in the spirit of Don Quixote, handing out printed literature to Palestinian men at a checkpoint, sitting in a Palestinian home in a remote West Bank village and interviewing the old people about their Jewish customs (laying *tefillin*, not lighting fires on Shabbat, circumcising male babies at the age of one week which is a Jewish custom not followed by Muslims, and so on).

Meanwhile one of the Hebrew University geneticists who participated in the research points out, not without humor, that even brothers pursue terrible feuds, and that the undeniable genetic link between Israelis and Palestinians may not be enough to bring us the yearned-for era of cooperation.

I look at it differently. I figure: Abraham's women in the bible, Sarah (the wife) and Hagar (the servant) had a nasty feud happening about whose son would inherit. Heaven knows that in our era, this sort of thing goes on all the time, and moreover supports legions of divorce lawyers and psychotherapists. But now there is ADR (alternative dispute resolution). Now we've discovered or rediscovered the art of mediation, which is a much less adversarial approach to conflict resolution than litigation. Arab culture has the *sulha*, with local and regional variations. Other traditional societies, including many aboriginal cultures, have their own analogs to the West's ADR. We can draw on these systems to create a

---

[27] Retrieved at: http://www.ireport.com/docs/DOC-279707# and see more at
http://mwiner.wordpress.com/2009/07/15/palestinians-of-jewish-origin/
Meantime Leah, a young Israeli blogger at www.mideastyouth.com suggested that Jewish origins should give all Palestinians a right of return to Palestine/Israel under Israel's (Jewish) law of return! Now, that's creative...

123

new, integrated approach to resolving this and other conflicts. Let's get with the new spirit of things, and end this vicious feud once and for all. If everyone in Palestine and Israel starts taking better care of the land together, there will be enough to go around for everyone.[28]

[28] In fact, co-environmental activism by Jews, Palestinians, Jordanians, and others has been in progress now for some years. This is where we should be investing our efforts together. For three examples online, check out the web sites of the Arava Institute for Environmental Studies and look at the water-related projects of the Israel-Palestine Center for Research and Information and Friends of the Earth Middle East.

Time's up!

Loyalty to an idea can persist long past the time when any neutral observer already knows that the idea is dead.

In her fascinating account of the development of an accurate way to enable mariners to measure longitude, and thus to have reliable information about their location and trajectory at sea, Dava Sobel points out that "any line drawn from pole to pole may serve as well as any other for a starting line of reference. The placement of the prime meridian is a purely political decision." [29]

And indeed, around AD 150, the prime meridian ran through what are now the Canary and Madeira Islands just northwest of Africa. Nearly two millennia and many changes of location later, Sobel recounts, after numerous cities had enjoyed the honor of serving as ground zero for the global timekeeping system, the prime meridian "settled down at last in London."

The lone genius who finally created a timepiece accurate enough to work in stormy seas, in varying temperatures, and despite a ship's motion, was an Englishman, John Harrison. But that does not seem to be the main reason the world calculates both longitude and time today using the city of Greenwich (outside London) as the baseline. The person credited with locking in the honor for England is Nevil Maskelyne, fifth Astronomer Royal of England. Maskelyne calculated longitudes from the royal observatory there in each of the 49 volumes of his *Nautical Almanac*, from 1767 to 1811. Everyone relied on those almanacs. Finally it seemed that the home base for figuring out where you are on this planet was going to be a British home base, forever after.

Meanwhile France—another country with a lot of effort invested in this field over a long period—was quite reluctant to cede this

---

[29] Dava Sobel, *Longitude: The True Story of a Lone Genius Who Solved the Greatest Scientific Problem of His Time* (London: Fourth Estate Limited, 1998, p.4).

honor to the rival English. Sobel relates that more than two dozen countries voted in 1884 to designate, once and for all, "the Greenwich meridian [as] the prime meridian of the world. This decision did not sit well with the French, however, who continued to recognize their own Paris Observatory meridian, a little more than two degrees east of Greenwich, as the starting line for another twenty-seven years, until 1911. (Even then, they hesitated to refer directly to Greenwich mean time, preferring the locution 'Paris Mean Time, retarded by nine minutes twenty-one seconds.')" (p.168)

French national pride sought for a long time to deny what the rest of the world could easily see: Greenwich, England had already won that particular race.

Such dilemmas are not all that unusual. They happen, with variations, all over the world. Possibly one of the few things sadder than a well-intentioned project that has morphed into something destructive and toxic, or merely ridiculous, is the human urge to cling to it anyway, long past the point of diminishing returns.

I would hope that Jewish Israelis and Jews around the world will be able to see that they are making the same kind of mistake about the current meaning and future potential of the Zionist movement. Because it grew from an unsustainable premise ("A land without people for a people without a land"), the Zionist enterprise was destined to face a hard choice somewhere down the line: reinvent itself, or crash and burn. I am one of those who would like to see it reinvent itself and, necessarily, rename itself as well, in some generous and creative way that brings the cousins back into the family.

126

Towards intelligent redesign

It is worth emphasizing that *Cradle to Cradle: Remaking the Way we Make Things* by William McDonough and Michael Braungart is a must read for anyone aspiring to help make deep, meaningful change in Palestine and Israel, or anywhere else. I mentioned them in Part I under "See the pattern," the first time I used the phrase "time to redesign." Their insights are too extensive to cover even a fraction of them in these pages. Let's make do with noting a few ways that I think McDonough and Braungart's ideas for addressing environmental and economic issues could be used or adapted for our quest for a future of partnership.

Imagine recasting the Israel/Palestine problem and other stubborn conflicts as design challenges instead of moral, political, historical, or religious ones. In nature, of course, nothing is wasted; whereas in dysfunctional inter-group situations like Palestine/Israel, vast resources are wasted.

Design challenges simply don't reference issues of blame very much; this is very much in the No More Enemies spirit. Even the best-intentioned analysts of the Middle East's problems too often frighten "the other side"–which ultimately is not really productive–because they always seem to need someone to blame. Now that the pendulum in world opinion is shifting away from Israel's perspective, does anyone think that Israeli Jews are less enraged and afraid when their interests are disparaged, than the Palestinians were all this time while <u>their</u> interests were being disparaged? Blame is a terrible waste of energy.

McDonough and Braungart redefine traditional terms in very interesting ways. For example, they offer the concept of "a product of service" instead of just "a product": This means that, instead of buying a television from a company, you could buy ten thousand hours of TV-watching but the TV would remain the ɔperty of the maker, who would worry afterwards about recycling (or, better still, "upcycling") its component materials.

The relevance of these ideas to Israel and Palestine is in the orientation toward rethinking what a transaction, or a situation, consists of.

What is sovereignty, for example? Why must there always be an exclusive, one-to-one relationship between sovereignty and geography?[30] Could land ownership be understood differently? – as land use, custodianship, stewardship, etc.? Does violent competition over land honor it, or the reverse? And so forth.

In making their case so brilliantly for total redesign approaches, McDonough and Braungart revamp the lexicon accordingly. In their environmental context, for instance, in the "product of service" concept: waste is viewed like food; materials in products are nutrients in a nutrient flow; and "products" are no longer "bought" by "consumers." Instead, "customers" purchase the "services of a product" for a "defined user period." The producer retains ownership of the nutrients and reuses them afterwards.

In their discussion of these and other concepts, the authors turn the customary economic incentives upside down. This sort of creative reversal is what's needed in conflicts like Israel/Palestine. The new model also encourages mutually beneficial, long term relationships between suppliers, producers, and customers. Everyone wins, including the environment.

I used to think of Einstein's dictum that "you can't solve a problem on the same level where it was created" as being about

---

[30] The idea of parallel sovereignty is treated in depth in two essays of mine online; see "Parallel Sovereignty for Israel/Palestine: Beyond the Onion of Blame" (2002) at: http://www.counterpunch.org/reich1030.html and "Calling All Semites" (2006) at: http://baltimorechronicle.com/2006/090506REICH.html . The Center for Middle East Studies at Lund University in Sweden sponsored research in the same mode, in its Parallel States Project in 2008-2010, with a phase II being considered at this writing (November 2010). A good overview of proposed alternative solutions for Palestine and Israel is available online from Howard Cort at http://www.approachestocoexistence.com/Approaches%20to%20Coexistence.html

128

physics and mathematics. Maybe it's also a design challenge–
which means that anyone with imagination can play.

Parallel sovereignty: why not?[31]

The notion of parallel sovereignty, or parallel states, for Israel and Palestine is a bold and forward-looking idea. There is an urgent need to bridge the disconnect between such creative new ideas and the leadership on the ground. Imagination is the main resource.

At the point when you are poised to begin mapping out the detailed implementation of a proposed new paradigm, that is not the time to retreat to old thinking. To do so would sink the effort. Instead, all kinds of assumptions must be reexamined so that new thinking can be brought into play, to support the process and inspire the people as they address implementation on the ground.

Here are three examples of what I mean:

One: There is a longstanding assumption that Palestinians and Jewish Israelis are rivals, adversaries, competing in a zero sum game. What if we decide instead to see them in a relationship of *hevruta*? Hevruta is the traditional study duo in a yeshiva, a Jewish institution of learning–consisting of a pair of students who study together, question each other, urge each other on to succeed, test each other and, in short, learn together. This particular idea has natural appeal for religious Jews who study using hevruta for many years and are familiar with its advantages: One never, for example, dismisses or belittles a partner's comments. Rather one listens, encourages and, when possible, assists. If the whole world were to run itself on the hevruta model, that would be dandy.

---

[31] These reflections on jurisdiction under a Parallel Sovereignty arrangement are a rewrite of the notes I made in preparation for the October 2008 closing conference of the two-year Parallel States Project at the Lund University Center for Mideast Studies in Lund, Sweden, where I had been invited to comment on the speakers' presentations on issues of jurisdiction. The session ran late so most of the comments were not delivered.

Two: We are all conditioned to think about social justice in terms of people's rights–individual rights, collective rights, human rights; and in terms of the denial of rights, restoration of rights, etc. We view this reality as a struggle from imperfect situations vis-à-vis rights, toward more perfect situations. What if we began, in addition, to give more emphasis to the people's potential *contribution*, rather than focusing only on their obtaining their rights? If people have energy to give (talent, work, commitment–all forms of energy), and if we have not arranged things, including provision of their basic rights, so as to evoke, permit, encourage, enable them to give their best energies–then we are wasting energy from the shared system, and robbing everybody of the potential benefits.

Three: Edward de Bono, the famous British author who has spent decades exploring better approaches to the teaching and learning of how to think more effectively, wrote a book called *Six Thinking Hats*[32]. He distinguishes different types of thinking by the color of the hat worn while engaging in each, and suggests a framework for using this approach in management and planning. Not only does it offer a way to make meetings more productive; it also decouples the thinking style (emotional, cautious, objective, creative, etc.) from personalities and defuses conflict in the meeting. This idea could be adapted for parallel sovereignty planning, maybe: to partially decouple the historical narratives, or at least the woundedness they signify, from the future.

There are other such ideas floating around cyberspace. The implementation of an innovative model like parallel sovereignty will falter if its proponents lose the courage to look ahead and not back. This is a special challenge in terms of jurisdiction and law, because the law is a field based so solidly on precedent. Economic teams may have an easier time being bold. Look at the

---

[32] Edward de Bono, *Six Thinking Hats* (New York: Back Bay Books / Little, Brown and Company, 1999 [revised and updated]).

131

upheaval in intellectual property ideas due to the Internet, the digital age, etc. No one knows precisely where all that is going, but clearly the new era won't be like the old era. Crafting jurisdiction solutions for a parallel sovereignty future will require boldness, too.

Jurisdiction solutions, like all the proposed solutions under novel sovereignty arrangements, will ultimately have to be solved by, and the solutions sold to, people of differing cultures, including subcultures within the macro societies. This challenge is best viewed, I think, as a design challenge. My inspiration here, once again, is *Cradle to Cradle*'s McDonough and Braungart. Their book addresses green design and building, not governance issues, but many of the principles are transferrable.

We all know that jurisdiction is an idea, and an unstable one at that—susceptible to differing culturally charged understandings, and therefore a fertile doorway to misperceptions and unintended consequences down the road. At the same time, cultural diversity around the meaning of various aspects of jurisdiction offers a very rich substratum of resources. These multicultural riches could be utilized to help round out the new package of innovative jurisdictional structures. Then, as time goes on, the same multicultural resources can help develop, elaborate, adapt, explain, translate, and ultimately "sell" this package to an exhausted populace wary of promises and afraid even to hope.

Even the term "jurisdiction" itself of course has a cultural bias. It is about the exercise and limits of authority, power, control, law. Some exercise it, some are subject to it. In a cultural milieu in which all parties—those governing and those governed—were linked in a more organic wholeness, a different picture would arise, perhaps, in which governing and governed are one, or anyhow co-arising, as a Buddhist might say. We would not speak of jurisdiction between a mother and child, probably. Where one party seeks to empower the other in partnership, the only jurisdiction that makes sense is going to have certain qualities: it is shared, mutual, interactive, interdependent, flexible, and changing over time as the parties grow and change.

I suggest that in looking at jurisdiction under novel governance arrangements, researchers and planners cast their net of inspiration as wide as possible—to tap into the largest range of avail-available paradigms from many different directions and fields. There is a lot of help out there, disguised as many other things. But potentially—help is out there, waiting. This sort of project could probably benefit from having an ombudsman or ombudswoman, with a background in anthropology or some other likely field and perhaps with a multidisciplinary background.

Ideally, all the civilians in the target area could be encouraged to think of themselves as participants in this fascinating project, rather than objects or pawns. "Parallel Sovereignty Project Associate" has more cachet than "resident of a permanent war zone" or "victim of an intractable hundred-year conflict," etc. If citizens could think of themselves as Project Associates, they could share in the world's appreciation of their courage and foresight in creating a new path, together.

Antonio Machado said it so well: *Caminante, no hay camino; se hace camino al andar.* Traveler, there is no path; the path is made by walking.

Given the terribly grim situation on the ground now (the end of 2010) in Gaza, the West Bank, East Jerusalem and, spiritually and politically, in Israel too—probably we should be running, not walking, to create our own path.

133

Yet another child with a gun

When I engage Israeli youngsters of army age (18-22) in casual conversation, as noted earlier, I like to ask about what they are doing in the army and what they think about it.

One morning at a café outside Jerusalem, there was a new young waitperson I had not met before. Call her Gal.

I asked how long she had been working here ("almost two days!") and what she is studying ("haven't had time yet–just got out of the army"). I always ask youngsters what they are studying as a form of aunt-ish encouragement: If they are working on a degree, I applaud that; if they are not contemplating continuing their education, I express my amazement–a youngster with so much potential, not planning to go to university?–and point out that they might reconsider. I do this in the firm belief that some-times all it takes to boost a youngster's self-esteem is one adult, even a stranger, who seems to believe in their potential. Anyway I can't see how it can hurt.

"So what did you do in the army, if I may ask?" I pursued, as always. (So far, no one's job has been so secret that they couldn't at least hint at what it consisted of.)

"Combat soldier," she replied. This is not the typical response from a young woman conscript.

"Oh, really?" I said. Such a little slip of a thing, such a young and open face… "Doing what?" (Maybe a medic? Or a commu-nications officer?)

"You know–carrying a rifle all the time–that stuff. And *milium* too"–annual reserve duty, which women are asked to do, along with the men, only if their army role is one that the new con-scripts can't do instead, or can't do well enough).

"Really? Whereabouts did you serve?"
"Egypt."
Egypt? "You mean, on the Egyptian front?"

A nod and a smile.

"So why did you choose a combat unit?" I pursued.

"You know—to give the most. To contribute my utmost. That's what you can do in a combat role."

That's what they all say. It's always about learning new things, stretching toward new horizons, testing oneself, meeting new people, all kinds of people who are different from the people back home... and, for those who are inclined to leadership, it's often about officer training and the path to leadership of one's peers. These are precisely the kinds of things that children in more fortunate environments cite as the benefits of going on to higher education, to college or university or art school or medical school.

This child, too, in some alternate universe, would be stretching her wings at college instead of at some border outpost in the desert, toting a rifle. She'd be giving her utmost in judo class or on the tennis team or in the *a cappella* vocal ensemble.

Another child with a gun. Every single one is one too many, in my opinion.

Standard terminology department

If he's one of ours and he's under 30, even if he's wearing a uniform and carrying a gun, he's a youngster or a boy: one of *our boys*.

If he's one of theirs, he's a terrorist, even if he's 12 years old and standing, with or without a rock in his hand, in a schoolyard.

This is how dehumanization happens: word by word.

Demonizing people may feel good, but it's dumb

Repeat after me: It's the paradigm, not the people.

Many attempts to vilify an entire national group, or any very large population group, are based on some kernel of truth because, in any large population group (including mine, and yours), most of the people will do mildly bad things sometimes, and some of the people will do really seriously bad things quite often.

The pendulum of world opinion has lately begun to reverse itself on the Israel/Palestine question: from blind support for Israel no matter what Israel does, to demonizing Israel, all Israelis, and Jews in general for the sins of Israel's government and the prejudices of some of its population. As the pendulum swings, there are some factors worth bearing in mind:

Millions—repeat, millions-- of Israelis choose to live abroad because they want no part of the violent, ugly reality at home *and they either have a second passport or are fortunate enough to gain residency in some other country on economic, professional, or family grounds.* Israel's population, of whom 20 percent are actually Palestinians, is officially 7+ million. My guess is that hordes of these folks who are counted as living here, are probably living abroad, de facto. Many who are still in Israel are still here only because they have no choice; no alternative; nowhere else to go. They are the least powerful and the most scared; they know they are trapped indefinitely in this death dance with Palestinians. The fear translates to aggression and plays nicely into the hands of the military-industrial elite that runs the country[33].

---

[33] On the concentration of wealth and power in Israel, see, e.g., "How do the powerful families affect your life?" by Ora Coren, *Haaretz*, July 21, 2010, retrieved at: http://www.haaretz.com/print-edition/business/how-do-the-powerful-families-affect-your-life-1.303126
Or "The Controversy Over Israel's Business Elite" by David Wainer and Calev Ben-David, *Bloomberg Businessweek*, October 7, 2010, retrieved at http://www.businessweek.com/magazine/content/10_42/b4199010761878.htm

So, dear reader, you can go ahead and vilify the ordinary Israeli, or anyhow the ordinary Jewish Israeli, if it makes you feel better, but you won't be moving us any closer to a just resolution of the dilemma of Palestine/Israel.

Better to revile the policies and refrain from demonizing the people. That leaves the door open to a paradigm shift in which Israelis could constructively participate, helping to reframe and redesign the Israeli-Palestinian relationship.

Now that the world's long-overdue outrage and solidarity on behalf of Palestinians is gaining momentum, it would be a tremendous lost opportunity to simply flip the game–switching the hats, as it were. This would only set the stage for another useless round of historical injustices in the other direction. We have an opportunity today to *change the game*. Let's go there!

In addition, as I am fond of pointing out, the vast majority of Israelis alive today had no role in the injustices of 1948 because they weren't born yet; and the vast majority of Palestinians alive today had no role in accepting, or rejecting, pre-State Jewish immigration or Zionist demands because most Palestinians now alive weren't born back then, either. What is the point of demonizing today's younger generations for choices made before they were born? Wouldn't it be more sensible to work with them to redesign the paradigm together?

No More Enemies.

Toward a polychromatic future

I have often wondered if the Jewish Israeli fundamentalists who want to expel all Arabs, foreigners, non-Jews, etc., and create a country with only people like themselves in it, have ever truly taken the time to look down the road at the ultimate outcome of what they aspire to do. The same is true, from the other perspective, of fundamentalist Palestinian ultra-nationalists. Imagine how the reality would look if these "us and us only" advocates (on either side) were ever to succeed. Their essentially sterile model of a monochromatic country with all its diversity flushed away could never work.

To begin with, the Jews of Israel are themselves a hugely diverse population with a vast range of geographic, linguistic, and religious traditions and lifestyles, some considered wildly heretical by other Jews in a way that offers very little ground for compromise. And this is before you even get to the fledgling movement for feminism within Orthodox Judaism. That movement features the courageous deconstruction of Jewish tradition to try to tease out the threads of social conservatism that deny women full partnership in religious life, while leaving the spiritual mosaic of Judaism intact and perhaps stronger for that effort.

If the extremist Jewish zealots' monochromatic paradigm is not rejected once and for all by Israeli society in favor of a much more universal and inclusive vision, then the moment these zealots get their longed-for objective of a country with no "non-Jews" in it, the conflict will simply shift into the "Jewish-only" arena and continue unabated, Jew against Jew.

The hard-line Jewish nationalists who want all others evicted can offer only an unsustainable foundation of discrimination against Jews who differ or who are different, or who are deemed "not Jewish enough." This approach offers thought control disguised as Torah learning, with the strictest interpretations of *ha-*

139

lakha (Jewish law) becoming the only permitted interpretations, and with rule by force complete with vigilante hit squads to enforce codes of modesty and so on. What a bleak picture!

But there is an even more profound basis on which to critique any such plan, and it has to do with the inherent value of diversity in the first place. There may be lots of diversity within the Jewish world in Israel and elsewhere, but designing a country around "us Jews and only us Jews" is nevertheless not a diversity-friendly program.

The simplest path to a healthy diversity is to stop labeling those who are different as the enemy, and bring them into the circle as full partners.

"Diversity," as McDonough and Braungart put it, "is nature's design framework." Instead of trying to minimize, or (how ridiculous it sounds!) even *eliminate* diversity, we need to be fostering it. Resilience is crucial for sustainability, and diversity is crucial for resilience.

The fantasy of finality

Most people my age can probably recall that, every decade or so when we were young, newspaper headlines would announce that some scientists somewhere had finally found what they were sure was the smallest particle of matter. Then, maybe a decade later, other researchers with improved instruments would find a particle even smaller. This scenario repeated itself with almost predictable regularity but, each time, the folks were certain that *now, finally* they had found the smallest, completely indivisible, particle in existence. This quaint idea appears in other fields, too: the end of history turns out not to be the end! And so forth.

I suggest, with the greatest respect to the devout believers in the various religious faiths, that the last prophet hasn't been heard from yet, either. There is something that doesn't compute in the idea that, somewhere out there, an omnipotent and compassionate Deity periodically sends humanity a prophet to help them find their way back to the high moral ground but that, at some point, He would stop sending any more such help.

I wonder if "this is the last word!" isn't a guy thing, maybe–at least in the West. Maybe in Western culture, the average guy tends to worry more about his legacy while a woman worries more about the kids' legacy. An Ursula K. LeGuin character once noted that men are afraid of women because, while men look at things in terms of what's good for this generation, women are looking at things in terms of what's good for the next generation. Meantime I once read that business decisions in Japan–in an earlier era, before the process was corrupted by the tyranny of the quarterly financial report and global stock markets–were taken only after considering the probable impact of each available option seven generations down the line.

Clearly pluralism, as a value, could go a long way toward rescuing Israelis and Palestinians from themselves. But pluralism has a time dimension as well as a dimension of thought and action in the present moment. The pluralistic orientation that can be comfortable with a diversity of ideas and interpretations now, could probably also allow for the flow of change to stream on into the future. If "this-is-the-final-word-on-this-subject" is permitted to damn up the flow, then are not stagnation and decline inevitable? Is the future of the Holy Land necessarily limited to copying the scenarios from the historical past? Is there some reason why co-operation and partnership among all the peoples who identify with this land cannot be the vibrant and fascinating story of its future?

No More Enemies.

Reframing *sumud*

Sumud is the Arabic word for steadfastness, and during the decades of Palestinian displacement and disenfranchisement, sumud has come to stand for an entire strategy, personal and communal, in the face of organized oppression and loss.

Over the years, Palestinians have achieved something else apart from standing fast, something important that has gone largely unremarked.

If by their steadfastness in refusing to be uprooted, Palestinians have proven, once and for all, that human communities ought not be displaced by force because that sort of arrangement is unsustainable and only leads to more suffering; if they have demonstrated conclusively that the long global history of migration and its unkind twin of expulsion, a history of the extension and rearrangement of sovereignty and hegemony by force, should give way to some finer and more consensual way of ordering human affairs—then Palestinians have done humanity a great service.

And in the same spirit: If by constituting or reconstituting a Jewish peoplehood based on a group identity centuries or millennia old, however historically accurate or historically inaccurate the idea of that identity is theorized to be, Israelis have proven once again that, in animating an ideal and inspiring great love for that ideal over the generations, myth can be even stronger than reality—then Israelis have done humanity a great service.

These two groups are natural partners to nurture a vibrant shared stewardship of the land they both love. Possibly the main thing delaying the realization of this vision is fear. The power that makes fear dispensable is love.

143

A translator's moment

At one point while I was working on this book, I was also doing a translation, from Hebrew to English, of a memoir written by a Jewish man originally from Riga, Latvia, telling the story of his and his comrades' lives just before, during, and after World War II. The narrative focused on their commitment to the Zionist movement as a path to reclaiming the ancient Jewish homeland in Palestine and redeeming Jews from 2,000 years of exile around the world. And it described their commitment to Hashomer Hatzair, a socialist Zionist youth movement that attempted to inculcate its young members with positive humanistic universal values, through a Jewish lens.

Since I have to earn a living, I decided to accept the job, despite the fact that most of my work in the last few decades has been a quest to escape both the Jewish Israeli narrative and the Palestinian Arab narrative in order to reach some kind of synthesis that could enable these two groups to create something new and worthwhile together. At the time I accepted the contract I thought, Well, I spend most of my time immersed in the Palestinian struggle for basic human rights; it might not hurt me, as a Jew, to spend some time immersed in the Jewish narrative again—the narrative that explains a lot about how the present impasse in Israel/Palestine came about.

And often, as I sat there working on the text, moving along in the first person with the narrator as he and his comrades navigated the horrors and challenges of encroaching fascism, wartime, expulsion, flight, danger, resistance, arrest and interrogation, escape, heroism, betrayal, endurance… I could not help thinking that you could lift some of this material right out of this story, change the names, and plunk it down right in the middle of the Palestinian narrative of the early 21st century, and it would sound quite natural.

In fact, the Compassionate Listening Project people[34] have told me that, when they bring groups to Israel and Palestine to meet with a wide spectrum of figures on both "sides," the recorded interviews by local Palestinians and local Jews resemble each other very much, sometimes almost word for word: "They hate us," "They don't really want us here," "They want the whole country for themselves and will do anything to get rid of us," etc.

Or, as Pogo might have said, we have met the enemy's narrative, and it is ours. The visitors from abroad find this ironic, and painful, and who can blame them.

Indeed, we are all part of God's great repertory company, sharing the available roles and periodically swapping them. Perhaps there are only one or two basic narratives and we all sit at different places along a basic timeline. I am where you will be tomorrow, or vice versa. This ought to enable people to develop some empathy for the other side, but mostly it has not (yet). Maybe people only need the idea pointed out to them in the right way.

No More Enemies.

---

[34] The Compassionate Listening Project home page is at http://www.compassionatelistening.org/

The Einstein-Goldstein fallacy

In looking at another society and comparing it to their own, people often fall into a trap I call the "Einstein-Goldstein fallacy."

Dr. Albert Einstein, the world-famous physicist, was a Jew all Jews can be proud of. Dr. Baruch Goldstein, on the other hand, was a Jewish physician from Brooklyn. He immigrated to Israel and lived in Kiryat Arba, the West Bank settlement that has made life all but unlivable for Palestinian residents next door in Hebron. Goldstein went amok on February 25, 1994—on the Jewish holiday of Purim—and took an automatic rifle into the mosque at the Cave of the Patriarchs in Hebron and began shooting Muslims who were praying there. He killed 29 worshippers and wounded well over 100 others before being killed by bystanders. The most extremist of right-wing Jews venerate Goldstein as a hero (for slaughtering "them") and made his grave into a pilgrimage site; most sane people, however, including the vast majority of Jewish people in Israel, in the West Bank settlements, and everywhere else, condemn his act and view both it and its perpetrator as deranged.

There is an all-too-common tendency to judge one's own society by its Albert Einsteins while judging some other society ("their" society) by its Baruch Goldsteins. Every society has its ultra-creatives, its Einsteins—and unfortunately, every society tends to have a few Goldsteins, too. You don't get points for comparing "our" oranges to "their" apples. It doesn't accomplish anything. It won't help. It won't work.

Look out for the Einstein-Goldstein fallacy. Don't go there!

Only pluralism can run a country today

Pluralism can contain particularity, but particularity cannot contain pluralism.

I think that pluralism gained a certain new legitimacy in Israel/Palestine during the 1990s, when the Oslo accords were signed. When the Oslo framework collapsed, one result was a kind of re-criminalization of pluralism.

Freedom from overt constraint is not enough. If Israelis and Palestinians don't have a new shared vision with a pluralistic goal, whatever freedom we might achieve is liable to degenerate into more conflict in a particularistic mode.

In my perspective, Zionism has tanked not because it was meant to be about racial superiority in the first place (I don't think the masses of Jews who became involved in the Zionist movement saw it that way), but because it's a particularistic vision from the 19th century–trying, more than a century later, in an utterly different world, to do a very tough pluralistic job: running a very diverse country at the start of a new millennium.

In a globally networked world, when you try to run a country without pluralism, you create unnecessary enemies every day.

Reading Thich Nhat Hanh in Jerusalem

Reading Thich Nhat Hanh, reading as an expatriate American Jew living in the confused space of Palestine/Israel, I realize what a simple yet eloquent affirmation of the No More Enemies paradigm it is, that I am reading his work and finding it transformative.

Thich Nhat Hanh, a Buddhist monk, is one of today's most brilliant, compassionate, and articulate souls. He grew up in the shattered world that was Vietnam in the latter half of the 20th century. He saw his country destroyed by a war between the USA and the Communist regime of North Vietnam and its sponsor, China. I saw it, too—from the American side.

Now, expatriate New Yorker, here I am in Jerusalem, reading his *The Heart of the Buddha's Teaching* and thinking: how ironic! Here is a man from a society that the US government of the time tried to persuade us was our enemy (or anyhow the northern half of it).

As I sit here in the Middle East, I like to think of him in his community of Plum Village in France, or traveling the world, telling people about the Four Noble Truths and the Noble Eight-fold Path, and urging people to seek peace and justice through mindfulness, without violence.

He says: "It is true that the Buddha taught the truth of suffering, but he also taught the truth of 'dwelling happily in things as they are' [in *Samyutta Nikaya* V, 26, and many other places] …If we touch the truth of suffering with our mindfulness, we will be able to recognize and identify our specific suffering, its specific causes, and the way to remove those causes and end our suffering."[35]

---

[35] Thich Nhat Hanh, *The Heart of the Buddha's Teaching* (New York: Broadway Books, 1999, p.23).

Our way, in Palestine and Israel, requires embracing a No More Enemies orientation. We have been enemies too long already.

I don't believe in sides anymore

I don't believe in "sides" anymore. Not for Israel, or Palestine, or anywhere else–except in sports, for fun. Not when it's life and death. In matters of life and death, there are only two sides and they do not pit me against any other living being. In matters of life and death, the sides are LIFE or DEATH. If you are on the side of Life, then all other living beings, by definition, are on your side. Once you begin making exceptions, it's an own goal–because only Death will profit.

"I'm on the side of Life, except for the settlers who have stolen our land"–Nuh-uh. No exceptions.

"I'm on the side of Life–except for the suicide bombers who target innocent civilians!"–Nope. No exceptions.

It is the acts that are abhorrent–not the people.

True, there are people whose grotesquely cruel acts seem to take them out beyond the farthest boundary of human sympathy–psychopaths, we call them. But often one man's hero is another's psychopath. Remember Dr. Baruch Goldstein–the man who signed the physician's Hippocratic Oath ("First, do no harm") yet, in a fit of rage, did fatal harm to 29 people, one after another–slaughtering them while they were praying in a mosque. And some people, people who term themselves religious Jews, venerate this man and make his grave a pilgrimage site. For me, this one is truly tough to figure out.

But I still say it's the act that was abhorrent, not the man. Before he ran amok, Dr. Goldstein was a dedicated physician and he healed people every day, including Palestinians.

When a dream crumbles

In the recent past, a despairing 83-year-old kibbutznik friend of mine, recently widowed, developed a sad habit of pacing around her modest living room while muttering darkly to herself: "They don't want us here. They just don't want us here." She means, "The Arabs don't want us here."

In her twenties, this lady worked in a DP camp in Cyprus where the British government was interning Jewish survivors of the slaughter of European Jewry. She dreamed her Jewish dreams and worked selflessly for many good causes over the years, including the cause of Jewish-Arab cooperation and coexistence within the existing realities of what Israel has become. It is hard for me to talk with her about Israel's historical misjudgments and missed opportunities for reconciliation with the neighbors; the greed of successive Israeli regimes for more and more land; the fantasy that Israel can buy collective Jewish security at the price of another people's dreams of independence and prosperity.

I know what I would like to say to her, but I can't bring myself to intrude. Maybe she will read this one day, and understand: Insofar as I can see, the main problem for the folks already here in Palestine when Jewish settlement was gaining momentum was not so much the idea of the Zionists' coming to *live* here; it was more the idea of the Zionists' coming to *rule* here. Exclusively.

Meantime, going on from where we are today in the region, one thing many Israelis and Palestinians have in common is their respective histories of displacement. If we could listen deeply enough to really hear each other's stories, we would discover many commonalities, including this one.

Don't chop up the baby

Once upon a time, there were two nations who claimed the same country.

This land is ours, said one.

No! This land is *ours*, said the other. We've been living here for generations! Look at our orchards and our fields, our vines and our gardens!

But our people were here thousands of years ago, said the other. And though forced into exile, some remained behind. We always had a presence here, all through the centuries. And now we've come back to reclaim our ancestral homeland.

What do you mean, reclaim? Look around you. You want to reclaim this olive tree that my great-great-grandfather planted?

(Pause.)

No... we do not claim the tree... only the land it is planted in. We will tear up the tree and you can take it with you when you go.

(This is chopping up the baby.[36] Don't go there.)

---

[36] The reference here is to a well-known biblical legend about King Solomon, renowned for his wisdom. He was called on to judge which of two women claiming a certain baby as their own, was in fact the true mother. He proposed chopping the baby in half so as to award each woman half the baby--which made it easy to identify the real mother when only one of the two women begged him not to harm the baby and offered to let the other woman have her child.

The obstacle is the opportunity

Many conflicts linger on because the parties or "sides" cannot grasp the idea that it is not altruism or religion or even international law, but rather their own long-term self-interest that requires them to cooperate.

Sustainable solutions can be achieved only by inducing all parties concerned to let go of enemy-hood in favor of joint problem-solving and joint decision-making. Management science demonstrated decades ago that stakeholders who do not participate in crafting a solution develop a vested interest in torpedoing it. This is not really so difficult to grasp. "Might makes right" is a very temporary dynamic. Better to think of it as "Might makes right, right now; later, might makes fight–again!"

Israel and Palestine provide a good example. Israeli Jews and Palestinian Arabs–the mainstream in each case–are in despair because each "side" views the other as an obstacle to the realization of its most precious dreams: independence, self-determination, cultural autonomy, economic development, prosperity and security. With a very slight adjustment, the "other side" can be seen for what it is: the repository of the crucial additional perspective that can help evolve a creative meta-solution to release all the constructive potentialities of both "sides" (and of all the many "sides" within each major "side," neither of which is monolithic or monochromatic). Then the old dreams actually become achievable, in somewhat modified or re-visioned form, with more room to grow and evolve and unfold in the sunlight of mutual effort and mutual respect.

I remember once, some years ago, my young friend Nireen, a Palestinian writer, said to me earnestly that in her honest opinion, anyone born in Palestine or what is now Israel has an unassailable right to live here as an equal citizen (for example: my children). But immigrants like me, she said, who came here as part of a movement or a program to seize control from the population already here, either displacing them or reducing them to disenfranchised serfs or unwanted citizens in their own country–those immigrants, including me, had no inherent right to stay and should be deported in the name of justice.

I had to take several deep breaths in order to remain calm while my Palestinian friend told me that if she had her druthers, I'd lose my right to live in Israel/Palestine. To my surprise, however, when I took those deep breaths and remained calm and began contemplating the idea in a disinterested way, it was much less threatening than I'd have expected. It was, first of all, her opinion–an idea–and not an edict (yet!). Nireen certainly has a right to her opinion, particularly in a conversation with me; after all, I came to live in her land, not the other way around. From her perspective as a Palestinian, born and raised in Palestine, it made complete and total sense. And she did not speak this opinion with rancor or hatred, but straightforwardly and with commendable honesty. The words were there between us; I did not instantly discorporate; the world did not end. More importantly, no blood flowed and no human beings died violently.

Later on, as a thought experiment, I began to try to imagine a mutually negotiated resolution of the Israeli-Palestinian conflict that would require me to go back where I had come from more than 30 years ago. I realized that while inconvenient in the extreme, it would not be the end of the world, either. I can already hear many single-minded immigrant Israeli Jewish readers screaming for my blood, even as I write this–but I ask your forbearance because I'm not done with this thought experiment yet.

Fortunately or otherwise, many thousands, even tens or hundreds of thousands, of Palestinians in Israel and in the West Bank and Gaza see things differently than Nireen does, and are in no rush to get rid of me. While they might not really mind very much if I and my fellow immigrants left the country, neither do they see it as imperative. They simply want the regime in Israel to stop treating them as having *less* of a right to be here than the people who have displaced them, and they want their independence, same as I do. Indeed, many Palestinians–probably a majority–evidently see the multifaceted synthesis that is already here (a synthesis of West and East, of African and Mediterranean and European and American and Asian and Australian, of Palestinian and Israeli, of Muslim and Jewish and Christian and Druze) as a potentially positive thing: providing, of course, that everyone would stand to benefit equally from its blessings, which is not the case today.

I remember something said to me once by Dr. Nazir Yunis of 'Ara, with whom I once worked on a grassroots project to create a shared Arab and Jewish school in the Wadi Ara area. Our group folded without having achieved its objective, but the school was created later by another, more determined and better organized group of younger parents, Jews and Palestinian Arabs together. One day I was sitting in their living room in 'Ara with Nazir and his wife Sanaa, talking politics, and he said: "Deb, we (Palestinian Arabs) have accepted you (Jews from abroad) here. What do you want to do–commit suicide?"

I had a hard time hearing this, partly because I knew that not every Palestinian Arab would agree that I am accepted here; my writer friend Nireen, for instance, would not agree.

At the time, I found the phrasing of his question quite bewildering. I thought: What does he mean, commit suicide? In the years since then, that question has increasingly come to seem like the real one, the most basic one. We (Jews) who currently hold power can choose to hoard it selfishly and harden our hearts, thereby guaranteeing our eventual doom (tyrants, as Gandhi said, always fall in the end); or we can open our hearts and bring "the other" into the circle to resolve our painful situation together on a basis of equality, dignity, and respect for all. This would have to include proper reparations where due, and formal apologies where due, and mechanisms of inter-communal reconciliation.

The other is not *an obstacle to* a solution; the other is *the key to* a solution. If we willfully, time and again, throw that key away–it begins to seem suicidal.

Murder/suicide

Some years after my conversation that day at Nazir and Sanaa Yunis's house, I read something eerily similar by Israeli author David Grossman:

"[F]rom the moment I started writing... I felt something I had not felt for years, certainly not in the political context: that consciousness, in any situation, is always free to choose to face reality in a different, new way...

"In this sense, writing... nonfiction... made me feel that I was reclaiming parts of myself that the prolonged conflict [between Israelis and Palestinians] had expropriated or turned into 'closed military zones.' Furthermore, I came to grasp the high price we were paying for willingly giving up on parts of our soul—a price no less painful than giving up land. I knew that we were not killing only the Palestinians, and I asked why we were continuing to accept not just the murder, *but the suicide too.*"[37]

The Israeli Jewish novelist and the Palestinian-Arab Israeli physician saw the same reality, from different sides of the looking glass, and came to the same conclusion.

Is it too late to change things here? I don't think so.

No More Enemies. Enemies no more.

---

[37] David Grossman, "Books That Have Read Me," in his *Writing in the Dark: Essays on Literature and Politics* (New York: Farrar, Straus & Giroux, 2008, pp.25-26). Emphasis mine.

157

Change is urgent

There is so much suffering today in Israel and Palestine.

Change is urgent, yet one cannot experience this urgency un-remittingly. The sense of urgency waxes and wanes.

What reignites my sense of urgency, day after day? Much of the time, my young friend Maha in Gaza does. The human psyche has an easier time dealing with the reality of one person's suffering than with the suffering of millions. For me, the person's face I see in my mind's eye, as she waits for change to come, as she waits for the Wall to fall, is often Maha's.

Maha and I first became acquainted when she translated my short story about the 1967 Six-Day War, "Dudu in Heaven," into Arabic. I thought she might find the story offensive because, even though it's about the human face of the enemy and I think of it as an "anti-war war story," nonetheless it's told from the perspective of an ordinary Israeli woman and I wasn't sure how much Maha could identify with that. When I asked her, she said: *It's a beautiful story, but it's far too sad. Next time, write a story that's not so sad.*

It was a woman-to-woman response and not a political response. And so we became friends and have remained friends, through Cast Lead[38] and all the other horrors since.

My friend Maha wants to live in freedom. Not when she's old. Right now! It doesn't seem like such an extraordinary wish.

---

[38] Operation Cast Lead was Israel's official name for its brutal military assault on Gaza, December 2008-January 2009.

Flowing with change (or not)

A friend sent around an email recently with a *New York Times* article[39] by Emily Parker in which the author quotes the prominent Japanese writer Haruki Murakami's comments on the changes in (some would say the corruption of) the Japanese language in the "age of English," cellphone novels, email, and so on:

"As Haruki Murakami, Japan's best-known living novelist, wrote via e-mail, 'My personal view on the Japanese language (or any language) is, If it wants to change, let it change. Any language is alive just like a human being, just like you or me. And if it's alive, it will change. Nobody can stop it.' There is no such thing as simplification of language, he added. 'It just changes for better or worse (and nobody can tell if it is better or worse).'"

I found this striking for several reasons. First, because I think Murakami's position is unusual for a literary figure: Those who love language may tend to resist its fluid, continual, and inevitable evolutionary changes as somehow heretical. After all, the evolution of a language is typically led by ordinary people, speaking or writing colloquially, which can sound to highly educated contemporaries as just "wrong"–although later generations may disagree (think of Shakespeare).

Beyond that issue, I have often wondered about the creative tension between respect for tradition and openness to change in the context of religion and society. Just as a language has its acolytes and its high priests who have a stake, or see themselves as having a stake, in fending off innovation–so too with religions, and maybe cultures in general.

---

[39] November 5, 2009: "Is Technology Dumbing Down Japanese?" by Emily Parker, *The New York Times-International Herald Tribune Sunday Book Review.* Retrieved at http://www.nytimes.com/2009/11/08/books/review/EParker-t.html?nl=books&emc=b

I thought about this a lot when I lived in a Muslim town in central Israel. Palestinians in Israel were and are a society plunged suddenly and traumatically into a confrontation with a very different society, the latter attempting in myriad ways, from subtle to brutal, to bend the former to its will. For Palestinians in Israel, that circumstance brought the ordinary tension between tradition and innovation to a painful peak.

And meantime I thought about the tension between tradition and change in Judaism. If Jews had totally assimilated over the centuries and merged—disappeared—without a trace into the cultures and religions of the diaspora; or if Judaism's sacred text did not compel every Jew to remember Jerusalem and aspire to return there, a core feature of Jewish tradition that was never relinquished even by secular figures (think Herzl)—how different history would have been. To paraphrase Murakami, we can't tell if the result would have been better or worse... but certainly different.

Then I think of the more universal aspects of the question: People roam, people have always roamed, and they land in places where the local culture is very different. Among the people already living there, the arrival of the newcomers typically stimulates a new dialogue—or struggle—between tradition and innovation. Is the tension thereby generated creative, or destructive?

The outcome used to be uncontrolled, a function of the accidental juxtaposition of the particular cultures involved. Now, when we are so much more sophisticated about the psychological and neurobiological mechanisms involved, now when we have global communication and an ability to share cultures instead of beating each other over the head with them... now we have an opportunity to optimize that encounter and make it as mutually beneficial as possible—seeing *all* the people as joint partners.

This is the sort of thing I'd like to see some of the new generation of scholars working on.

Partnership is the new affinity group

Question: What made the difference between my response (repulsion) as a student in New York in the 1960s to the left-wing calls for a "secular democratic state" in Palestine, and my response today (receptive) to the idea of a confederation, or parallel sovereignty, or some other variant on shared governance in Palestine/Israel? Or between my response (indignation) to the massive post-1948 boycott against Israel promoted by Arab countries back then, and my sympathetic response to the Palestinian call for BDS (boycott, divestment and sanctions) today, a campaign supported by a growing number of Israelis in Israel and abroad, including me, even if with a heavy heart, knowing that every other strategy to assure justice for Palestinians has been tried, and has failed?

Answer: The difference is... several decades of getting to know Palestinians personally, living with Palestinians, working with Palestinians, and seeing with my own eyes that we can build something worthwhile together, if given half a chance.

The world has changed beyond recognition since Israel's founding, and the situation in Israel and Palestine has changed, too. There is even less room today than sixty-odd years ago for a new country defined as the state of only one group, whatever it may be. The Palestine so longingly remembered by displaced Palestinians no longer exists; many of the razed villages have not been built on, but others are now airports, highways, university campuses, high-rise neighborhoods. Nor is the romantic vision of a modern Jewish (meaning all Jewish, or Jewish only) political sovereignty attainable or reasonable anymore. The "Jewish" state is full of citizens who don't fit the definition (probably at least a third, if you count all the citizen groups who are "other" in some way). Myriad states elsewhere also find themselves in a new multiethnic era in which traditional nationalisms no longer speak to

161

the reality we live in. This change simply cannot be avoided or denied, even if doing so were desirable.

To me, the continuing campaign to woo affluent Western Jews to make aliyah (immigrate to Israel to fulfill themselves as Jews in the ultimate Jewish space) is as anachronistic as if someone were to start wooing families from the East Coast of the USA to travel westward in covered wagons and settle the frontier (and the "savage redskins" be damned). As the rest of Israel struggles mightily to come to terms with the challenge of reframing its entire worldview to make room for a newly emergent reality, every year several hundred of these enthusiasts for the old fantasy continue to arrive by airplane and descend to the tarmac and kiss the ground of the dream world they want to believe is here.

Meanwhile, something possibly even more inspiring than that hollow fantasy is trying to be born here–a partnership of erstwhile enemies–and that's where all the cool people are going with their energy and their enthusiasm. For the new Jewish *olim* (immigrants making aliyah), I feel deep sympathy. But they don't want my sympathy and when you talk to them about the reality gap they are facing here, they mostly get very angry, and who can blame them? They were sold a seductive fantasy. Now what? (Well–join us! Join the NME team, get with the new program, and get in the game.)

One thing the privileged group under an oppressive regime clearly has in common with the disenfranchised group living next door is that, in a situation of inequality and oppression, neither group is making anything like their best or fullest contribution to their children's shared future.

Peaceful resistance: scary!

At one time or another, Jews in Israel and abroad have confronted me angrily, demanding to know: Where are the peace activists on the other side? Where is their peace movement? Meanwhile, these same critics would also vilify any Israeli or Jew who works for peace with Palestinians. And as the grassroots Palestinian peace movement has earned more visibility, most of these hostile and angry Jews apparently have not warmed to it; quite the contrary.

In recent years, as nonviolent peace activism has gained traction among Palestinians, there has been increasing harassment, arrest, and abuse of its practitioners—Palestinians, Israelis and people from many other places who come to help ("internationals"). Sometimes the abuse is lethal. Evidently peaceful resistance is the most terrifying kind for the authorities because it is, in the end, invincible.

The day the grassroots movement for a free Palestine segued from a reliance on "armed struggle" to a reliance on "international law" (at least, on the West Bank, so far) was a good day for Palestinians and for the rest of us, too. Except it wasn't "a day"— it was "a process"—right?

So hop on the No More Enemies train, folks. It's heading for a good place.

Regime change

I do not want regime change by force. I do not want regime change by stealth. I do not want regime change by violent insurrection, and certainly not by terrorism.

In places ruled by the enemies paradigm through its puppets (the jaded and impervious elites–political and/or economic and/or military), I would like to see regime change. Yes! I would like to see it happen as an inevitable sequel to a massive paradigm shift in which the notion of enemies suddenly becomes as obsolete as the Flat Earth Society. That will be a massive tectonic shift of ideas, and the enemies-driven leadership mentality will be left outside the new playing field unless those old leaders can adjust, and fast.

Moving easily up and down and around the new playing field, to the cheers of the crowd, will be emerging young cadres of post-enemies leaders: women and men who understand how to tap constructively into the new energies released by the exit of the enemies paradigm.

Remember the fellow in the (imaginary) village of Helm who said, maybe a hundred years ago: *If I were Rothschild, I'd be richer than Rothschild. –Oh really,* says his buddy, *how would you manage that? –Simple,* says he: *I'd do a little teaching on the side.*

So, as they might have said in Helm: When we get the No More Enemies paradigm shift happening, we'll get a little regime change on the side. Maybe more than a little.

Flashback: another conference on equality

(My notes from 2007)

As we appear to be sliding ever closer to some final, unimaginable chaos, does everyone else wake to this massive dread, this wash of foreboding, as I sometimes do in the morning? Or am I tuned somehow to a frequency no one else is receiving?

Three of us from Wahat al-Salam~Neve Shalom drove up to Nazareth last week for the annual Sikkuy conference, reporting on implementation of the Or Commission recommendations to redress the structural discrimination of Israeli society that privileges Jewish citizens over Arab citizens [40]. At the conference, we learned (no surprise) that progress toward equality for Palestinian Arab citizens of Israel is—how to portray it?—unbearably lagging. Yet somehow we all bear this.

Our little delegation from WAS~NS comprised two Palestinian Israelis who between them have clocked nearly 40 years of walking their talk as residents of this country's only intentional Jewish-Arab or Arab-Jewish shared community, plus this author, longtime colleague and friend and [at the time] also a nonresident staff writer, editor, and translator in the WAS~NS village administration.

The damning data from speaker after speaker washed over an audience of the usual NGO-sector suspects, seated and listening politely in rows of white Keter plastic chairs. They were suited and tied or neatly trim in skirt and blouse, redolent of aftershave or perfume with an under-scent of shared frustration and disappointment and, yes, anger. Somehow, said one of my companions quietly, it all seems so k'eelu. The word k'eelu all by itself is a many-splendored Hebrew idiom that translates, in this richly unhappy context, as "ersatz," perhaps. The literal Hebrew meaning is "as if." Close

---

[40] The Hebrew word *sikkuy* means "prospects" or "opportunity"; the organization's full name is Sikkuy: The Association for the Advancement of Civic Equality in Israel. See their reports in English at
http://www.sikkuy.org.il/english/reports.html

enough. The littlest words, like the visible nuclei of enormous clouds of unseen context, invisible to outsiders, are always the hardest to translate.

As speaker followed speaker, reporting the grim details of little or no progress toward equality in education, health, employment, Bedouin rights, land use policy, and all the rest, we listened politely and had no trouble distinguishing the common thread: The necessary funding was never voted, or it was voted but never allocated, or allocated but never disbursed, or disbursed in Jerusalem yet somehow never actualized in "the field" where 1.1 million Palestinian Israeli citizens are still waiting for a fair deal in their underfunded and neglected separate communities and neighborhoods. The famous 4-million-shekel budget for parity, touted several years ago by the government, translated into—what? Some progress on the ground, but not much. The appearance without the substance: k'eelu. In Arabic it would be even more harsh: kalem fadi (cheap talk; literally, empty words).

There cannot be a sustainable and just solution in Palestine and Israel until we move to a new template. A regime change is much less urgent than a paradigm shift.

Symmetries and asymmetries

Power?

Israel's Jews are supposed to have the power all sewed up. That's a crock! Long-term, Goliath is always at risk. No wonder that Israeli Jews, deep down, are so afraid. Brute force is never more than a temporary advantage in power. Eventually, someone else comes along with greater brute force: your adversary, or your adversary's grandchildren, or some strangers who covet what you have, or dissidents from within your group. Real and sustainable power comes from empowering the maximum number of people in the society to lead productive, fulfilled lives. On that standard, how does the Israeli regime score? Badly! And the Palestinian leadership? Not much better—but these days, at least, they can more persuasively claim extenuating circumstances.

Survivor's guilt?

In Israel, we all have it. The Jews have the Holocaust. The Palestinian Arabs in Israel have the Nakba, the expulsion of 1948 and the fact that they are still here, while the others are refugees. Ordinary Palestinians in the West Bank and Gaza can feel guilty by comparison to the martyrs and prisoners. Diaspora Palestinians? Ouch! Too prosperous!

What brought some of this home to me was a public email dialogue circa 2009 between two dedicated and well-known Palestinian human rights activists—one residing in the USA, the other in the West Bank—exchanging views on the Right of Return and unable to resist the entitlement competition: "You live in comfort in the USA!" accused one; versus "You live off foreign grant money!" retorted the other. How sad is that?

This sort of unsightly warp in the fabric of life will fade somewhat, probably, when there's a sustainable agreement in place. After that, there will be new and different warps in the fabric. Such is life.

From Isaiah to Thich Nhat Hanh

The women's peace movement in Israel embraces both Jewish Israeli women and Palestinian women with Israeli citizenship. In hindsight, the very fact of their cooperation, which is already longstanding, was a significant precursor to the strategically significant campaign dubbed "We refuse to be enemies" as described in Part I of this book.

Rela Mazali, feminist and longtime peace activist in Israel, is credited by her peers with originating the phrase "We [women] refuse to be enemies." It came into being as a slogan to give shape to the women-initiated campaign of protest and solidarity in the fall of 2000. Palestinian-Arab citizens of Israel (one-fifth of Israelis) and Jewish citizens of Israel mounted a vigil together, to decry the deeply institutionalized and entrenched government discrimination against citizens who are not Jewish, and to protest Israeli violence toward Palestinians in Israel, as well as in the West Bank and Gaza (who, at least at this writing, are not citizens of Israel). The women's campaign was part of a broad wave of social outrage at a situation of ongoing, indeed escalating, injustices in Israel/Palestine, which culminated in the death that autumn of 13 nonviolent protestors (12 of them shot by police) who were taking part in street protests or, in some cases, simply watching them.

It is not the details of this particular conflict, or this particular protest, or even those particular tragic and unnecessary deaths, which drove me finally to write this book. It was rather the realization that the idea of ordinary people *refusing to be enemies* has tremendous power and is broadly applicable to conflicts in lots of other places. I have lived in Israel most of my adult life, and my fascination with the idea of refusing to be enemies is certainly about Israelis and Palestinians and the desperate need for all of us to stop pondering the Israeli-Palestinian "conflict" and begin actualizing the Israeli-Palestinian "relationship" (as veteran grass-roots dialogue activists Libby and Len Traubman of San Francisco have brilliantly advocated[41])—but it's about a lot more than Israel and Palestine.

The idea must be repeated endlessly until it enters the global public consciousness: Refusing to be enemies, and embracing partnership instead, is part of the Next Big Thing for all of us. We are all on our way to a different level of interaction as a species, and the path from here to there leads through the door that is opened in our awareness by (among other things) the notion of refusing to be enemies.

To my mind, if there is any power in the biblical prophecy of Isaiah that "from Zion shall go forth the law, and the word of the Lord from Jerusalem," then the Israeli women's peace movement campaign in the year 2000—"We refuse to be enemies!"—presages the fulfillment of the prophecy, or at least the beginning of its fulfillment: *And they shall beat their swords into ploughshares, and their spears into pruning-hooks; nation shall not lift up sword against nation, neither shall they learn war any more.*

Visionary Vietnamese Buddhist monk and teacher Thich Nhat Hanh, visiting Jerusalem some years ago, said that the task of Israelis and Palestinians is to learn how to make peace *as Israelis and Palestinians*—and then to tell the rest of the world how they did it. The same would be true, of course, in all the other conflict hot spots around the globe.

Maybe the time has finally come, with the idea of *refusing to be enemies*, when we can all seize the task of learning how to live together with our neighbors, co-creating a better world wherever we are; not only Israelis and Palestinians, but everyone.

No More Enemies.

---

[41] Libby and Len Traubman blog at:
http://traubman.igc.org/global.htm

Deep listening

Some deep listening is called for, if we want to heal all the war-torn places.

In Palestine and Israel there are many groups actively searching for the way to reconciliation and justice. Two in particular should be mentioned here, in tandem: The Bereaved Families Forum and Combatants for Peace.

The Forum is a group of Palestinian and Israeli families who have lost close family members in the conflict. They have paid the price and they have understood that violence will not bring us to a resolution. They meet together and share their pain, and they lecture together in schools and other venues to spread the word. Their shared goal is that no other family will have to experience a loss like theirs.

Combatants for Peace are a group of former Palestinian and Israeli fighters–militants and soldiers–who have come to see that there is no military solution to the conflict and that only a determined and sustained dialogue of equals can bring a better future. Such dialogue, they say, is sometimes harder to do than shooting and bombing, and requires more courage.

These two groups are like two poles of the energy that could transform us and transform our children's future: the shared grief of the bereaved, all of whose murdered children, as Nurit Peled-Elhanan has repeatedly said, are together now under the ground; and the shared, bitter disillusion in the ranks of the killers–former soldiers who have put away their weapons of war, knowing that there is no future down that road.

The shared message is this: Let us listen deeply to one another, and draw our conclusions, and then, together, let us walk a different path.

This is its signpost: No More Enemies.

Part III – Living behind the lines
(a time out, for stories)

I think we should go to our house, and open its doors.

--Ursula K. Le Guin, **Tales from Earthsea**

A note about Part III

Dear reader,

Most workshops and seminars give participants some free time to mingle and talk together outside the organized sessions, certainly at coffee breaks and at meals. These less formal encounters provide unscripted opportunities for learning and growth, and often turn out to have been as illuminating as the organized sessions themselves.

The collection of personal stories in Part III is meant to fulfill a similar function for readers of this book. I wanted you to have a chance to meet and get to know some of the people whose life stories are interwoven with the tapestry of ideas presented in Parts I and II. You can think of this as an informal break from the regular sessions, to which we will return in Part IV.

As elsewhere in the book, the names and identities of most of the people mentioned in Part III have been altered and disguised to protect their privacy. The exceptions are people with existing public profiles as community leaders, civic activists, and the like. The stories themselves are all drawn from my actual experiences with friends, neighbors, and colleagues between 1981 and 2010.

--Deb R.

All are welcome

The house of No More Enemies is a place of many tales; many rooms.

You are unconditionally welcome here. No one will interrogate you about the doubts you may be harboring on your arrival. You can leave your anxieties on the doorstep, for a time. If you have weapons, likewise: just check them at the door. You will need no weapons in this house.

Please visit at your leisure and sample the stories here. You may discover a room where you feel at home. You may discover many.

If you seem to be getting lost, most likely you will encounter someone already oriented, someone from one of the stories, who can help you get your bearings. That is why they are here.

I am a visitor here myself. I write what I see, but please do not think I am the mistress of this house. The house belongs to all of us who come to it on our journey—those who are long gone, and we who are here now, and those yet to enter.

Beyond that is mainly mystery, but one thing is certain:

You are welcome here.

Haunted

Some women will tell you that there is no pain greater than childlessness. Other women will tell you that there is no pain greater than losing a child.

Imagine, then, a woman who has experienced both: first, the barren years; the dismal prognosis. Then success: a beautiful child. Then the sudden loss.

Even the two children who came afterwards, both healthy, growing up nicely *and may Allah protect them*, might never erase that earlier trauma.

Imagine that her family teases her gently sometimes, calling her "scaredy-cat." She lives every day and every night with the ghostly memories of her firstborn and the pain of her loss. Nothing that happens now, however joyful, can quite expunge this dark shade, but she wants to be brave and she carries on.

Even later, as the mother of another daughter and a son, she will never quite banish the shade. Her husband is very tender, very understanding and forbearing as she continues to see reality through this lens of woundedness to which she has become accustomed now. Imagine her joy when their daughter is engaged to be married to a wonderful young man.

Perhaps one day the first grandchild will finally close the wound. I doubt it, but only time will tell.

The four-ton hummus

After I moved in 2007 to Al-Qaryah, a very small Arabic-speaking Muslim village in the Jerusalem hills, I discovered that one of the bonuses of living there was the proximity of good restaurants. When I am working on a deadline, I don't cook much, and it's great to have somewhere close to home where I can get a tasty meal at a reasonable price. Just over the hill from Al-Qaryah is the village of Abu Ghosh, a tourism hot spot famous for its great restaurants.

With friends who would come to join me for a leisurely meal at one or another of these great eateries, I used to joke that Abu Ghosh is the center of the universe. But the joke was on me one day in 2009, when a representative from the Guinness Book of World Records organization came to town to certify the largest platter of fresh-made hummus in the world: four tons.

The media hype began weeks beforehand, reprising the ongoing competition between Israelis, of whatever ethnicity, and our neighbors to the north, the Lebanese. They have been very vocal in their outrage at the hubris of any Israeli, Arab or Jew, who presumes to claim hummus as their own traditional (or worse yet, national) dish. Everyone knows it's a Lebanese dish, say the Lebanese. In 2008 they made it into the Guinness Book with a two-ton hummus platter and quite a lot of hype.

Abu Ghosh has its own impresario of hype, not to be outdone by anyone, anywhere: Jawdat Ibrahim, an enterprising restaurateur who seems to enjoy celebrity for its own sake, for the fun of it, as much as for the business it attracts. His celebrity also makes him a target of gossip, but he must be used to that by now. The Ibrahim family is one of the two major families in Abu Ghosh and Jawdat is by far its most famous pop culture scion. I've shaken his hand at the establishment where he presides benignly in the evenings, but I don't really know him. The tales of his deeds, however, abound, and I've heard many, at least half of them probably apocryphal.

They say he went to the United States as a very young man and was fabulously successful in business. Not only that, but he won the lottery in one of those states with the giant jackpots ($12 million? Florida? $17 million?) and came home a wealthy man. The envious and the gossips claim he never won any lottery and that the money was a windfall from one of his many business deals: a distinction without much difference, really. I'm told that he married an Asian beauty queen, possibly Thai, possibly not, and they had a beautiful daughter (*may Allah protect and guard her*). He is said to hand out college scholarships left and right to deserving young people, both Arab and Jewish. The Jawdat detractors claim it's all hype, but I believe it.

Jawdat evidently could not resist taking up the gauntlet so dramatically thrown down by the Lebanese, with their record two-ton hummus platter made by 50 chefs, at least some of whom were photographed in their white chef's hats mashing all the chick peas by hand, from scratch. One day we heard in Al-Qaryah that Abu Ghosh would attempt to wrest the record away from the Lebanese with a mammoth four-ton hummus. The media spotlight appeared on cue and hovered hotly. Abu Ghosh made the headlines in the national press in Israel, and beyond–in Lebanon, no doubt, too. All my friends knew I lived close by. Emails starting coming in from everywhere, asking if I'd heard. By then it seemed as if everyone on earth had heard.

A huge industrial-sized satellite dish was lent by Globus-Golan, the film production company headquartered up the road in Neve Ilan. The dish was set up several days in advance on a humongous platform in the parking lot of Jawdat Ibrahim's restaurant, alongside the main road through the village. Driving by one day on my way home to Al-Qaryah, I saw it there, buttressed by scaffolding underneath and stabilized by a network of wires, a giant empty nest awaiting its chickpeas.

179

Word went around that a major section of the main road through the commercial and residential center of Abu Ghosh would be closed to vehicles on the Friday of the event, from 10:00 AM to 3:00 PM. That was sure to cause pandemonium because Friday is a big tourism day for all the local restaurants and the hummus hype would only exacerbate it. I decided to stay away on the Friday. Mass events tend to make me feel claustrophobic. Meantime, everyone seemed to be stocking up on bread and milk in advance, as if a hurricane were bearing down on us.

According to the media and to my neighbor's son Ahmad, age 15, who provided an eyewitness report the next morning, the event was a big success. Even the weather cooperated, with blue skies and balmy sunshine in December. Hundreds of people thronged to the precincts of the nested satellite dish to watch the pots of hummus being weighed and added to the platter under the watchful eye of the Guinness guy. There was music and dancing and people surely forgot their mortgages and their overdrafts for an hour or two. The Guinness rep eventually certified the outcome and declared Israel the new record-holder for the largest platter of hummus in the world. *Mabrouk!*

The unseasonably warm and cloudless weather that had insured a good crowd and a smooth production also meant that the hummus itself sat under a burning sun for hours and hours. The local Health Department therefore declared the hummus unfit for human consumption, and a huge sanitation pump was activated to slurp all that record-breaking hummus straight from its platter into the sewer. There was something not right about the waste. On the other hand, no one would have especially wanted to eat hummus from a giant satellite dish parked outside in the hot sun all day.

Amid all the congratulations and brouhaha, a few hardline Jawdat detractors were heard to insinuate that not all 4,000 kilograms of the record-breaking hummus was home-made. Not only is that idea insulting to an upstanding local businessman and philanthropist; it doesn't even make sense. Surely, I thought, the

180

Guinness guy is no fool and he would have been on to any ir-regularities quicker than you can say "mash those chickpeas!" Meantime Ahmad, the young math whiz next door, insisted that the satellite dish could not possibly have contained four tons. "But I heard that they weighed it all, in plain sight," I protested mildly, not liking to challenge him. He shrugged. In a better world, a kid would not be so cynical at 15.

One thing has surely been proven beyond any shadow of a doubt. Jawdat Ibrahim is clearly a world-class impresario, and also—an unusual combination, perhaps—the owner of a robust sense of humor. There's a story told in Al-Qaryah about the time a trio of VIPs from abroad came to Jawdat's restaurant one morning without benefit of an appointment and asked the hand-some fortyish guy in a grubby tee shirt who was energetically mopping the floor if they could speak with Jawdat Ibrahim, whom they had (evidently) never met. Impromptu visits by VIPs are not unusual for Jawdat, but the timing of this one was way off. Caught underdressed and without his aftershave by a trio of pilgrims, the Three Kings arriving in Bethlehem on the wrong day, Jawdat leaned on his mop and fixed the three with a com-miserating gaze. "Unfortunately," he is supposed to have told them, "you've missed him. He's at a meeting with some govern-ment minister in Jerusalem today."

The doctors were wrong

After she and Ra'ed were married, my neighbor Reem told me, they tried to have a child right away, without success. They tried for seven years.

Reem told me this not long after I'd moved in next door, on a small side street in Al-Qaryah. It was one of the first things she told me about herself. Reem had quickly adopted me as the older sister she had always wanted.

They went to lots of doctors, she told me. They consulted specialists. The doctors were not particularly encouraging.

When they became engaged thirty-odd years ago, Reem and Ra'ed were a well-matched young couple. They married with the blessings of their elders but were also marrying for love. They never imagined not having a family of their own together. In a child-centered, family-centered, traditional small community like Al-Qaryah, not having children is among the worst disasters any-one can experience. Along with the inner sense of loss is the crippling social handicap: everyone pities you, and you know it.

One day, more than two thousand days of disappointment lat-er, Reem found herself pregnant. The young couple's prayers were answered. Reem in due course gave birth to a daughter and they named her Tibah, which means *goodness*.

Shishbarak

Shishbarak is a dumpling dish I first tasted in Al-Qaryah: tiny bits of spiced ground goat's meat wrapped in dough and swimming in a creamed soup of stock, olive oil, labane (sour white cheese) and seasonings. Each miniscule dumpling is only about the size of the end of your little finger: one delectable bite.

Making shishbarak is a labor-intensive process best done in a group. First one has to make the dough and prepare the ground meat. Then it's pleasant to sit, perhaps three women together. One person can roll out and cut up the dough while the other two stuff, close, and pinch, arranging the finished dumplings side by side on a large floured round tray. They look like a collection of elegant miniature seashells.

When the broth of seasoned stock and labane is ready, in go the dumplings to cook. You know they're done when they plump up just right.

One of Reem's aunts is famous for her shishbarak, and she always comes over to pitch in when Reem is planning to make it.

When I learned to shape the dumplings properly after a lot of trial and error, Reem was generously proud of me—and maybe she was also just a bit peeved that a woman who plies a keyboard for a living should prove such a quick study in the realm of dumplings. Or anyhow that's how it seemed to me. I understood her perfectly. Each of us likes to think of ourselves as an artisan in her own world.

Wadi Ara: the skirt

When I was a community service volunteer in a Muslim village in the Wadi Ara area of north-central Israel in 1981, we had a clear dress code based on the axiom of respect for the host culture. For men: no short pants, no sleeveless undershirts, no outrageous or immodest-looking fashion statements. For women: skirts well below the knee, sleeves well below the elbow, no low necklines, nothing transparent. The dress code is actually quite similar to what you'd find in an Orthodox Jewish community and lots of other conservative communities, no doubt. I went shopping in Manhattan before I left to join the program in Israel. One of my budget-friendly acquisitions was a colorful calf-length skirt, inspired by some unidentified South Asian or Mediterranean tradition, with patterned panels and wide horizontal bands of color in strong tones of burgundy and turquoise.

In the Wadi Ara Muslim communities, people wanted to know what village or town this dress represented: a perfectly logical question for rural Palestinian women to ask circa 1981. They could tell it wasn't from anywhere in Palestine. Traditional Palestinian women's garments are always embroidered with a distinctive pattern of stitching and colors that tell the initiated at a glance what region or town the wearer is from. This skirt of mine looked as if it was *from* somewhere in particular, but somewhere distant. The notion that I could be wearing it, yet be clueless as to its origin–a person like me who was essentially, in their terms, rootless–this both fascinated and repelled my neighbors in the village. They were too polite to say so, but I could read it clearly in their faces.

This was my favorite skirt and I wore it a lot, so I had many opportunities to ponder the various lessons that one simple article of clothing could teach.

184

Yaara goes to first grade

The quiet side street where my little flat in Al-Qaryah is located has a genuine princess in residence. She is Kemal and Noor's daughter Yaara. Kemal is my neighbor Ra'ed's second cousin. Little Yaara is one of those children who seem to have been sprinkled with magic fairy dust at birth. By age six, she had unusual charisma for such a young child and a definite aura of natural royalty. September 1, 2009 was to be her first day of first grade at the Jerusalem Hand in Hand bilingual school where classes are taught in Hebrew and Arabic and the students include both Jewish and Arab children.

When I first moved to Al-Qaryah in 2007, Yaara at four-and-a-half was quite tiny and rather bashful and reticent. On the infrequent occasions when she could be coaxed over to my end of the street to visit, she would sit shyly and twist the ends of her shirt between her fingers. She would sit only with Rawan, Reem and Ra'ed's daughter, who was then about twenty. Rawan has a way with children. Now suddenly Yaara has grown into a much more self-assured version of herself.

She and her parents and I were guests for the *iftar* meal (the evening meal breaking the daily Ramadan fast) at Reem and Ra'ed's house the night before Yaara's first day of school. She was barely able to contain her excitement. I glanced around the table: everyone's eyes were on Yaara and everyone was smiling: Reem and Ra'ed, their daughter Rawan and son Ali, Reem's sister Najla and brother-in-law Fuad, and Yaara's mom and dad, Noor and Kemal. We heard all about Yaara's new book bag and pencil case and a lot of other things (in Arabic) that I didn't catch. I promised her that I'd be up the following morning in time to come outside and see her leave at 7:00 AM.

And in the morning, there she was in the bright sunshine of what could almost be called a crisp morning here, as autumn ap-

185

proached at last. The air was fresh, the birds sang, and a regular multicultural gallery of fans was there to bid Yaara good luck: Hanan and Ella (the young Jewish tenants next door) and their toddler Yali, who at one-and-a-half was already Yaara's devoted shadow; Reem and Rawan; the proud parents Kemal and Noor themselves, of course; and me. The whole world seemed to sparkle and shine for Yaara's first day of school. Bursting with pride, she showed us her brand-new Barbie book bag (on wheels) with a lot of pink and white everywhere. She undid the top, some new-fangled design with a stiff hinged flap that opens and closes in one easy motion. Relishing the drama, she unzipped the main compartment and gleefully exhibited a multi-pocket Barbie pencil case obviously made for serious work: It must have weighed half a kilogram all by itself and was stuffed to capacity with implements of first-grade adventure: regular pencils, colored pencils, markers, erasers, a ruler, a glue stick...

Yaara was dressed in a very spiffy pair of blue-gray pencil-thin jeans and a pink and white shirt that went well with the Barbie book bag. Noor had done her shining brown hair in a neat pony tail. Her enormous grayish-green eyes sparkled and she was radiant with anticipation. She attended the same school last year, as a kindergartener, so it wouldn't be like going into the complete unknown. She wasn't scared; she was hyped on the thrill of it all.

The whole scene took me back very powerfully to the days when my own kids were young. Something turned over in my chest. If only the world doesn't make her feel smaller than she is, I thought. She's a girl, and an Arab in Israel, and a Muslim, and the path ahead is littered with obstacles. If only her world will let her be whole and feel entirely and utterly wanted, included, and able. If only they know what a gift she is.

What mattresses say

I don't think I'd ever seen a foam-rubber mattress until I came to Israel the first time, when I was 17. At home in middle-class suburban New York where I grew up, beds had box springs underneath and seriously thick built-up mattresses covered in striped ticking or flowered patterns. (Can it be that there were buttons on the mattress, tacking this upholstery in place, like quilting, like furniture? That's what I remember.)

My initial encounter with a foam-rubber mattress, then, apart from gym class, would have been on the first Israeli kibbutz (collective farm) I ever lived on, in 1967. All the kibbutz beds in those days, on every kibbutz I visited, consisted of a simple iron frame, a plywood plank with a few round holes in it for ventilation, and a foam-rubber mattress, maybe three inches (about eight centimeters) thick, encased in a brightly colored cloth cover. Not luxurious. Practical, sturdy, inexpensive, and serviceable, like most things on a kibbutz in the 1960s.

It was in Wadi Ara, in the first Muslim village I lived in, that I was later introduced to the notion of a private household's stash of foam-rubber mattresses. Every family had a stack of these mattresses, sometimes thinner than eight cm, and somewhere to store them. They served as furniture for sitting on, and as beds for sleeping on—on the tiled floor or on top of woven straw mats. A family with numerous relatives elsewhere kept a larger stack of mattresses, so that when the relatives came to visit, everyone would have a bed. That was true for a great many families who had been scattered in 1948 to different towns and regions, while either trying to avoid battle zones or expelled outright, and for families in which one or more sons had taken a wife from another village. A stack of mattresses was one of the things a bride had to have when she married. She would have her own household now, and her own family visitors, *insh'Allah* (God willing).

187

The Wadi Ara family in whose home I lived back then could cite those same familiar reasons for having relatives living elsewhere. Faiza, the mother of the house, was from a small village near Jenin in the West Bank; her husband Eyas was from Wadi Ara. The family on both sides surely had relatives elsewhere, though almost certainly they could not all come to visit, since some were in Lebanon or Jordan or even Syria, and unable to enter Israel (because Israel wouldn't let them, or their home countries wouldn't let them, or both). I don't remember ever discussing this at the time. But I remember the sizeable mound of cloth-covered foam mattresses stacked on a special platform that was stored upstairs in the part of the house my flatmate and I lived in, in a corner of a large living room rarely used but handy for life cycle events like engagement parties. Eyas and Faiza did not have all that much furniture. They were not wealthy people, in material terms.

I remember looking at the stack of a dozen or so mattresses and thinking that a culture like this, in which assuring a place to sleep for every visiting relative is a leading priority in the purchase of home furnishings, is a culture I could respect and admire. The close family connection, the unbreakable family solidarity, and the generous hospitality: all were evident in the emblematic stack of mattresses piled on a platform in a corner, ready for the long-awaited, long-dreamed-of family reunions.

Tibah was a special baby

Reem and Ra'ed's firstborn, Tibah, was by all accounts a precocious baby. She crawled early; she sat up early; she stood up by herself early; she began vocalizing ahead of schedule in ways that seemed intelligible.

Tibah was the miracle baby, born to parents who had waited a very long time for her.

Reem would come into her room in the morning to raise the shutters and Tibah would be talking to her, babbling really, but it seemed very intelligent! Standing there in her crib, the picture of health, she always radiated her special charm to the aunts and cousins whenever they came to pay court. Everyone in Al-Qaryah agreed that Tibah was a very unusual baby (*and may Allah guard and protect her*).

Seeing Ramzia happy makes me happy

When I go to visit my old friend Ramzia up north these days, I am filled with satisfaction just to contemplate her life as it is now. Her handsome, modern, two-story house in a pleasant neighborhood in a suburb of the large Muslim town of Umm al Fahm has a fabulous garden. Two late-model cars are parked outside. Ramzia has a kind, generous husband who still seems to be in love with her, and whose career has blossomed. And they have six wonderful, bright kids, three girls and three boys, from elementary school age to just graduating high school. In this idyllic picture, Ramzia's long-widowed mother occupies a special place of honor: cared for, treated with respect and indulged.

Everything Ramzia and Abdel Hadi have, they have worked hard for. Both of them.

If I think back to Ramzia's life when I first met her, the transformation is almost unimaginable.

When my fellow volunteer Melanie and I came to live and work in Wadi Ara in 1981, Ramzia was living with her mother and father and her brother in the most modest of cement-block homes. I remember it as two small rooms. The living-dining-kitchen area, which doubled as a second bedroom at night, was unpainted. The furniture was sparse: mattresses and cushions. The kitchen equipment was exceedingly basic. There was one electric light hanging from the ceiling by its cord, which was fairly typical in modest homes, whether Jewish or Arab, in the Israel of that era. There wasn't much else.

Ramzia's father died some years thereafter, and her parents' family connections were no good to her, as far as I could make out. No financially solid uncles stepped in to help support the household, to see to Ramzia and her older brother's future, to provide some kind of backup, some security. Ramzia, having already graduated from the local high school, was working as a secretary in Hadera, a nearby city. Her brother was not a significant earner and had scant formal education. The little family must have been living mainly on what Ramzia earned. But she had made up her mind early on that life—her life—was going to be much more than these inauspicious beginnings promised. Ramzia had energy, intelligence, curiosity, a robust spirit of adventure, discipline, and drive. She had no sense of entitlement and wasted no time bemoaning her circumstances. She applied herself to the role of family breadwinner and pursued every opportunity to learn new skills, encounter new and interesting people, and broaden her horizons.

I first met Ramzia through Melanie, my flatmate and fellow volunteer. I don't remember how Melanie and Ramzia became friends, to begin with; probably Ramzia came to one of our organized activities, or came to our house to visit us, or perhaps someone introduced them. Melanie was in her early twenties and Ramzia would have been nearly the same age at that time. She was a striking-looking young woman: handsome rather than pretty. She had a dark Mediterranean complexion, strong features, dark eyes, and very black, thick hair which she wore, as I recall, cut short—a bold statement of independence from tradition. Her clothing was unexceptional: longish skirts, modest blouses. Sometimes she wore jeans. The trend to more Islamic garb had not yet arrived; that would come later. She wore no head covering, which was not terribly unusual among Palestinian women in Israel in those days. On the other hand, the act of going outside the village to work, alone and unmarried, independently, all on her own, was still quite rare for a woman from a traditional Muslim village in the quasi-rural Wadi Ara area. This did not faze Ramzia.

At a certain point, Ramzia's older brother became engaged to a young woman from a neighboring town. Part of the bargain he made, as head of his family, was that Ramzia was betrothed to his bride's half-brother, who had few prospects. Ramzia was given no say in the matter. She had no option but to move to the young man's home as demanded, but they lived separately and she was able, eventually, to obtain an Islamic divorce. She moved back in with her mother, went back to work and went on with her life.

Eventually, Ramzia was courted by Abdel Hadi, a quiet chemist some years her senior from a neighboring town. He had studied in Italy and come back home with his academic degrees and a cosmopolitan outlook. Within a short time he was working as the director of a medical laboratory in the district. He met Ramzia through a mutual friend and decided that he wanted her for his wife, and when he proposed, Ramzia accepted him. Because of her divorce, his family was not enthused, and some of the relatives actually boycotted the wedding, which took place when I was working abroad. Later, when I first visited Ramzia in her new home, in a small corner of her husband's family's multistory compound, I could tell that things were stressful.

Meantime as their family was growing, Abdel Hadi was doing well in his career. They saved up and bought property in an outlying suburb, and built a very fine house. Ramzia's mother was installed there with them, and Ramzia applied herself to grooming the garden and making the house over, gradually, into a splendid and comfortable residence. Sometimes she also held down a job, while raising six kids.

On the ground floor underneath the main house, two rooms and a bath were eventually added. At different times this suite has housed a young male physician interning at a local hospital; a novice Argentinian chef, also male, who was interested in studying Arabic for fun while learning about the local cuisine; a grocery store; and a young American female translator, Andie. Ramzia liked having foreign young people in residence to help her children understand that there was a wider world out there beyond Wadi Ara, beyond Hadera where they went to the mall, and even beyond Israel and Palestine.

The Umm al Fahm municipality opened a high school for gifted students in time for Ramzia's children to attend it. Her middle daughter Nura went on a high school exchange program in the UK last year, and at one point switched host families because she was very unhappy with the first one. At Ramzia's request, Andie and I had some small part in the correspondence in English with the people in the UK, but Nura probably could have managed all right her own. She's smart, strong, assertive and determined, like her mom. "I'm a feminist," she will tell you, grinning, and she seems to feel that nothing further is required to explain herself.

Ramzia and Andie visited me in Al-Qaryah once and I'm ashamed to say I took them to a restaurant in Abu Ghosh for lunch in order not to have to produce a meal that would embarrass me by contrast to what Ramzia always prepares. Fortunately Ramzia accepts me unconditionally as I am (including being too lazy or incompetent to cook a serious meal on short notice), which has no effect, of course, on my Jewish guilt (unassuaged).

When I go up north to visit periodically, I am always made to feel entirely at home, which I do. I am greeted joyfully and fussed over: a wandering aunt who finally makes a long-overdue appearance. The kids tell me their latest news and I get to inspect their current friends who come over to hang out, and to admire their newest jeans and listen to their latest plans. I always bring everyone chocolates. I sit in the kitchen and keep Ramzia company while she assembles a meal, and she asks after my kids and we catch up on each other's news–in English mostly, because her English has by now far outstripped my Arabic. We could talk Hebrew together since we are both fluent, but maybe because it's the first language of neither of us, most of the time we don't.

Sometimes she even lets me chop some vegetables. When you've been friends for thirty years, you have perks.

193

Reem's road accident

In the mid-1980s, when little Tibah was not quite six months old, Reem was nearly killed crossing the street, by a hit-and-run driver who was never identified. She had serious internal injuries and had a very hard time. She was expected to make a full recovery eventually, but the doctors advised her not to get pregnant for at least a year, to let herself heal properly and regain her strength. The young obstetrician at Hadassah Hospital in Jerusalem who was part of her medical team was sympathetic and encouraging. He reassured her that all would be well and urged her to take her time and let herself heal completely.

I heard the whole story of that road accident one morning in 2007 when Reem and I were sitting together and stripping zaatar (hyssop) leaves off their stems in Reem's summer kitchen. There was a mountain of zaatar to process, which gave us time for a good long talk.

For Reem and Ra'ed, who had waited so long to have a family, it was a huge setback, but they coped. The main thing was, Reem was going to be all right again. It was *min Allah* (God's will). They would wait. Meantime Reem's mom was there to help with Tibah and the cooking.

Healing was slow but steady. After a few months, once she was up and about again, Reem put her energy into raising Tibah. Happy in her marriage, she enjoyed keeping house in the new home that Ra'ed had built for them, two minutes' walk from her mother's house. The seasons came and went. Life was good.

The shadow of bereavement she had known in childhood, losing her father when she was very small, had receded somewhat into the background after her own marriage. Reem's mother was a strong and determined woman, lovingly and singlehandedly raising her two daughters, Reem and Najla. Reem's mom gave

194

her girls a solid sense of security. If she herself was lonely, she never spoke of it.

Meantime, Reem's family was also getting over the pain of having had much of their land expropriated by the state for a road improvement project along the southern boundary of their orchards. Thirty years later, Reem would still be able to recite a list of the fruit trees that had been uprooted, could still smell and taste the plums and apples and pears and apricots she had eaten straight from those trees, as a girl. But Al-Qaryah prospered and everyone understood that progress exacts its price. The neighborhoods abutting the improved road were safer for the children, with proper sidewalks and proper grading.

Some things are lost and other things gained. Life goes on.

And meantime there was Tibah, delighting everyone who saw her, charming, adorable and happy, doing everything ahead of schedule, galloping forward into life almost as if it were a race she was determined to win, while the onlookers cheered.

Parenting lessons

When I lived in Wadi Ara as a volunteer, our team of two or three women at a time lived in rented housing on the second floor of a family's home. A similar number of male colleagues lived on the other side of town, a ten-minute walk from our place, in another rented apartment. The family who were our landlords lived on the ground floor—the mom, Faiza, and the dad, Eyas, both in their mid-thirties then, with six children under the age of ten.

That was an era when Wadi Ara villages very clearly had one foot in each of two worlds. The old ways were still very much in evidence: traditional village social customs prevailed. There were few cars, many unpaved streets, no sidewalks. Both girls and boys went to school, and high school graduates were increasingly going on to university, but few married women worked outside the home. There was television but there were no telephones: The infrastructure for land lines had not yet been provided to most Arab communities, although nearly every Jewish home in Israel had a telephone by that time. The cellphone era was still to come.

Despite the absence of a telephone infrastructure, social visits were sometimes made by prearrangement, but mostly they were spontaneous. You just showed up, and hospitality dictated that you be made welcome, however convenient or inconvenient your timing. We learned to read the signals fairly well, though, so that we sometimes could guess when not to stay, after all. By decoding the cues, you could usually infer when the hosts were about to go out themselves, or when they were expecting other guests any moment, and so on. Sometimes we made embarrassing mistakes, overstaying our welcome without being aware of it until afterwards—but our hosts always tried to cover for us. This is a culture in which cordial social interaction is a supreme value, and making a guest welcome has been raised to a fine art.

196

Looking back, I realize that Faiza's family was very brave, and also evidently needed the extra income, else they would not have let their second floor to a program for young volunteers from outside the village, most of them Americans with little knowledge or experience of how to conduct themselves in a different culture.

Eyas had injured his shoulder in a work accident before we came to live there. Seeking an alternative livelihood, he had opened a small convenience shop in a hastily erected concrete-block structure next to the house, where he could be found most days sitting with a few friends and relatives, all men, passing the time of day between customers. Like many such small neighborhood groceries, it was not heavily trafficked during the off-peak hours and did not provide much of a living, but it was better than nothing, I imagine. At least you saved money by eating your own profits instead of buying groceries from someone else. Many years later, my friend Ramzia in the Umm al Fahm suburbs did the same thing for a while—ran a little grocery shop in her ground floor front room—while her children were young.

Most of the community did not really understand what our little group of volunteers was doing there. Some thought we worked for the Israeli security services and had been sent to spy on them. (This was by no means a baseless suspicion, apparently. Future Israeli secret agents were routinely sent to enjoy home hospitality in Arab villages to perfect their command of spoken Arabic dialects. Only later, when one of those same young people reappeared in an official capacity, would the former hosts realize how they had been duped.) Meantime, we had our supporters, fortunately: people who understood the idea of our program's mandate—which was to promote joint Jewish-Arab grassroots community projects between schools, women's clubs, sports teams, and other groups in their village and those in neighboring Jewish villages. They understood that we wanted to help reconcile Jews and Arabs in the area. They could tell that we meant well, certainly. In hindsight, I think that they also realized that we

197

had no very solid grasp of the enormity (not to say impossibility) of the task, given the pervasive structural inequality of Israeli society. We must have seemed terribly naïve as, indeed, we were. But people were welcoming and did what they could to make our projects successful. We also taught English conversation in the local elementary schools and that, at least, was greatly appreciated. The welcome we typically received in the neighboring Jewish communities was less enthusiastic. There was too much fear and mistrust.

When my roommate Melanie and I were not away at meetings or conducting programs or out visiting people, our landlady Faiza would invite us to hang out with her during the day while she did her housework. Sometimes she had the patience to teach us cooking. Now and then we helped her peel potatoes, dice cucumbers and tomatoes for salad, strip the pods off peas, peel and chop onions, sort through bulk-purchased uncooked rice for small stones, and all the other jobs that had to be done endlessly to feed a family of eight with meals constructed from scratch. We practiced our rudimentary spoken Arabic and laughed a lot together. When the muezzin's call to prayer was heard, Faiza would excuse herself and open her prayer rug in a corner of the room, and pray. Faiza knew her Qur'an and took it for granted that I, as a Jew, knew my Torah just as well. Alas, I had to fake it a lot.

On a typical evening, Melanie and I would be invited to join the family in their sitting room, which was arranged in the traditional way. Devout Muslims do not hang visual art unless it is sacred visual art, so the white-painted walls were bare, aside from a framed, ornate calligraphic rendering of the *Fatiha*, the first verse of the Qur'an. There was a television on a small, low table. Simple, cloth-covered foam mattresses were ranged along two of the other walls, with straw mats like tatami mats in front of them. We sat in a relaxed way on the mattresses on the floor, with soft pillows behind and hard pillows as armrests, our feet tucked under us or stretched out on the straw mats. If Eyas or any of the male cousins were present, they sat along one wall and we women sat along another wall, facing the television. The women always sat with a blanket or a shawl draped over their legs, for modesty.

Melanie and I generally dressed in long skirts in deference to local custom, but we did wear jeans sometimes. Either way, when we came downstairs to join the family in the evening, we were each given a shawl to cover our legs too, so we could sit any which way and be comfortable, the requirements of modesty satisfied. The younger children ran around expending energy before bedtime; the two oldest, Rabab and Mufid, sat a little apart, doing their homework while the adults talked, watched TV, and went through piles of sunflower seeds. I never quite mastered the trick, performed so effortlessly by all locals, Jews and Arabs alike, of putting a whole roasted sunflower seed in one's mouth, cracking the shell and spitting it out while chewing and swallowing the little seed. But not for want of trying.

When little Soraya, Faiza's youngest and still only a baby, was tired, she was nursed and then put to bed right there on a mattress alongside her mother. Then one by one the others, as they ran out of steam, were sent off to brush their teeth and came back to lie down alongside their siblings, be covered gently with a blanket by one of the adults, and fall asleep. No fuss, no tantrums, no whining, no negotiation necessary. The kids were always bathed in the daytime, as I recall, never in the evening when they were tired and cranky. In hindsight, most of the really useful things I've learned about childrearing without stress, I learned during those eight months in Faiza's household, watching her parenting.

Breastfeeding without borders

In 1987, just after my son Amos was born, when I was married and living in Karkur about fifteen minutes down the road from Wadi Ara, I went back to the old neighborhood for a visit. We were only recently returned from a couple of years overseas and I had somewhat lost touch with my Wadi Ara connections, but I wanted to take my baby son to meet the family there. The reunion was very warm, with a lot of excitement, hugging and kissing, and admiring of one another's children and how they'd grown. Faiza, her cousin's wife Rasha from next door, and several other neighbor women oo'ed and ah'ed at my infant's undeniable charms: blond hair, dark eyes, a plump and happy baby.

I sat around with the women and we exchanged stories for a while, and when Amos started fussing, they all wanted to watch while I nursed him. It felt weird: like, let's see how the Jewish woman does it. I hesitated. I was not yet adept at this game and the baby did not always latch on properly right away; to minimize distractions, I usually nursed him in a very quiet and private space. Then I thought—well, why not! I had often seen this same sort of innocent curiosity in Jews who came to Wadi Ara and met Palestinian Arabs for the first time: What do they eat? How do they eat it? What kind of towels do they hang in their bathrooms? I suppose that, when Palestinians who visit Jews infrequently come to a Jewish home, they must feel much the same curiosity; it's only natural. Today it was: Hmmm… does this Jewish woman nurse her baby the way we nurse ours? So although I felt a bit vulnerable, I hiked up my shirt and undid my bra and nursed Amos right there in Faiza's living room, surrounded by several interested breastfeeding veterans.

They all wanted to share their best advice about the most ef-fective way to hold the breast, position the baby, angle the nipple—the works. Mothers all, most with several children, they were sure they knew more about this business than I did. They were probably right. I was busy trying out the new angles for a considerable time afterwards.

Tibah is gone

Five months after her accident, hardly ever in pain, and thankful to be functioning normally again, Reem went into Tibah's room one morning to raise the shutters and Tibah was, uncharacteristically, not already standing up in her crib to greet her.

Tibah, what's wrong? Tibah habibti, why are you still sleeping?

Tibah was gone–she wasn't breathing. She felt cold. Colder than cold.

Reem remembers gathering Tibah's little body in her arms and, still in her nightgown, stumbling along the street to her mother's house bearing her dead daughter, screaming for help, tears running down her face. *Help! Mama, help!* But no one could rewind the film and make this precious child breathe again.

A week or two later, Reem went back for a routine follow-up visit to the young obstetrician who had talked with her after her injury. He had already heard through the grapevine about Tibah.

Reem came into his office and sat down, and the young doctor began to cry. The two of them sat there together, tears streaming down their cheeks, comforting one another.

A good-looking suit

I am sitting at the little laundry establishment on the main road near Al-Qaryah on my way home one evening, talking with Malik, who is half the staff. He alternates shifts with a coworker who is very untalkative, or maybe just shy. Malik is sociable enough for both of them.

We are drinking, from little red plastic cups, the cardamom-spiced Arab coffee that Malik made fresh when I arrived. In his mid-thirties, Malik is tall and wiry and energized, sociable and humorous. He has a well-developed appreciation for the value of customer service and an open, congenial way of dealing with every customer as a friend and an equal: a natural people person. He and his wife have three young sons. His mom lives in Amman and he misses her. Whenever she's due for a visit, he goes around with a huge, idiotic, neon grin all over his face for days ahead of time. They lived in Argentina when he was a boy: part of the vast Palestinian diaspora. Somehow he made it back home and got papers, but his mom only made it as far as Jordan.

As we sit there drinking our coffee, a good-looking fiftyish man comes in, smiling a greeting. I pick up on his vibes right away: that warm Mediterranean *je ne sais quoi* that so many Israeli and Palestinian men seem to have, much more often than the law of averages would predict. I am very susceptible. In fact, my ex is half Iraqi, on his father's side, but the other half is American, with Russian roots farther back, which kind of pasteurized him somewhat, in my opinion. But that's another story.

Anyway, in comes this obviously affluent guy, or anyhow very comfortable. He's not too tall and not too short, trim and spiffy but not prissy, wearing a jacket and trousers. He is unmistakably a family man; the pheromones never lie. He's also very attractive.

The two of them start chatting inconsequentially as Malik goes to fetch the man's dry-cleaning order off the rack of plastic-protected hanging garments. This is apparently an old and favored customer.

Malik brings him two jackets and a couple of pairs of trousers, and the guy–let's call him Meir; come to think of it, he looks sort of Kurdish, maybe–after a cursory glance at the clothing, Meir says in some surprise, "Malik, this old jacket isn't mine. Mine was from a really good-looking suit."

"Well," says Malik, "that's the one you brought in the other day, with the rest of these things. It all went to the dry cleaner's together–I took it myself–and it all came back together. Who else's could it be?"

"But it's not mine, I tell you," insists Meir, getting a little irritated.

"It matches the number of your stub," points out Malik, looking at the number stapled to the jacket and keeping his cool.

"Yes but, Malik old buddy, it's not the jacket I brought in, I tell you…"

I sit quietly observing and they go on like this for a bit, each sure that the other is mistaken, but the mystery gets no clearer. The idea of monetary compensation is floated briefly and I could see that Malik is feeling that his good name is at stake. Meir makes noises signifying that to impugn Malik's good name is the farthest thing from his intention, but that he wants his jacket to materialize as usual. Malik makes courteous but unyielding noises in reply.

Impasse.

Into a delicate pause I suggest, gently, that maybe Meir could double-check at home to see if his jacket is maybe still there, in the closet? Maybe–and here my irrepressible associative tendencies come in handy, for a change–maybe somehow he inadvertently brought in the wrong jacket? Maybe it was an old one of his own, or a house-guest's, or the one his brother-in-law had left there last Shabbat, or after the last bar mitzvah in the family, or something similar? Something that could explain the mystery of how this jacket here, identity unknown, has found its way into

204

Meir's own dry-cleaning order while the jacket he'd meant to bring in is nowhere to be found?

Somewhat mollified but clearly still skeptical, Meir leaves, promising to check and let Malik know the outcome. We hear the tweet of the automatic lock opening Meir's car outside, the *chunk* of the car door closing, and the sound of the engine turning over.

As Meir drives away, a charged silence settles on the little shop. Malik sits back down behind the little counter and we resume sipping our coffee. "I'm sure, one thousand percent, that's the jacket he brought in," Malik says to me, grinning wryly. "It's really unfortunate that he doesn't remember."

Shrugging, I suggest that we wait and see... If Meir finds his jacket at home, I point out optimistically, gathering up my keys, then the problem is solved.

"Insh'Allah," says Malik cheerfully, and on that note, we part.

A couple of days later, my cellphone rang; it was Malik.

"Malik who?"

"Malik from the laundry! You know!"

I laughed. I know only one person named Malik. "What's up, man?"

He laughed, too. "I just thought you'd like to know that Meir found his jacket at home," he said, his satisfaction unmistakable. "I know you were a bit concerned."

"You're too right," I said. "He sounded like it was custom-made in London or something. What if you'd had to replace it?"

"No chance!" he said, and I could picture his grin.

"Nice of you to call and let me know," I said. "So whose jacket was in the shop?"

"His!" crowed Malik delightedly. "An old one."

"Nah–really?"

"Yeah. And he apologized."

I should think so, I said to myself. All's well that ends well, we agreed, and rang off. I thought how typical it was that Malik had bothered to call and let me know what happened–to satisfy my

205

natural curiosity, to establish that he'd been right after all, and to show his appreciation for my moral support. I like that young man.

A few months later, I stepped into the elevator at the mall in nearby Mevasseret, and there was Meir. After a moment or two, simultaneously, we realized where we'd met. We laughed about the Mystery Jacket.

"It was my mistake after all," he confessed.

"I know, Malik mentioned it," I said. We shared a "well, that's life" moment. The elevator stopped; the doors opened; we went our separate ways.

A very good-looking suit. And very married.

The universe gives a boost

Periodically I need to print business cards, now that I'm freelancing full time again. Neighbors in Al-Qaryah told me there's a good print shop in a village across the highway, not far away. It would be a lot simpler than going into Jerusalem, especially now that they've torn up half the city's downtown for construction of the new light rail system.

The thought occurred to me that, while I was at it, I could get some cards the same size with Yousif's picture on them, and a caption, and then we'd have something to give people when we ask for donations. Yousif is my friend Maha's teenage nephew, in Gaza; he and his brother Mohammed suffer from CGD, an inherited immune disease. They have lots of medical expenses which I help raise the money to pay for.

I found the print shop easily. The printer introduced himself as Farraj. He looked to be in his middle thirties and his place looked spiffy and well organized. About half the space was furnished as an office with two large plain desks, each with its desktop PC, and some chairs. The front part of the shop was stocked with school supplies and home office essentials—pencils and notebooks, copy paper, file folders, kids' backpacks, and a photocopy machine, obviously serving the local market of nearby villages.

I introduced myself and asked about business cards. Farraj showed me a digitally printed, colored plastic sample and we talked price. I preferred the more traditional ivory card stock with black lettering and he said it was more expensive, but he'd give it to me at the same price as the plastic. Nothing I wear, and certainly not my aging Hyundai chariot parked outside, says "financially secure"; and of course the hair going gray gives me that grandmotherly look. The overall effect seems to bring out the chivalrous in people like Farraj, a small business owner with a soul. I told him, Thanks, but I'll pay full fare on the business cards because I have another little project I want your help on; let's save the discount for that.

After I explained about Yousif, I asked him how much he could discount it for me, and he said, "I've got it." –A nice young man with clear brown eyes and probably a couple of kids to support. "Thank you," I said.

It's just as the books say: You take a step in a good direction toward a worthy goal, and the universe gets behind you and pushes.

We emailed the artwork back and forth till we were on the same track and I approved it for printing. I told him to do 500 business cards, not 1,000, because that would save me $15 and I've never yet managed to use 1,000 business cards before the current movie ends and something changes–my address, or my work, or the country I'm living in, or something.

When I went to pick up the cards, Farraj wasn't there, but I saw my stuff rubber-banded on a shelf and introduced myself to a different young man who turned out to be Farraj's brother, Nadim. The cards looked great and I said so--my five hundred business cards, and the extra ones with a color photo of Yousif. We chatted for a while because Nadim wanted to hear Yousif's story. Finally, figuring he probably had work to do, I took out my wallet.

Nadim–gazing at me with the same clear brown eyes as his brother's, framed by the same sort of laugh lines–held up both hands near his shoulders, palms facing me, and smiled. It's a universal gesture and it meant: *I'm not going to take any money from you for this.*

I raised my eyebrows: Not even for my business cards?

Nope. Not for them, either.

What could I say? I said thank you. I took my cards in a small plastic bag–it had started to drizzle–and walked out of the little shop. I took a deep breath and looked up at the sky and let the rain fall gently on my face. It was not so much about the money, although every little bit helps. It was the sense of not being in this thing alone. There are people out there who want to help; people who care.

That's a really good feeling.

Reem and Ra'ed have more children

Not quite two years after Tibah's death, Reem and Ra'ed's daughter Rawan was born: a blessing indeed. And about two years later, there was a son: Ali.

Today, when you see the infinite care, the endless patience, the gratitude, in Reem's ministering to her family's needs, day in, day out, you cannot help but be struck with admiration for her, every time. Not so much because she has more reason than many other mothers to be aware of the miraculous gift that her children represent—but because she infuses all her work as a co-parent and homemaker, and as a wife to the father of her children, with that awareness, every single day.

Reem is also a worrier—she's famous for it, in the family—but no wonder. Ra'ed, I've noticed, has deep reserves of patience for her habitual anxieties, although he often teases her when she voices them at the dinner table ("After all, if something happened to Ra'ed, I'd be all alone—no parents, no brothers to take care of me," etc.). Ra'ed's sensitive balance of patience and humor seems a well-calibrated antidote to her fears. I understand you, my dear (he seems to be saying), but, hey—the radar of life is full of sometimes fatal blips and we might as well get used to it.

This, from a man whose bottomless love for his children is evident in every little affectionate pat he bestows, for any reason or no reason; in the way he worries about their future but tries not to let on that he worries; in his hard work as family breadwinner; in his loyalty and devotion to the family as a whole.

Being Reem's shabbos goy

When Reem called me over one day to come and taste the ground meat and rice filling for her stuffed green squash, I was rereading Edward T. Hall, the anthropologist.[42] "Reem" in Arabic is a woman's name meaning "gazelle." Reem, who thinks of me as her older sister, is (like me) more solidly built now than in her graceful youth, but she has a noble and gazelle-like soul.

I was sitting here at my keyboard wondering why it is that, when otherwise normal-seeming groups of people lose their bearings and behave in terrible ways, we try to prove that they're evil people. How can we learn to focus instead on the underlying paradigm? Hall says we must and, moreover, seems to believe that we can.

Scholars in many disciplines have theorized about, and even experimentally demonstrated, how easily normal people can come to behave monstrously (think of Stanley Milgram's elegant electric-shock punishment experiments in the early 1960s at Yale[43]). We know that the capacity for such behavior is latent in ordinary people like you and me and that it can be provoked by circumstances. I found an old monograph somewhere entitled *The Problem of Partition*[44], which discussed four or five historical cases, including that of Palestine. Chopping a country in half rarely, if ever, fixes the underlying problem.

Probably when there is an "intractable conflict," what is actually intractable is something about the underlying paradigm. When people are asked to do the impossible—to behave differently, yet retain the troublesome underlying paradigm that generated or exacerbated the problem in the first place—they are unable to

---

[42] Edward T. Hall, *Beyond Culture* (New York: Doubleday, 1976).
[43] Numerous web sites, including Wikipedia, provide full descriptions of the original Milgram experiment at Yale University.
[44] Thomas E. Hachey, *The Problem of Partition: Peril to World Peace* (Chicago: Rand McNally College Publishing Company, 1972).

comply. So probably we need to empathize with their dilemma rather than judge, punish, ostracize, bomb, tear-gas, slaughter, kidnap, wall off, deport, or abandon them. Empathizing is easier if we see our ultimate long-term interests and theirs as aligned rather than opposed.

The *enemies* paradigm simply does not promote good solutions. The "other group" is the partner you need in order to fix what's broken. Labeling that group as your enemy just about guarantees that nothing will get fixed in a way that benefits both groups. An enemy is someone I can legitimately aspire to outmaneuver—*defeat*—in a negotiation, so that my gain comes at their expense. The solution will thus have a winner and a loser and will therefore be temporary, at best. The axiom that sustainability requires win-win solutions would seem self-evident by now.

It was while I was thinking about all this that Reem yelled from her summer kitchen next door for me to come help her by tasting something with ground beef and onions for tonight's *iftar* (the meal that ends the daily Ramadan fast). She reminded me yet again that she can't taste it because she's fasting and a practicing Muslim, but I can taste it because I'm Jewish and only fasting by choice, out of respect for local custom. No problem, I thought, except that it will make me really hungry. (We did this exercise yesterday and the day before and the day before that, too). She worries about added salt because of husband Ra'ed's high blood pressure (I knew that). Does the beef need more salt?

Absolutely not. Tastes great. Doesn't need more salt. I tell her it's delicious, the compliment richly deserved, and she's pleased, reminding me that I'm coming for *iftar* again tonight. Back to work. Dinner at 7:18 tonight, after the *muezzin* proclaims *Allahu akbar.*

Sure enough, my stomach rumbles as I sit down at the keyboard again in my little apartment overlooking the *wadi*. On the other hand, a growl or two from the tummy is really not that much of a hardship, given that Reem is cooking everyone's dinner including mine, while I write.

I thought of all those generations of *shabbos goyim*, non-Jews doing the various tasks on the Jewish Sabbath that their Jewish neighbors were religiously forbidden from performing: replenishing the wood or the coal, lighting the fire, turning the lights in the *shul* (synagogue) on and off... As the official taster, I guess I'm this Muslim family's *shabbos goy* for Ramadan.

Cool.

Fear of "them"

Fear of "them" is a strange thing. It can happen all at once, but it can also infiltrate your system slowly, gradually. It can go unnoticed for a long time and then suddenly make itself evident. It can zap you when you're not looking.

When I first went to live in Wadi Ara, a 33-year-old single female Jewish volunteer from New York taking up residence in a Muslim Arab village in Israel, I had very little fear. In hindsight, such fear as I did have was mainly not fear of Arabs or fear of Muslims, but fear of the unknown, fear of failure, fear of committing some colossal faux pas and appearing ridiculous—the usual fears people have anywhere, before undertaking anything new in a new environment. I was an English major at college and I'd worked as a writer and editor; what did I really know about community work? After some minimal training: not so much. My Hebrew was more or less functional; my Arabic was skimpy.

Unmarried, self-supporting, I was about to enter a conservative, traditional culture where every woman's status was mainly if not solely determined by the man or men with whom she was associated: father, brother, husband. Arab feminism in Israel, today a well-established movement, was still completely under the radar back then. To raise feminist issues in Wadi Ara would have been perceived as an attempt to impose an alien culture, not as any form of female solidarity.

In New York, I'd lived through the emergence of the new wave of feminism of the late 1960s in my teens and early twenties, an impressionable age. "Leave your Western ideas at the door when you go into Wadi Ara," we were told now, in our training for cooperative community work. "Especially let go of your feminist ideas," they told us. "Don't judge. Don't evaluate what you encounter by the standards that applied back home. This is not your community and you are guests here." I saw the

214

sense of this, but was ambivalent. Either women are entitled to equality as a fundamental human right, or not; if so, how could a society which denies or ignores it be exempt from the standard? Or maybe the point was simply not to rock the boat, since our status as Jewish residents in an Arab community would be anomalous enough already.

All of this uncertainty left plenty of room for missteps. Any fear I was aware of feeling was mainly about all that. If I harbored primal fears of the Arab as "other," I had pretty fully repressed them. Consciously, at least, I looked forward to meeting these others. I knew that the boundaries of my world were about to expand exponentially. I was ready and eager.

Another Jewish woman I met at about that time who was also working in a joint Jewish-Arab program had a lot of fears about sexual assault, all mixed up with fears of the "other." Some years earlier, she had been raped in a familiar home-town setting by someone of a different race and had decided that an interfaith, multi-ethnic, cross-cultural work experience might help her recover. As a Jew working with Arabs, she hoped to become desensitized to the perceived threat posed by the "other."

I did not know what to say to that; I had no comparable experience. I've never been raped. Living in Manhattan as a single woman for twelve and a half years, I was never even mugged. Somewhat naively, maybe, I always prided myself on my street smarts. I knew the difference between a safe neighborhood and an unsafe neighborhood, and it was not about race but rather drug use, the nature of the public spaces, and so forth. I knew how to walk alertly, swinging my arms slightly in a relaxed way, with a lot of chi streaming out of my fingertips, sending a message to a potential assailant: *Don't even try it.*

At the same time, I knew that avoiding a mugging or an assault is not necessarily about precautions or courage, but may also be about luck and timing. I knew that my Manhattan street smarts would not entirely prepare me for life in a conservative Arab village in Wadi Ara. Still, I worried much more about inadvertently

215

insulting people by behaving inappropriately in their context, than I did about inadvertently endangering myself. I had no very particular concerns about the men there. Guys are guys everywhere, was my view: for better or worse. And by and large, I must say, that view was borne out by subsequent experience.

Meantime, our training had taught us that living in a family's home would extend to us the protection of that family's *hamoula* (clan). Moreover, hospitality in general is still a primary value in traditional Arab society: the guest is sacrosanct. However naïve or ignorant of local custom a visitor may be; however partial or inaccurate her grasp of Palestinian history or Palestinian aspirations: a guest is a guest. So it seemed that we would be doubly protected from harm: as family, and as guests.

While I was actually living in Wadi Ara, I always felt safe. I felt the village wrap itself around me, seeming to sense my intentions—benign—and respond accordingly. How much of that was real, and how much my fantasy, I have no idea. Looking back now, I wonder if I really understood at the time how little reason a Palestinian inside Israel might have to welcome a Jewish volunteer into their community, much less into their own home. Nearly everyone in Wadi Ara had close relatives or friends displaced or exiled in 1948 or 1967; nearly everyone's family had lost land to conquest or confiscation by the new Jewish state; many people had friends or family who had been jailed for political activism. And in 1981, anyone in their early twenties or older could personally remember living under an Israeli military government in their own village or town, because only in 1966 was that system discontinued, while secret surveillance persisted and indeed persists to this day. And yet, the people I encountered seemed glad, even grateful, that someone cared enough to commit two years of their life to try to do something positive about the situation.

It seemed to me that I was, on balance, a lot safer in smalltown Wadi Ara, surrounded by Arab neighbors who took a lively interest in my activities, than I would have been in anonymous big-city Tel Aviv, surrounded by a couple million fellow Jews

216

minding their own business. This feeling persisted even though I knew that it was inconceivable that everyone in the village was favorably disposed to Israeli Jews in general, or to cooperation with Jews, or to the concept of our cooperation program in particular. Apart from recent history, every community has angry people, hotheads, radicals, people with drug problems, personality disorders, who knows what. No town is paradise.

As things turned out, I lived without incident for about eight months full-time in Wadi Ara. Whether or not our work there was effective in any significant way in advancing the cause of peace is anyone's guess. But living there felt good. I still sometimes meet people from the village who were children when I was a volunteer there; they remember us. They remember that we wanted to help change things. They remember us as Jews who cared. I suppose that's something, anyhow.

Interestingly, the fear came later, when I was married to an Israeli Jew and living down the road in Karkur, and raising our children. I had an acquaintance, call her Liora, a native Israeli Jew whom I'd met at the local mother and child clinic when we were both pregnant with our first. We kept bumping into each other in the waiting room there and we developed a friendship. Subsequently we both gave birth to boys, and we began getting together periodically so the kids could play. Liora had grown up on a kibbutz north of Wadi Ara, spent her youth in Jerusalem, and moved to Karkur after her marriage. To go home to visit her parents on the kibbutz, she had to drive up Route 65 to the Megiddo junction—right past all those Arab villages. While I experienced Wadi Ara as a friendly environment, Liora did not. She had been raised from birth in fear of Arabs; Arabs were the people all her menfolk had fought repeatedly in successive wars ever since she could remember.

At that time, I considered Liora's fear deplorable but understandable; still, I felt that it had nothing to do with me. I did not have her baggage. I had felt at home in Wadi Ara. And yet at some point after I had been living for several years in Karkur, a

217

Jewish mom in a Jewish family in a Jewish town in this extremely polarized country, I began to sense that I was developing fears of Wadi Ara, fears of a village in which I had happily lived and which I considered a second home. This encroaching fear was like a kind of formless fog; it was hard to pin down; it seemed to seep into my consciousness and cling there.

Quite suddenly I understood that everything about living in a Jewish environment in Israel was gradually planting in me a fear of Arabs as a collective, almost as an abstraction: the constant media barrage, the outlook and opinions of the people around me, and my unexamined desire to belong, as a Jew, among Jews. My visits to friends in Wadi Ara were becoming more sporadic and my friends there rarely ventured to Karkur to visit me. The connections grew dimmer and more distant. As I grew to feel more securely at home in Karkur, I began to feel less at home in Wadi Ara. It was almost as if one had to choose: us or them.

At some point I realized that I was not going to be happy with this phenomenon and made up my mind to do something about it. The decision brought a sense of relief. I understood that I could not sit passively and do nothing while the environment tugged at me, taking me to a place I did not want to go: a place of distrust, of alienation from my Palestinian Arab neighbors. At that time, I was still visiting Arab friends periodically and inviting them to visit me, but I could see that just visiting occasionally was not going to be enough to counter the insidious undertow of collective distrust all around me. Something more assertive, constructive, and proactive was required.

In 1996, when Amos was nine and Maya five, I began working on a project to start a Jewish-Arab school in Wadi Ara, modeled on the one at Neve Shalom- Wahat al Salam which had been in existence for over a decade by that time. I resolved that I would dive back into the warm waters of easy companionship, without false barriers.

And guess what? From the standpoint of my inner world, at least, this proved very effective. As I began meeting and mingling regularly again with Palestinian Arab friends and colleagues, the creeping sense of fear and alienation receded, never to return. My feeling of belonging in Karkur, on the other hand, would never be complete. (Meantime, we didn't succeed in establishing a joint Jewish-Arab school at that stage, but another group of parents managed it, several years later.)

I learned that our human connections are always in flux. I understood that you can never simply turn your back on fear because it will inflate itself silently while you're not looking; only a frontal engagement can really banish the fear. I saw that, as the years went by, ties of friendship across strong social barricades can be both delicate and resilient, and are rarely simple. What we make of all that is up to us.

Ali goes to an experimental preschool

Reem and Ra'ed's family was thriving. Rawan and Ali were happy and healthy kids. Ra'ed was doing well, working in construction, as his father had done. His father, Abu Ra'ed, owns several dunams of land, with olive and fruit trees, and has always been honored in his community as a man of great dignity and good sense, a quiet man, an amateur historian, a creative thinker.

Ra'ed admires his dad and takes his advice in many things. Abu Ra'ed worked with both Jews and Palestinians all his life and has many connections in the world outside Al-Qaryah and in Palestinian communities in the diaspora. Dignitaries would come periodically from distant places to consult with him.

Ra'ed himself is less outgoing than his father. He is a man of few words and deep thoughts; both are qualities I admire. He brings great intelligence and excellent taste to any project he undertakes. I told Reem once, about a week after I moved in next door: If you are my sister, I said, then Ra'ed is my kid brother. She laughed and hugged me, but I knew that we had just sealed a bargain that accomplished something important: We had made an acceptable space for me in their family circle that permitted me to be friends with Ra'ed as well as with Reem, in a non-threatening way.

Rawan as a toddler had been enrolled in the local preschool, and she was happy there. When Ali was ready for nursery school, however, his dad was thinking of sending him to a new preschool outside the village, at the first-ever bilingual, bicultural, Jewish-Arab experimental school in Israel or Palestine, called the Oasis of Peace Primary School. It was built originally to serve the children of Neve Shalom-Wahat al Salam, an intentional multi-faith, binational community about half an hour from Al-Qaryah, next to the Latrun Monastery. The community was not large enough to support a school all by itself and had lately opened its doors to children from the surrounding villages and towns.

Ali liked the idea, and so away he went, out into the wider world via a minivan, together with a few other local kids, at the age of four. This step would set the direction of Ali's future–looking outward and working for a more just society; looking inward and seeking to understand. Now 24, he has held a variety of day jobs in telemarketing and the like, to support his artistic addiction: He writes lyrics for popular songs in Hebrew. ("I don't aspire to be literary," he says.)

Ali's other great love is chess. He traveled abroad once with a mixed Jewish-Arab junior chess club. They played in Moscow. He would go again in a minute if he had the chance. He admires chess champions because, he tells me, *chess is a beautiful game in which anyone can compete, no matter their color, nationality, size, age, mother tongue or religion. It doesn't even matter what kind of personality you have. You just need a brain, a memory, and a lot of perseverance. That's why it is a great game.*

I wonder

The women my age, when I lived in Wadi Ara as a volunteer, were married with young children. Otherwise they ended up like our friend Khulud, resolutely single, living in a small studio flat in her eldest brother's house, with a life circumscribed by a web of elaborate do's and don'ts, and very little wiggle room. In this respect, what made us dissimilar was less the Jewish-Arab divide than the fact that I had lived in Manhattan on my own, unmarried, working, and self-directed, for the preceding twelve years. In a Wadi Ara community there was no such social category because it was a *village*. The issue wasn't just what was and was not permissible behavior for a female adult. It was also that an individual life had its truest meaning only as part of an elaborated collective. No one was alone, sailing their ship solo on the high seas of life. Such a pattern was completely foreign to the village's residents.

If I had been born there, among those villagers, I would have come at all this from the other side of the mirror, of course. I wonder how emancipated in the Western sense I would have become, in that milieu, in that place and time, in that life?

Kitchen thoughts in Wadi Ara, 1981

Cooking here is done in a kitchen located indoors or out. Some are fully equipped with modern appliances in Western style, while others are a hybrid of modern and traditional–with marble countertops, say, but a camping-style gas ring for cooking. In poorer homes, the appliances are older and more basic but I notice that the competence of the cook bears no relation to these material circumstances.

I visit homes where, in a kitchen full of gleaming, spotless counters, the family's women will dice and chop all vegetables while squatting casually on their heels in the middle of the kitchen floor–because that is more comfortable and familiar than standing at a counter.

Does this seem backward to you? Think again. Time after time I watch respectfully as a housewife reduces an onion or a tomato to neat, almost surgically diced cubes–working over a bowl with only her two hands and a good, sharp knife: in the air, without benefit of cutting board or chopping block. I never tire of witnessing this culinary sleight-of-hand. I soon let go of my semiconscious assumption that modern is always better, or anyhow more advanced. The perfect tiny squares of diced tomato cascade gracefully into a clean plastic bowl sitting on the spotless tiled floor between the artist's knees, as I silently revise some of the patronizing preconceptions I hadn't been aware of harboring.

In most of the homes I visit, I can most readily access the kitchen and the women's world in general if I come in the morning when the menfolk are at work.

On visits during the afternoon or evening, however, particularly if I am accompanied by a male colleague, typically I am treated like an honorary male and kept in the salon, to be formally entertained by the head of the household and the older children. I confess that I enjoy being treated as an honorary male; at least, I enjoy it some of the time. I am plied with good conversation along with the unvarying succession of soft drinks, fruits in season, cakes and cookies and baklawa and candies, fragrant Arab coffee with cardamom in small porcelain cups, and tea with mint or sage in delicate glasses. The women do not join us and the kitchen work proceeds without my admiring observation. I am stranded in limbo between the two worlds. My categories of reality are almost meaningless here. This, too, is educational.

More about Ra'ed

After graduating from high school, Ra'ed went off to Netanya with his father's blessing to work in the hotel industry and see something of the world. He learned the difference between a steak knife and a fish knife and a lot more about what makes people tick.

Ra'ed was a top student in high school, back in the day. I heard this from other people, including his children, but not from the man himself; too modest. I asked him once if he would have wanted more education, if he'd had the chance, like some of his younger siblings: one sister is a pediatrician, one brother is an accountant and another is a physiotherapist. Ra'ed shrugged. He wasn't particularly interested in books, he said, and he preferred working to sitting in a classroom. I have a strong feeling that part of his eagerness to work had to do with making sure that the family would find the money to pay for higher education for his younger siblings, but it's not a topic I feel comfortable raising with any of them.

Ra'ed impresses me as an empath and a born multiculturalist, curious and non-judgmental about how other people live, skilled at reading between the lines of what people say, to get what they actually mean. Our area was full of people from somewhere else and, judging from his infrequent comments, he seemed to read them all quite easily. Some of that skill he may owe to his early exposure to the world outside Al-Qaryah, traveling with his dad to jobs all over Israel, as well as to his time working in the resort hotels of Netanya. Ra'ed has tremendous balance, great dignity, and a generous heart. I cannot remember, from our various conversations, that he ever had a disparaging word to say about anyone.

I am glad for Reem that she has a life partner like Ra'ed, and vice versa. *May Allah protect them, their health, and their family.*

Al-Qaryah, a quiet backwater

Like many neighboring communities, the village of Al-Qaryah is Muslim and Arabic-speaking. It has an unusual history, however: The earliest residents of whom anything is known today were not from the area, nor even from Arab communities elsewhere in the region. They came from a distant place, somewhere in the Balkans, perhaps; or perhaps from Turkey. No one knows for sure. And despite a certain amount of intermarriage with local Palestinian Arab Muslims over the years, the older generation in Al-Qaryah will tell you quite straightforwardly that they are not "really" Palestinian, although they are Muslims. The younger generation identifies more strongly as Palestinian.

There is no documented explanation concerning what moved the first residents of Al-Qaryah to settle where they did. But the village has been in its present location for at least three hundred years and possibly longer. Up in the hills and off the beaten track, Al-Qaryah has remained a quiet backwater.

Few people have ever heard of Al-Qaryah. Its near neighbor Abu Ghosh, on the other hand, is quite well known. The original Muslim inhabitants of Abu Ghosh were also not local. They came from somewhere in the Caucasus Mountains in Eurasia. Again, no one knows for sure what prompted the original Abu Ghosh progenitor to uproot his family and travel thousands of miles to settle in the Middle East. All that is known is that, when he brought them to this likely spot on a ridge at Jerusalem's western edge, they settled down and took possession of a strategic pass on the road linking the coastal plain with the ancient city of pilgrimage on the hill. Thereafter, from all travelers he collected a toll—a travel tax—for the privilege of passing through. In due course the place acquired a name, after its founder. The economy of Abu Ghosh, then, was built originally by a man who knew how to make the most of possibilities: a natural entrepreneur.

Today, the town's economy rests largely on tourism, with a main street several kilometers long lined with successful restaurants and bakeries. The founding entrepreneurial spirit lives on.

I spent nearly three years living not far from Abu Ghosh in Al-Qaryah, in a small rented apartment, a lovely little flat with a tiny terrace, a miniscule garden and a great pastoral view. I got to know the neighborhood fairly well and shared in the life of its residents. Some of their stories are recounted here.

Rawan knows what she wants

When she was four going on five, Ali's sister Rawan had entered preschool right down the road in neighboring Abu Ghosh. Even if she had had a different option (she says now), she would not have wanted to travel a long way on a bus every day to anywhere else. She was happy right there at home with the friends she'd always had.

Although later, as a young woman, Rawan would study architecture in Jordan, this venturing abroad to attend a foreign university would not change her basic direction. She was not interested in spending her life in Jordan, nor in meeting a potential husband in Jordan—neither a Jordanian nor a Palestinian expatriate. When the time came, she wanted to meet someone from Al-Qaryah or maybe Abu Ghosh, someone who wanted, as she did, to settle down right there, near her mother and aunts and cousins. She would find work in Jerusalem, or she would freelance. Marrying outside, in her view, would mean raising her own family in some far-off Muslim town in the Triangle or the Galilee or even, heaven forbid, abroad. She had no interest in that sort of future. She had never seriously considered living in a city, either.

Rawan explained all this to me quite straightforwardly, and I still marvel at the clarity she can bring to the business of planning a life! I wish I could wave a magic wand and make all of her dreams come true. The one about finding a wonderful guy close to home, in any case, has already come true. *Allah karim.*

A Day in Tel Aviv

Mid-September, 2009. I am sitting at Greg's Café, the espresso bar next to *Tzomet Sefarim* ("Book Crossing") in Dizengoff Center, the original Tel Aviv mall. Its first store opened in 1977.

The women of Reem's family are wandering up and down Dizengoff Street looking for a dress for Rawan's engagement party next week. She was hoping to have found one a long time ago, but the right dress just seemed to elude her. And because stress always seems to come in bunches, next week her intended will also be sitting for his university placement exams. Zahi, the groom, is a real sweetie. I finally met him the other day, a few months after Rawan did, and I like him very much indeed. He has *mensch* (a good guy) written all over him.

Rawan and Zahi met in a traditional way, in what we might call a quasi-arranged match: His family approached her family to propose a union. Both families are thoroughly modern people and while all the elaborate formalities were observed, they left it strictly up to the young people to decide. It was sheer good luck that they found each other fascinating from the first meeting and the rest just fell into place. Rawan's grandfather Abu Ra'ed was very much in favor, and he is both a man of the world and a person of great insight who is devoted to the welfare of every member of his extended family, so I was inclined to think that this match probably has a lot going for it.

Now we're at the shopping moment of truth; Rawan must have the perfect dress for her betrothal. Since I was never an avid shopper, I find myself sitting here writing while the other women canvass the boutiques.

They wanted to start at Kikar Hamedina, an upscale *haute couture* enclave. I lived in Tel Aviv once upon a time, so I managed to find my way to the right area by following my nose and by consulting another driver at a stop light–a young man who gazed curiously at our carload of Jewish driver plus Arab passengers while he thought about how many more traffic lights we would pass before the next turn I needed to take.

"Two wives," Reem told him, laughing, just as we drove away.

"What?" I said absently, watching the traffic.

"You know—our father had two wives," she chuckled. "I wanted to relieve his curiosity!"

Reem loves this sister thing and I am careful now not to contradict her, ever since the day at the furniture shop at the Bilu junction when we were negotiating for her new dining table and chairs. We told the Jewish salesman, Ofir, that we were sisters and he looked us up and down skeptically: one in trousers and a short haircut, the other in a long dress and wearing a Muslim headscarf. He said, But are you *really* sisters? We answered simultaneously, both laughing: Reem said Yes and I said No—a quintessential East-West moment. (What is "real"? A birth certificate, which after all is just a piece of paper? Or what you have in your heart?)

So Reem, Rawan, Reem's sister Najla and Najla's daughter Saida all came in my car together to Tel Aviv and we began at Kikar Hamedina because Reem and Rawan wanted to. I was pushing for Dizengoff Street so I could park under the mall there and then hit the bookshop and a café while the others strolled around the shops along both sides of Dizengoff without me. It turns out that the glitzy *couturiers* at Kikar Hamedina have morphed into regular clothing chains sometime in the recent past, so we got right back in the car and went to Dizengoff Center after all.

By that time, what with all the driving around in city traffic and parking at Kikar Hamedina only to get back in the car and drive away again, my focus was a little diffused. I was thrilled to arrive at the Dizengoff Center parking entrance without having wasted too much time navigating all the one-way streets downtown. While busy congratulating myself on my driving acumen, I pushed the button and took a ticket from the machine at the entrance to the underground parking and drove heedlessly past the

230

security guard's little post opposite, without even noticing him. When he called out to me to stop, I didn't even hear him. Reem and the others hollered to get my attention. I braked abruptly, a couple of meters beyond where I was supposed to be. The guard, now very alert, told me brusquely to back up and then asked in a business-like tone for all our ID cards.

I got out of the car and launched into a series of apologies and explanations as I realized belatedly that from his standpoint, I had tried to sneak or bluff my way past his guard post into the parking lot with a carload of…unexamined Arabs.

Oh hell, I thought, going around to the back to unlock the trunk for inspection and mentally casting around for a fix-it strategy while assuring him that I was so very sorry and that I just had not seen him. The guy was not amused. I leaned into the car at Reem's urgent gesture and she whispered that Rawan had forgotten her ID card at home. I rolled my eyes. *We'll say that she's only 14* (two years underage for an ID card), I improvised, thinking to myself even as I said it: Okay, that's not a great plan if he bothers to check. Luckily, she was not wearing a sign saying "Just Got Engaged."

I knew the guard would most likely never have heard of Al-Qaryah, so I tried the magic words "Abu Ghosh": "We're all one family; we're from Abu Ghosh," I said, as he examined first my ID and then the other three (glancing meanwhile at the four passengers, one after the other, trying to see which one was the "child," I guess). I pulled out my checkbook which luckily was one of the newer ones with my Abu Ghosh post office box printed on it and waved it in his face and said "See? Abu Ghosh." (Al-Qaryah has no post office.)

Abu Ghosh is considered a "friendly" Arab town by Israeli Jews and something bordering on a treasonous enclave by not a few Palestinians, because in the 1948 war, its residents (like those of Al-Qaryah) did not physically resist the Jewish forces. The people of Abu Ghosh, immigrants from Eurasia once upon a time, had lived in Palestine under the Turks during the Ottoman

Empire and under the British during the Mandate period. If they were now to be living under the Jews, they would deal with that, too. The reed that bends with the prevailing wind, does not break—something like that. In consequence, despite the village's strategic location and unlike hundreds of other less fortunate Palestinian communities, their homes were not blown up by the Jewish army in that war and their mosque was left intact. They have continued to maintain a kind of dignified neutrality ever since. The younger generation identifies much more closely with Palestinian national aims than their elders seem to, but at Israeli checkpoints, the phrase "Abu Ghosh" is still something akin to a magic password.

Somewhat mollified, the security guard at Dizengoff Center inspected the baggage compartment and waved us on through, including Ms. Just Got Engaged without her ID card.

I won't say my hands were trembling by that time, but neither was I really breathing normally. Imagine the bad karma if the guy had hauled us off for further questioning on the day we were shopping for Rawan's engagement gown. Reem wondered aloud why he wanted to see their identification and I told her, Listen, I'm as sensitized to racial profiling as the next person, but this time I think it was my fault and it wasn't (mainly) because there are Arabs in the car. This time it was because he thought I was trying to drive through without stopping to let him do a security check on us.

I didn't want to ruin the mood before the day had half started. I was so persuasive, I almost believed me, myself.

We drove around the gloomy underground labyrinth a while and found a parking space and I remembered (for a change) to memorize the location so we could find it again later.

The girls went off with their moms to shop the Dizengoff Street boutiques while I sat down at Greg's Café right next to the big bookstore. Time flowed pleasantly as I sipped my coffee, my pen pinning part of reality to the page while I waited for the others to come and meet as arranged.

232

I predicted on the way into Tel Aviv that Rawan would find a great dress for not too much money and that she would buy the very first one she tried on, after then trying on a few dozen others, to be sure. So I phoned just now to see how they are doing. Did she find a dress? Yes, she did. Is she pleased? Yes, she is.

And was it the first one she tried on? --Yes!

You're kidding! --No!

Now we'll see what it cost them. They sound pretty happy.

Andie has her baby

I got an email from Andie, the Jewish translator who before her marriage had lived in Wadi Ara as one of Ramzia's downstairs lodgers and then married a nice Jewish boy from Tel Aviv and moved to the big city. Good news: Andie's baby was born and they named her Rachel!

Thinking of Andie always has pleasant associations for me. I met her at a Sikkuy conference in Nazareth; she was sitting at the same lunch table, and we began talking. She was looking for help to find an Arabic-speaking environment to live in for a while. I introduced her to Ramzia and Abdel Hadi, who eventually rented her a ground floor room in their home in the Umm al Fahm suburbs for a year or so while she learned Arabic. Ramzia and Andie are still close friends.

That was the same luncheon at which I first met Bedouin feminist and social activist Amal A-sana Alh'jooj and heard her tell, in person, about her discovery that working in partnership is so much more productive than running on anger: *After I first met Jews committed to justice and equality*, she said, *I began cooperating on joint projects with them instead of just being angry. I was amazed at how much more I could get done that way, and I stopped struggling alone from a place of anger.*[45]

Unsurprisingly, Amal is a graduate of a School for Peace change-agent training course at Wahat al Salam~Neve Shalom. She also did her M.A. in community development at McGill University in Canada. She went on to become a highly effective activist for Bedouin rights and for women's rights in the Negev. Her transformation transforms others every day.

---

[45] In a personal conversation. Amal A-sana Alh'jooj is a Co-Executive Director of the Negev Institute for Strategies of Peace and Development and the founding director of AJEEC–Arab Jewish Center for Equality, Empowerment and Cooperation. See them online at
http://www.nisped.org.il/info/english/about/Aboutus.htm

Maybe by the time Andie's little Rachel grows up, she won't have to be a soldier, after all.

Yaara turns seven

Noor and Kemal's daughter Yaara, our precocious and beautiful young neighbor in Al-Qaryah, who is a first-grader at the Jerusalem Hand-in-Hand bilingual school, turned seven yesterday. Birthday parties are not traditional in Palestinian Arab culture, but the custom is catching on in some circles lately—thanks to television, perhaps. And of course Yaara goes to a multicultural school where her Jewish classmates doubtless have birthday parties.

Thus, a few days ago Yaara appeared at my door one evening with a handwritten invitation to her party: obviously the result of painstaking effort. For her Hebrew-speaking Jewish friends in the neighborhood, she had done the text in Hebrew block letters, with a thick colored marker, on a small lined sheet of paper torn from a spiral notebook with a Bank Leumi logo in the corner. I can imagine the scene: *Mama, can I have some paper? --What for, Yaara? --To make party invitations... --I can help you with that, honey... --No, no, Mama, I want to write them myself! —Do you want some paper with lines on it? How about using this pad?*

The invitation, in red ink just to make sure it got proper attention, and embellished with two rows of balloons, or maybe lollipops, said (in Hebrew):

> *SUNDAY*
> *AT YAARA'S HOUSE*
> *AT 06 O'CLOCK*
> *Q Q Q Q Q*
> *YAARA'S BIRTHDAY PARTY*
> *Q Q Q Q Q*
> *[BANK LEUMI LOGO]*

Neither Noor nor Kemal works at Bank Leumi, so probably they bank there. Or maybe the high-tech company where Kemal works counts Bank Leumi among its clients. Anyhow, the logo definitely gave the whole thing a somewhat official look: very cool.

I was flattered to be on Yaara's list and asked her who else was coming. She had invited a bunch of neighbors including Reem and Rawan, but Rawan was already back at school in Jordan. The birthday girl's parents had invited the usual suspects—mainly their own siblings and cousins whose children are near Yaara's age.

Picking a gift wasn't hard. I found a little silver necklace that said *shalom ~ salaam* ("peace" in Hebrew and Arabic), just the right size, and polished it with some toothpaste and spritzed it with a little scent and found a little gift box for it. "Is this party," I had queried of the birthday girl in advance, "a dress-up type of event?" "If you want to," shrugged Yaara, not wishing to commit herself either way. Very tactful! So at the appointed hour, I changed into something more formal—meaning, a clean top and some presentable slacks—and walked the few steps over there with Reem.

Yaara grinned at us and clapped her hands with excitement, then skipped over to usher us in as we came through the gate: a royal welcome, just for showing up. Children are never certain, I think, that their significant grown-ups are going to take their affairs seriously. Although the air was already nippy with evening coming on, Yaara had made no concessions to the weather. Holding herself like royalty, she was resplendent in a thin calf-length white party dress with a gathered tulle overskirt, a heart-shaped bodice and spaghetti straps. This was matched by elegant white patterned tights and soft white party shoes like ballet slippers. Everyone else present was much more warmly dressed, and I laughed inwardly, imagining the mother-daughter argument, or anyhow dialogue, that must have prefaced the decision about what to wear. (*The white party dress from cousin Mahmoud's wedding, or something warmer?*) Yaara, predictably, had won that one. She

237

looked every inch a princess, her naturally tan skin glowing, her huge green-gray eyes shining with excitement, her long dark brown hair caught at the crown and cascading down her back in waves. A natural star, and aware of the impression she was making, as how could she not have been? If, to my mind, the overall effect was maybe more appropriate to a young woman of at least nineteen, it's nonetheless the way girls her age dress these days–but that's another conversation.

There was a reasonably nice-sized turnout of friends and relatives (most of the friends ARE relatives)–young professionals like Yaara's own mom and dad. The women with babies sat around in the living room, chatting and supervising the rug rats: a bunch of cuties. This old woman enjoyed herself with the babies. I played peekaboo with a charming little guy called Yousif and didn't try to learn all the other kids' names, since I would just forget them right away in any case. The ones Yaara's age ran around outside and let off steam. One or two dads were also there. They sat with Kemal on the back porch next to the kitchen and drank coffee and talked guy talk, bestirring themselves occasionally to shift chairs or tables or keep an eye on some of the kids or perform the odd chore when called upon. Meanwhile Noor and her sister and a couple of other youngish women sped back and forth from kitchen to porch to living room to a big side veranda, where the children's party table was, serving fruit and tea and coffee and munchies to everyone.

So we ate and drank and made small talk, and the kids played Pin the Tail on the Donkey. We all sang Happy Birthday (in English!) and Yaara blew out the candles and everybody congratulated her and had some of the cake. It was a chocolate layer cake with whipped cream filling and white icing from Farouk's Bakery, next to Hisham's Sweets Shop down on the main street in Abu Ghosh. The cake was tasty and the kids enjoyed themselves and none of them swallowed any pieces of the balloons that they kept trying alternately to blow up and to bite into, scaring the heck out of me. All's well that ends well.

238

In the good years, time flies. When I moved into her neighborhood originally, Yaara was a very shy four-year-old. It seems like only yesterday, to me. Yet now, at seven, she is suddenly so grown up and self-confident. Nothing fazes this child.

May her world appreciate her, and may the future be kind.

Happy seventh birthday, Yaara!

Our little multicultural enclave

Reacting to my description of my neighborhood one time, a friend emailed me that I had clearly managed to find a "little multicultural enclave" here in Al-Qaryah, in the Jerusalem foothills. The rest of this region tends to separate very sharply, or be separated, into "us" and "them"–but our little corner of it has a different ethos. Here–if not in every way, nor all the time, yet certainly on many levels and in many contexts–we are all "us."

This particular little multicultural enclave evolved in recent years, as local families began renovating their basements for rental, or fixing up a grandparent's old one-room house for rental after building a much larger and more modern family home next to it. At my best guess, between Al-Qaryah and Abu Ghosh with a combined population of more than 7,000 Muslims, there are at least several dozen (and possibly many more) outsiders renting apartments, both in the more crowded older areas and in the more spacious and newer sections: that is to say, both "downtown" and in the "suburbs."

Within a few hundred yards of my front door are four other rental units. One is a young Jewish man from the Galilee, Oren, an art student, a really nice guy. He has a tiny dog called Kutya (which means "dog" in Hungarian) who is very well behaved, and not too big. In fact if Kutya were any smaller, he could be mistaken for a rodent. Kutya is friendly and well-behaved and, unlike many dogs his size, does not greet every passerby with hysteria. I like Kutya. Aside from which, Oren's landlady wouldn't rent to anyone with a big dog again. Arabs in this society do not customarily keep dogs as house pets, to begin with. And there was a Ukrainian lady, a retired pharmacist, renting a flat in that same courtyard for a while, who owned some kind of huge furry canine from the frozen steppes of Siberia. Despite this dog's calm demeanor, he scared the heck out of everyone and Oren's landlady swore that was the last dog, period, but she relented for Kutya. Kutya has a great personality.

On the other side of Oren and Kutya is Guy, also a twenty-something Jew and, like Oren, easygoing, friendly, not noisy, and gainfully employed: in short, a good tenant and a good neighbor. Guy has no dog but, like Oren, drives an old falling-down car. Every time I see Oren or Guy's basic wheels parked outside, I am reminded of my long-ago youth. Besides being nice young people, they have this nostalgia factor in their favor.

So much for our little street. We follow the typical pattern in Al-Qaryah: the owners are Muslim and their families have lived here a long time; most of the tenants are Jewish and relatively transient.

Next door, Ra'ed's cousin Kemal and his wife Noor have two rental apartments in their yard. One is home to a growing young family of four, a Jewish family: Hanan, a photographer with a good job working in an elite media agency; his wife Ella, who works as an animator and private children's tutor, although she studied biology at university; their daughter Yali, about two years old now, very cute and bilingual because she spends her days at in-home daycare with Rabia, an Arabic-speaking neighbor; and Yuval, Yali's new baby sister.

I have become very fond of Hanan and Ella, not only because they're charming and intelligent and friendly and cheerful, but also because they offer an invaluable neighborly service that translators cherish: They are willing to be interrupted most hours of the day or night when I have a question about an unusually complicated Hebrew passage in a translation I'm working on. Both of them speak excellent English so I can lapse into my mother tongue whenever I like; neither of them speaks much Arabic. They have a large terrace and they barbecue there on weekends sometimes in the warmer months. When they entertain friends, it's never boisterous. Rather than being disturbed by the noise when they have company, I find it puts me in a good mood to hear them having fun. I did my laundry over there occasionally, before I got my own washing machine; they wouldn't let me reimburse them for the detergent or the water and electricity. They let me make silly grandma noises at their kids whenever I want to. What more could I ask of neighbors?

More on our neighborhood

One sunny day when Hanan was sitting outside his front door smoking a cigarette, I came outside to consult him about an incomprehensible passage in the memoir I was translating into English, the one about the young Eastern European Zionists trying to get themselves and their surviving friends out of postwar Europe to Palestine. Hanan said: "You know, Deb, that's my grandfather's story."

I imagine a lot of people in many parts of the world would connect with this story in their own way, but it is unlikely to be published in English, since Zionism is not a popular word these days. My translation was privately commissioned, by a friend of the author's widow, so that the family abroad who do not read Hebrew could get to know this part of their own history.

Aside from Hanan and Ella, Kemal's other tenants on the other side of the house are a couple of doctors: Sonia is an internist and she is a Russian Jew; Amir, who is Palestinian, is an orthopedist from the Galilee who went to med school in Canada. They have one child, a little girl called Lily, now almost a year old. They met at the hospital where they were both working at the time, and fell in love. Marriage across the Jewish-Arab divide in Israel is rare and can be a very iffy life choice, but at least in Sonia and Amir's case, their families have not given them a hard time. Amir's parents are living abroad now and decided not to make an issue of his choice. Sonia's family in Ashdod took the position that they are happy about the marriage because Sonia is happy, and they love Amir.

Intermarriage is not a bad thing in my eyes. In some ways, all marriages are intermarriages in the sense that they unite two entirely different worlds into one union. I do not view a child as disadvantaged because her parents profess different faiths or have different ethnic origins, but I am a realist: In Israel in our day, the child of a mixed Jewish-Palestinian marriage faces a great many awkward moments and will be shunned entirely in some quarters. It was inevitable that Sonia, Amir and I would become friends, I guess, because we have a lot of interests in common and also because I have no trouble relating to them as just folks, rather than as some kind of weird aberration.

Sonia and Amir want to buy a house and Sonia asked me where I think they should look, and I said: Abroad. I was only half kidding. Why should Lily have to feel like a freak here when she could be accepted as totally normal in Paris or London? Meantime, they were scouting out a neighborhood near where they are currently working–an almost exclusively Jewish neighborhood, as it happens: French Hill, which Palestinians and international law define as an illegal settlement and most Israelis define as "ours." Recently she was discussing all this with a woman colleague at the hospital where she works, Sonia told me. The colleague (Jewish) said to her: "But wouldn't you and Amir be *more comfortable living with Arabs*?"

Now what would be an appropriate answer to that question? I was stumped! Maybe we could ask Oprah.

When this young couple was preparing to register their child's birth, they had some soul-searching to do. In Israel, a new citizen is not registered as "Israeli"–despite a longstanding struggle by citizen activists to obtain precisely this option. There is no such category of identity as "Israeli" in Israel. A newborn child is registered by religion (and until recently, in a practice discontinued under pressure, he or she would also have been registered as either Jewish or Arab on the ID card). An Israeli citizen's passport may say "Israeli" in English, but on his or her Israeli identity card, in Hebrew, there is no such designation.

In the present case, Sonia cannot register her daughter as Jewish because she herself is not Jewish enough for the authorities: Sonia's father is a Russian Jew and Sonia was raised as a Jew, but her mother is Christian. Hence baby Lily is not Jewish according to Israeli law, which follows the traditional (halakhic) matriarchal definition of Jewishness. So the baby could be registered as a

Christian, or a Muslim (like her father), or else as a "blank"–that is, as having no religion. After much thought, Sonia and Amir chose "blank"; when she is old enough, they told me, she'll decide for herself. They're not sure they would have registered her as Jewish in any case, even if they'd had the option, because of all the social and political baggage that comes with that choice in this country. The authorities, meanwhile, don't care how adorable Lily is, or how smart, or whether she is going to grow up to be the next Marie Curie or Eleanor Roosevelt or Meryl Streep. They see her as a Demographic Blank. Isn't bureaucracy wonderful?

On the other side of the village, Ra'ed's father has a small studio flat in his yard. He rents it to a young Arab pediatrician from the Galilee who is working at Hadassah Hospital in Ein Kerem. I'm sure this young man and Amir are not the only Arab tenants around here, although most of the renters I meet seem to be Jewish.

So here we all are, Jewish, Christian, and the occasional Muslim tenant too, living side by side in this Muslim village, with Muslim families as landlords: a bunch of young professionals with young kids, some singles, and the neighborhood grandma (me). There's a lot of warmth and friendly conversation over the back fence, as it were, sometimes in Arabic or even English, most often in Hebrew. Kemal and Noor's Yaara (first language, Arabic) and Ella and Hanan's Yali (first language, Hebrew) are both growing up bilingual, with both Arabic and Hebrew: a great head start for a multiethnic future. Sonia and Amir's baby is also learning English and Russian at home.

Yaara still attends the Hand in Hand School in Jerusalem, so she's not around much during the week. She's in second grade now, very personable and still ahead of the curve. She comes over to my place occasionally and I take out my stash of crayons and markers so she can make me some new refrigerator art. Her Hebrew is already better than my Arabic. We understand each other pretty well, despite the language gap, the culture gap, and the age gap.

Truly, we have a special community mosaic of our own here, probably temporary because tenants, including this one, tend to move on eventually. Meantime, life is very pleasant.

It's not rocket science. It's just friendship.

Your money or your car

My neighbor Ra'ed's cousin Badira lives with her widowed father and keeps house for him. Badira, who is single, had a job once upon a time, and has a driver's license and owns a car. She gave up her job to look after her frail and elderly father when her mother died. Consequently Badira is eligible for a modest income supplement from the National Insurance Institute, and she has to report weekly (by fingerprint, to a machine).

When the global economy tanked a few years ago, donations to Israeli nonprofits fell off sharply and I was downsized from my staff job at Wahat al Salam~Neve Shalom. In due course, after filling out the relevant forms in triplicate and supplying the copious documentation demanded and waiting on line a lot to have my forms processed, I started getting unemployment compensation: my first time ever. Unemployment compensation here, these days, runs for six months. So Badira and I were to be on public assistance together for a while.

One day I took Badira with me by car to Jerusalem to the National Insurance offices, since I had to go there too, to sign for my unemployment. Usually she goes by bus, which is not a simple proposition because her dad's house is nowhere near a bus stop. So she was glad to have a ride, and in addition we had a chance for a good chat, just the two of us.

Driving into Jerusalem, Badira mentioned that, in case I didn't know, she actually owns a car herself: the one that's always parked in the yard of her dad's house. People receiving income supplements from the government, however, are not permitted to drive, she told me. "What, not at all?" I was amazed; that would never happen in California, I thought. "Not even someone else's car?" I queried. Apparently not.

The logic, I guess, is that if someone can afford a car, and insurance, and gas, or even has friends who can afford all that, then

247

they don't need an income supplement from the government. On the other hand, it would be convenient for Badira to be able to drive her father, who has limited mobility, to wherever he needs to go, including to the doctor at the local clinic, or grocery shopping. If Badira were caught driving, however, she'd lose her benefits. Theoretically her dad could still drive but evidently is not too eager to do it anymore. And what about when he is no longer able to drive at all?

While I understand the government's point of view, it seems a rather harsh and rigid rule. Badira will doubtless care for her father until the end of his natural life, saving the state a lot of money. And the older he gets, the more it would be helpful if she could chauffeur him around as the need arises. Of course there are other family members who can help out in a pinch; still, it seems dumb. What is she supposed to do if he needs to get somewhere in an emergency, and no one is around to help out: call a cab?

Accustomed to finding random instances of discrimination under every rock I turn over, I asked Badira if this policy is just for Arabs receiving income supplements, or for everybody receiving income supplements. She sighed. Then she laughed at me. It's for everybody, she assured me.

Great, I thought. We can all be ground up together, everyone on an equal basis, by the ponderous and indifferent wheels of government bureaucracy.

On the other hand, I probably should not complain. I did get unemployment compensation for six months while the government tried, theoretically, to help me find new work–but since unemployment compensation is apparently not considered an income supplement, no one told me not to drive my car.

248

Central Bus Station, Jerusalem

I got to know the Central Bus Station in Jerusalem quite well while I was collecting unemployment, because the office where I had to report every month is located in the adjacent mall. These days, you report yourself as present and available for work by having your fingerprint electronically scanned by a big machine like an ATM. When I went to report the first time, they needed to take my sample print for future matching, but my index finger did not scan, for some reason. The clerk told me to try my middle finger. Sure enough, that worked. So every subsequent month until my coverage ran out six months later, I reported to the National Insurance Office, Unemployment Division, at the mall at the Central Bus Station at the entrance to Jerusalem, and gave them the finger. In exchange, I got some meager percentage of what I had been earning. I am not one to look a gift horse in the mouth, however. And this was two gifts, actually: a modest stipend, and a chance to let the whole system know what people think of it! Double the pleasure.

On a Sunday morning at the Jerusalem Central Bus Station, in the fast food area, you will find an interesting microcosm of to-day's Israel. First of all you'll notice that there are an awful lot of soldiers around (on their way back to base after a weekend leave), and secondly you'll notice that most of the establishments are kosher, or glatt (very strictly) kosher, or kosher l'mehadrin (even more supremely strictly kosher).

In the cul de sac by the stairs up from street level at the main bus entrance to the terminal, I found Crepe Café (kosher l'mehadrin); Holy Bagel Café; Pizza Home; China Town (kosher); Schnitzli: The First Hebrew Schnitzel (kosher); Pita Plus Schwarma & Felafel (kosher); Breakfast Health Bar (kosher l'mehadrin); and Burgers Bar (kosher l'mehadrin). At nine in the morning, all were open but the pizza and the Chinese place. Of the approximately 35 people sitting at the tables, all but three or four were soldiers. Most of them wore knitted kippas (skullcaps), some were bare-headed, and one or two had pe'ot (long side-curls worn by strictly observant ultra-Orthodox Jewish men).

Everyone was in olive drab except two guys in dress khaki sitting alone to one side; maybe officers? Or air force or navy? I have never served in the Israeli army, having come to live here permanently at the age of 33, at which point they would not have been too interested in having me, even if I'd been interested in joining up. My ignorance of the Israeli armed forces and all their insignia is complete and this has put me at no real disadvantage except, once in a while, as a translator.

I walk along the adjacent corridor looking at the food shops there, and find: a Kosher Express MacDonald's; a Taboun Bakery (kosher l'mehadrin); and Pinati Schwarma (kosher).

This certainly is the face of today's Israel, at least in Jerusalem: lots and lots of religion, and lots and lots of soldiers. Most of my secular Jewish friends in Jerusalem feel not only that they are gradually being overrun by people who actively despise their way of life, but that the process is very far along. Who can argue? (The Orthodox, of course, feel a similar sense of alienation and believe that secular people despise them—which, some of the time at least, is all too accurate.) In a word: polarization.

An in-depth look at the friction between the Orthodox lifestyle and the secular lifestyle requires a book in its own right. The way I see the problem, in a nutshell, is this: With religious issues as with other issues, pluralism can contain particularity, but particularity cannot contain pluralism. What that means is that, when the religiously orthodox are in charge, the space in which secular people can live a secular lifestyle tends to shrink—continually. Public spaces and municipal arrangements are increasingly adjusted to accommodate the requirements of orthodoxy: Proposed sex segregation on public transportation, for example, is currently a hot-button issue in Jerusalem. Whereas when the secular citizens are in charge, generally the religiously orthodox are free to live the lifestyle they choose—but not to impose it on others.

The reality, of course, is a lot more complex.

Meantime, if the moderate secular mainstream on both sides of the Wall could only get together, they could jointly reaffirm the value of an open, pluralistic, egalitarian society where the spheres of religion and state are not commingled. They could forge a vital new partnership with a secure space for everyone to live as they wish, including the religiously devout of every faith. No more hostility. No more coercion. No More Enemies!

Who knows? Sanity could break out here any day now.

Life in Al-Qaryah: snap, crackle and sizzle

This is my third year living in Al-Qaryah, and I feel as much at home here as I've ever felt anywhere else.

Nearly every morning, I wake up to the muted clatter of Reem organizing her family's main midday meal in her outdoor warm-weather kitchen next door. The winter's been so mild, thus far, that she continues to cook down here. She's hoping it will get cold soon, I think, so she can start cooking more of the time upstairs in her newly renovated, state-of-the-art main kitchen.

On the other hand, downstairs she has her trusty old free-standing baking and roasting system: an enormous circular hinged aluminum pan, something like a hugely overgrown waffle iron or sandwich maker. She uses this almost daily to make traditional foods like *kuraas izaatar,* a large flat circle of wheat dough stuffed with fresh leaves of zaatar (hyssop) and liberally basted with olive oil. The downstairs kitchen is also equipped with her old gas range and electric oven, green Formica cabinets mellowed to a deep olive tint, and white stone sink with its marble countertop over a row of more olive green cabinets. All of these were in her kitchen upstairs prior to its recent renovation and had been there ever since she and Ra'ed were married, 30-odd years ago.

The old dilapidated equipment had been driving her crazy upstairs in the house for years, and it was a happy day when the old kitchen was finally gutted. Somehow, though, it all looks homier on the ground floor, where the kitchen is roofed but still more or less in the open air.

Reem rises early, whereas I tend to work at night and get up later in the morning. Lying in bed after the alarm goes off, contemplating the importance of my morning calisthenics which I should on no account skip, as skipping is a slippery slope, I listen to the cheerful bustle of pots and pans clanging, just audibly, next door. The clanging is muted because Reem tries to minimize it if

252

she thinks I'm still sleeping. Her whole orientation is caring for and caring about the immediate circle of her family and cousins and then the surrounding circles of kin, friends, and neighbors. I'm the resident neighborhood artist, or maybe the resident eccentric; the older sister who writes until midnight and rarely rises early. Reem would never question this and tries not to disturb me.

Sometimes she is quick-browning chicken parts that will then be baked in a *makloubeh* (a traditional "upside-down" casserole with chicken or lamb or goat meat, carrots and potatoes and cauliflower, rice, oil, and spices) or some other fabulous dish. Reem does not stint on feeding her family. I can hear the snap, crackle, and sizzle of the hot oil as it grabs each piece of chicken and goes to work on it. Her frying is done in a dedicated aluminum pot over a separate gas burner sitting like a camping stove on a little strip of earth at the edge of the yard, where splattered oil poses no problem. When it rains, the oil that has dripped or splattered on the dirt and weeds roundabout is washed into the earth: a low-maintenance cleaning system of which I highly approve.

I have tried in vain to wean Reem away from deep-frying as her preferred flavor enhancer for meat and vegetables. A cook's preferences are deeply rooted. On the other hand, I never thought she'd cut back on salt, either, but she's doing it because Ra'ed has developed high blood pressure. At some point in the past, I was introduced to sodium substitutes, so when I started to get Reem's reports on Ra'ed's blood pressure problems, I bought her a container of low-sodium salt at the supermarket at the mall in Mevasseret: Try this, I said. So she did. As far as I know she is still using it for cooking. The Arabic word for "vegetarian," by the way, is *nabetiyye*, as in the Nabateans, an ancient people who lived in our general area and who traveled the Spice Route to the Far East. You can see some of their history at a tourist park in the Arava in southern Israel. In Arabic, that part of the country is called Al Araba and it is thought of as southern Palestine, of course. We live in parallel universes here.

The basic meaning of the Hebrew word *nevet*, which gave us both "vegetarian" and "Nabateans," is "sprout." Something good is definitely sprouting here in Al-Qaryah, a little Bohemian backwater in the Jerusalem foothills, where all kinds of people are living harmoniously together and no one makes a very big deal out of it.

Rawan's betrothal

Next door, things are humming. Tonight is Rawan's betrothal. In a few hours, there will be a big feast, an absolutely huge feast, a sit-down dinner of several courses for the extended families on both sides. There will be roast lamb and roast chicken and huge platters of Persian rice garnished with ground meat and pine nuts, and many Middle Eastern salads and condiments and side dishes, and a great variety of soft drinks and fruit juices. Afterwards they will clear the tables away and everyone will sit around in two circles of chairs, one of women and one of men, while the bride opens gifts from the groom, to the cheery approval of the admiring guests as platters are handed round with baklawa, cake, fresh seasonal fruits, dried fruits and nuts, and someone will circulate with trays of black tea with mint, and then coffee with cardamom. Later on, there will be dancing.

Throughout all the feasting, most of the immediate family members on the bride's side will be working as servers; that's how it's done. Rawan's brother Ali will be the catering crew chief for the duration. The men do all the heavy lifting. Reem and the aunts have been cooking for three days. Now as the preparations next door intensify, despite my status as an honorary member of the bride's family, I am not helping. I am across the way in my little flat, in bed, desperately fighting off the flu. I will have to make a supreme effort very shortly and get up, shower, and dress. There's no way I could not put in an appearance. Rawan will be wearing the gorgeous gown from Dizengoff Street, the one she swears she never would have found if I hadn't been with them. Strictly speaking, I wasn't with them; I was sitting in Dizengoff Center at Greg's Café, writing about life in Al-Qaryah with her family and our various other neighbors. Rawan has a generous heart.

I take a headache pill and linger in bed a little longer, thinking that if I don't do any work on this party today, I'm going to have to redeem my good name tomorrow somehow, like by pitching in on the cleanup in a very big way, but that's okay. Maybe by tomorrow morning, I'll be feeling human again.

The first stage of the engagement ritual solemnizes the agreement that Rawan has been promised formally to Zahi's family as his bride. Zahi runs a production control center for an Israeli media conglomerate and is studying something scientific and complicated at night school. He wants to build a house, marry Rawan, pursue his career, settle down in Al-Qaryah, and have a family.

Zahi is a real mensch, a mensch with a sense of humor, so I'm greatly pleased for Rawan. This is just what she wanted, a nice solid reliable kind of guy from her home town so she can raise her own family right here near her mom and her cousins. In another three years she will, *insh'Allah*, finish her professional apprenticeship requirement to the satisfaction of the Israeli Ministry of Science, Industry and Employment. She will receive her architect's license. Then she will get a good job somewhere nearby, or start her own business. This will launch her into the most exhausting and demanding decades of her life: juggling career, marriage, and children. Fortunately Rawan is a hard worker and, with any luck, will manage it all with her usual faultless composure and a lot of help from her mom and the aunts.

The ceremony begins just as I am walking over, somewhat revived by a long hot shower, from my place to Reem's. The men from the groom's extended family, as many as could be mustered, have come to meet the men of the bride's family to formally request this bride for their young man. I hurry indoors, exchanging winks on the way with Ali, brother of the bride-to-be. He is looking especially handsome in a very well-cut suit. The men are gathering on the front veranda of the bride's house. Men only! Apart from the ceremony of the formal request, they will read aloud the first verse (*fatiha*) of the Qur'an in solemn ritual, and they will solemnize the prenuptial financial agreement, while all the women, including this writer, sit in the house waiting. Reem is busy with the aunts and cousins, putting the final touches on the dinner preparations. At this stage of the ceremony, the women are not even allowed to peek at the proceedings outside; it's bad luck.

Formally, the financial arrangements must specify what sum the groom brings to the marriage and the details of compensation in case of a divorce. The bride's side is expected to supply major appliances and some of the furnishings for the couple's home. Once these matters are finalized, it's about the feast thrown by the bride's family for everyone. Reem, delighted with her role as mother of the bride-to-be, is nonetheless a complete nervous wreck. Who can blame her?! In her religious tradition, as practiced here, a betrothal is considered almost as final and binding as a wedding. As soon as the couple is formally betrothed, they can go everywhere together unchaperoned, visit friends and entertain as a couple, and spend time alone together. Once there has been a betrothal ceremony, there is really no going back. Plus the food has to be fantastic, of course.

The feast surpasses all expectations. For me it passes in a slightly feverish haze but I smile a lot anyway, with vicarious maternal happiness. Afterwards, when everything has been cleared away, platters of sweets are handed around, the groom's gifts to the bride are opened and admired, there is music and dancing until midnight, and everyone consumes more sweets and fruit, and drinks tea, and did I mention eating sweets?! Long after I have made my excuses and gone home to bed, the young couple will still be dancing on a small stage to Arab music and Western music and fusion and world music, with their siblings and close friends taking it in turns to join them. A photographer with a videocam will capture everything digitally, and Rawan will never sit down once during the entire time.

I heard all about it in due course, after redeeming my honor by doing a couple of hours on dishwashing detail the next morning. Later, I was privileged to see some of the uncut footage of the video. Meantime, when she got out of bed the morning after, Rawan could barely stand up, never mind walk. Reem must have been even more exhausted, but you would never have guessed. Everyone agreed that it had been a thrilling evening and a lovely celebration to be remembered always.

Now, while Rawan completes her degree and Zahi pursues his education while also working for his media company, their house will be a-building. Then—maybe next summer—they can finally get married and move in. They'll be living one street over, on the Abu Ghosh end of Al-Qaryah, almost within sight of Malik's laundry. And then, *insh'Allah*, Reem will be the happiest mom on this earth, and Ra'ed the proudest dad.

Part IV - Reader's toolbox
(your invitation to action)

Will it make any difference? Will the slaves go free?
Will beggars eat? Will justice be done?

---*Ursula K. Le Guin,* **Tales from Earthsea**

Dear reader: Accept this invitation!

Hop on the No More Enemies train! All aboard! Plenty of room for everyone here!

If you sometimes get discouraged, depressed, or afraid of the future, I have written this action-oriented section especially for you. It restates key ideas from Parts I and II in a more operational mode, and introduces some new ones.

If you live in a conflict zone or you are worried about people you love who are in one of the world's conflict zones–or you worry that maybe your town or your whole country or half the planet could become a conflict zone, maybe next week–read stuff from this book aloud with your friends, or mail them a copy. You'll feel better afterwards. And then look through this last section and see if any of the suggested actions might work for you, and recruit your friends to join you in trying them out. It doesn't matter where you start. Just begin!

True, what I have been telling you in these pages about moving beyond the *enemies* paradigm won't fix all problems in the world instantaneously. It won't even fix all my problems or all your problems instantaneously. But actively joining in the effort to shift the public conversation and public policy toward NME can liberate you to see your issues, and the world's, in a new way. Seeing things differently makes us feel different, and acting on that new insight makes us feel changed, because it changes us. Change that we own as ours is empowering. Actualizing this empowerment is invigorating. To restore your energy and enliven your days, to revive your capacity for hope, start flexing your capacity to experience yourself as co-creating better and more sustainable solutions in this world–with partners you rescue from oblivion, by recycling enemies into comrades.

Part IV offers more than fifty ways to look again at the NME ideas in this book–from the standpoint of how to actively use them, apply them, breathe life into them. In other words, let's say you buy into the whole NME paradigm shift thing, or at least are ready to experiment with it–what happens now? Now we get to work!

The first entry in Part IV encourages you to create an actual physical toolbox for yourself, where you can store your NME ideas and plans. After that, there are nearly seventy more entries in this section, but some are ideas that appear a second time with a different emphasis: "Decommission just one enemies relationship today," for example, is quite similar to the subsequent entry called "End the day with one less enemy today": the first one stresses the idea of "decommissioning"(with its association to nuclear decommissioning), whereas the second one focuses on that moment in the evening when we look back on the day just ending and give thanks for having done our best.

Part IV is designed to be read easily and lightly: Troll for the entries that best speak to you, and use those.

No More Enemies! Go for it!

Find a little red wagon

What does "refusing to be enemies" involve? What does embracing the new partnership paradigm, now emerging in place of the enemies paradigm, involve?

First I want to explain what I mean by a *toolbox*, because I intend that an important benefit of reading this book is that you create your own custom-tailored NME toolbox. The items in the toolbox will be mainly symbolic. Their basic purpose is to encourage you to go out and DO things to promote partnership and healing in the world by reclaiming chunks of it from the *enemies* mindset.

Often when I read a book with great ideas in it, I'm left afterwards with no very clear way to apply them. I may periodically think of the insights I gained from reading the book—usually just before I fall asleep at night, when the day is over and I'm already in bed, in my pajamas: not the greatest time for implementation. Or I may pester my friends with a series of emails or chat messages filled with moving quotes from the book, which they graciously acknowledge (in the best case) and then delete. But I've always felt that there ought to be a better way—a way to reinforce the insights we harvest when we read a book, and to encourage us to turn the insights into action. This toolbox section aims to provide that.

In this final section, we will explore a very mixed bag of NME ideas together with an array of simple suggestions for actively reorienting ourselves and others toward a no-more-enemies paradigm. Pick out what works for you. You will notice that all the subheadings in Part IV are phrased as suggestions. Try whichever ones you like. You are also invited to think up your own tools and strategies. The aim is for you to develop a sense of ownership of this paradigm shift process. Put everything that comes to mind—your random thoughts, your notes, photographs and draw-

265

ings, small physical objects, icons or tokens representing your ideas–put it all into your toolbox. If any entry in this section doesn't speak to you–turn the page and try the next one.

Think of the toolbox section as a kind of game. It should be fun, but it's also meant to be useful to you afterwards. You can label everything, if you want, or keep a list or an index for yourself. If you enjoy being very well organized, you could cross-reference your tools to the discussion in the book that gave you the idea. When you're done reading the book, you will have a custom NME toolbox, assembled by you, for you, with your chosen tools in it and some kind of roster of what's in there, and you'll be ready to rock 'n' roll.

To begin with, then, why not pick some kind of toolbox *container*. Something to hold the tools that you will, we hope, acquire or invent as you read this section. Probably it should be something fairly sizeable: a nice sturdy basket or carton; an old gift box; maybe a shiny little red toy wagon. In fact, if you're a parent, appropriating something your kids don't need any more is allowed, and even encouraged, because the spirit of play is an important aspect of what we are doing here. You can choose something funny, or quirky, or decorative, but let it be something that has pleasant associations for you.

Later on, if you get SO MANY useful tools from reading this book that your container is too small, you can find a bigger one. (Optimism is also a tool.)

We're on the honor system here. Go and find a container before you turn the page. When you sit back down, set the container down right in front of you. This is a special moment, and an important beginning: your new No More Enemies toolbox is right there, waiting to be filled. If you have a little hand mirror around, you can put it in there already, and we'll talk about it later: Tool #1.

Wow. Okay. Let's begin.

For the toolbox: a small hand mirror.

266

Think "Rumpelstiltskin"

I want this book to be a Rumpelstiltskin phenomenon for you: transforming (i.e., *spinning*) the idea of "enemies" into something infinitely more valuable. And I definitely do not mean "spin" in the corrupted modern sense of manipulating reality for PR, but rather in the much older sense of spinning thread from wool: taking appropriate primary materials (with thanks to the ones who grew them) and forming something worthwhile with your labor, one day at a time.

You don't need to be any kind of scholar or certified expert. Bring your list of enemies and use what you read here to spin them into something worth their weight in gold. Spin your enemies into partners. Start today. (You can put your list of enemies into your toolbox.)

Rumpelstiltskin, in case you never heard the story, is a figure in an old folk tale revolving around a maiden in distress whose foolish dad bragged that his daughter could spin straw into gold, although of course she had no clue; a greedy king who wanted to marry her and be rich; and an opportunistic elf whose marketable skills happened to include spinning straw into gold. The elf volunteered to spin for the maiden on a rush overnight basis, in secret, but he wanted her future firstborn child as his reward someday, and he wasn't prepared to teach her how to do the spinning for herself, either.

Luckily, in our case the situation is a little different. I'm not an elf; I hope you're not a clueless maiden in distress; and I don't want your firstborn child as a prize (thanks, but no thanks—I already raised two of my own). Moreover, I'm doing my best to walk you through the steps so that you can learn how to do this transformative gig yourself. Once you get the idea, you can take it from there, and you don't have to marry any avaricious old monarch, either.

It took me about 40 years to figure out for myself how this particular transformation process happens. I always had a vague suspicion that it was possible. So I read a lot and listened to other people who were working on similar ideas. I spent a lot of time thinking and experimenting. And possibly I'm also channeling valuable information from some parallel universe; I certainly would not rule out the possibility. Moreover, I've done something that's still fairly uncommon, although I'm by no means the only person to have tried it and it's becoming more popular every day: I've gone and lived with the folks who were supposed to be my enemies–on purpose–for long periods. Twice! Think of it as field testing or, as it might be termed in certain faith communities, as bearing witness.

Lately I've been thinking over what I've learned. I've been processing it into a collection of user-friendly narratives and suggestions, easily understood and assimilated. That's how this book was conceived.

Are you ready to let go of your designated enemies and transform them into partners instead? Or at least, to experiment with the process? No one can tell you the answer to that; it's up to you.

If you are ready to go with this, one bonus is that, as you reimagine your supposed enemies as partners, you create a space for them to transform themselves while meantime you are also transforming yourself: a kind of co-transformation.

My conviction is that just about anyone–sufficiently motivated–can learn to spin enemies into partners. The main requirement is a willingness to be a little adventurous. You need to be a little adventurous because, if you want to start spinning enemies into partners, you will probably have to move out of your comfort zone somewhat. It's a bit like learning to ride a two-wheeled bicycle. If you've been accustomed to using training wheels to think with–by which I mean, having a guru or a spiritual adviser, a teacher or a parent or a best friend tell you what you think and, especially, tell you who your enemies are–you may have to let go of that. Riding the new way feels weird at first, and maybe a little scary—but once you get the knack, it's no big deal.

Eventually you'll feel as though you always knew how.

Toolbox: A copy of the tale of Rumpelstiltskin. And don't forget to put your list of your current enemies in there, too.

Recast your designated enemies

Whom do you define as your enemy these days? Few are the people who, when asked, will say that they have no enemies. Most people can come up with someone they will agree to label as their enemy. This is unfortunate, unnecessary, and increasingly inimical to human survival. So I am asking you to reconsider. The whole notion of "enemy" is destructive. We need to move beyond it.

In practical terms, your designated enemy is someone whose potential contribution to human welfare you are helping to lock up uselessly, in a mutually destructive dynamic of fear, hatred, or oppression.

Many people want to kill their designated enemies. In many times and places, society at large, and its leaders and opinion shapers in particular, openly define killing an enemy as noble, patriotic, or necessary—sometimes all three.

Unfortunately, killing other humans is not just morally wrong; it is also wasteful. When someone or some group of people kills a human being or obliterates a whole group of human beings (as in war), they destroy not just the person or group but all the potential contribution to human welfare that was latent in that person or group. They take all that vibrant energy out of the game of life, without ever having utilized it for the common good. What a waste!

If you take part in systematically oppressing or disenfranchising or discounting a whole group of people over a long period of time, you are not merely helping to deprive them unfairly of the ability to exercise their basic human rights. You are also helping to bind up most of their vital, mysterious human energy (and much of your own) in a sterile and ugly cycle of joint struggle, suffering and death.

Finding ways to help release the positive energy of your adversaries in a mutually beneficial manner is the transformative key to a prosperous and secure future for your grandchildren—and theirs.

In our time, now, today, we are right on the cusp of a broad global movement to liberate the latent cooperation bound up in dysfunctional relationships of "enemies." Once this movement gets rolling, it will soon tap into the greatest storehouse of energy imaginable: the human potential of those whose optimal contribution to the wellbeing of our world has thus far been welcomed and utilized only very minimally, if at all.

The most fundamental resource we can have is energy. Energy underlies all the other resources we think we need to get a job done. Any job. Quite possibly, there is more than enough energy in the world to create a paradise on earth… but meantime, a huge percentage of this energy is misused, wasted, or channeled at cross purposes to itself, while we cling to this unexamined notion of "enemies." If each of us will now set out courageously to locate these systemic leaks in the world's positive potential energy and repair them, the sum of all our efforts can create a more just, humane, and beautiful world filled with laughter, boundless creativity, and good fellowship… and sooner than we think!

If your main response to this thesis is "Yes, but…" then please look in the mirror. (You need to have a little mirror in your toolbox.) You will see your own worst enemy there! Remember Gandhi's axiom: *Our only true enemies are in our own hearts, and that is where all our battles should be fought.*

Meanwhile, your list of designated enemies, if you made one, is like an agenda, a task list for you. Those people are the raw material of your proposed transformation. If you didn't make a list yet, do it now.

Toolbox: A list of enemies, the raw material of transformation.

Refuse to be anyone's enemy yourself

The *idea* of refusing to be enemies is simple enough, but perhaps not as simple to practice.

If I am going to refuse to be enemies, then am I going to refuse to be enemies with anyone–no matter what?

I'm not sure, but I think the answer is yes.

I may, on the other hand, not succeed in being *friends* with everybody.

If some group, or some person, is out to get me, it would be rather extreme on my part to view them as friends. But that doesn't mean I have to view them as enemies.

The alternative status, the third option, somewhere in the middle, I would like to call "potential future partner in cooperation."

I believe that I can reasonably take the position that everyone who is *not yet* my partner–my partner in co-evolving this world of ours–is a potential future partner. That gives me an incentive to work really hard to understand where these other folks are coming from. If they are angry, there may be some way to defuse their anger by addressing, and redressing, their grievances–rather than be seduced by their anger into giving up on them. If they are poised to bomb me or shoot me or otherwise injure me or my loved ones, evasive or defensive action may be required. Of course! But the inward act of labeling them "enemy" is not required. I still have all my options, even while I'm dodging their bullets.

I'm willing to go so far as to think of such people as *"misguided* potential future partners" or even "potentially lethally misguided potential future partners"–but not enemies. Refusing to be enemies, as a philosophy and a modus operandi, could propagate fairly rapidly around this earth, I should think–but we are going to have to get behind it and push. We are going to have to give it everything we've got.

Toolbox: You can write "I refuse to be anyone's enemy" or "Enemies are my potential future partners" on a card, and put it in there with the mirror and the list.

Reach for the wisdom of displacement

Displaced people and relocated people and expats and bi-culturals and multi-culturals all have their minds expanded, willy-nilly. People displaced involuntarily, and even those displaced by choice, may often wish that they could go back to the status quo ante and lead the lives they once had... but mostly they cannot. Their reality has moved on, and there is no going back.

Still, a shift in horizons has its own compensations for those travelers brave enough to accept them. (I'm not talking now about people who are being systematically starved, murdered, violated, warehoused, and abandoned, but displaced people with some modicum of stability and enough to eat—including refugees, where applicable.)

Involuntary displacement engenders suffering, of course: but not only suffering. I have met displaced people who, it seemed to me, had been able to harvest some good things from their experience, apart from their suffering: Their hearts were opened, their souls stretched, their vision extended, the dimensions of their understanding multiplied. Their own suffering and the suffering of family and friends made them more compassionate and more aware, not less.

In his book *Voluntary Simplicity*, originally published in 1981, Duane Elgin makes a point about the subjective nature of material prosperity, with an example of two men riding a bicycle to work: One is poor and could never afford a car, but wishes he could; the other is an environmental activist who rides a bike by choice, as an intentional contribution to greening the earth. Compare the subjective experience of those two men on their bicycles, he suggested; imagine how different their feelings are. I always thought that if the man living in poverty could see himself as an environmental activist too, his experience would be completely transformed. (Maybe he already does, and it already has been.)

Certainly a person displaced involuntarily is going to have a different subjective awareness than a person who voluntarily relocates. Nonetheless, both of them can choose to think of themselves as a wise resource for the rest of us. For each of them, in their different ways, taking that step could open doors that they did not even know were there. They are uniquely qualified to undertake the NME transformation because (among other reasons) they already have the tools to see reality from multiple perspectives—a basic step in the paradigm shift that orients us toward NME.

If you are not already a displaced person, you might try voluntary relocation to some other interesting place for a while. It's incredibly instructive. Among the other things that you may learn, is a very deep empathy for refugees and migrants.

Toolbox: A world atlas or a small globe of the earth could serve to remind you of the alternate realities you would see in our world if you were gazing on it from somewhere else on the planet, as a displaced person or an expatriate.

Be a conscientious objector to the enemies paradigm

After many years spent in Palestine/Israel working toward reconciliation between Jews and Arabs, Palestinians and Israelis, I have come to one main conclusion: The struggle here is not unique, the terrible pain and suffering–though devastating–are nevertheless not unique, and the lessons we need to learn here are universal. What many Westerners revere as "the Holy Land" gets more than its share of press, true–but many of its problems are similar to the problems people have in other places. Tribal wars that last a hundred or a thousand years have happened in other places, too. So while we're at it, we might as well look at the big picture to see what commonalities there are, and maybe figure out how to resolve more of the world's conflicts with a more systematic approach.

The undeniable fact of conflict does not force us to accept the notion of "enemies." We can conscientiously refuse to accept the paradigm.

Friends and lovers, siblings and partners often find themselves in conflict. Conflict comes in many forms and there are positive as well as negative ways of resolving conflict, transforming it, or learning to live with it. The notion of "enemies" arises when, in addition to being embroiled in a shared conflict (or even before there is a conflict), people are deeply afraid of one another. Their fear leads to hate, anger, suspicion... and more conflict.

Fear may have its legitimate evolutionary history in human biology, to help differentiate friend from foe, but at this point in the human story, fear is a very poor guide to both policy and action in an overpopulated world.

Many people–perhaps the majority of people on earth–are still captive to the destructive notion that they have *enemies* and that these *enemies* are people who must be repulsed, oppressed, controlled, occupied, deported, incarcerated, or otherwise crushed.

Again, all that negative strategy requires and uses–indeed, misuses–a lot of energy.

This lethal misdirection of human energy–the energy of both oppressor and oppressed–may be largely responsible for most of the ills on earth.

To repair the world and open the way to a more enjoyable, healthier, more secure and more prosperous, more just and more sustainable future, we can start the process right now of liberating ourselves and our adversaries from this mutually destructive dynamic.

We can begin by refusing to be enemies and, in my experience, there are always plenty of folks on the *other side* ready to do likewise, at the first opportunity.

Let us be conscientious objectors, together.

Toolbox: You're thinking about becoming a NME conscientious objector? Refusing to be an enemy of someone? Tell yourself: Well done. Put a gold star in there.

Audit your dream

"Cradle to Cradle," apart from being the title of an invaluable book by William McDonough and Michael Braungart, is also the name of a basic principle of global ecology: that nothing can be thrown "away" because there is no such place as "away" and that any project, to be sustainable, must include viable plans for what happens "afterwards."

More and more of us may be learning to think this way about the environment, but how often do we apply this mode of thinking to our dreams and aspirations? I'm guessing... not that often. We need to start doing that.

Political movements are a splendid case in point. Take Zionism. Is it, or was it originally, a noble national liberation movement or a racist excuse for ethnic cleansing? (Opinions differ.) And so on and so forth, *ad nauseam*. Moreover the movement has passed through several stages in the last hundred-plus years since its founding, and as it has morphed, its impact on the world around it has also morphed: for better or worse. From the standpoint of those who, in its name, have found meaning and achieved something positive in their own lives, individually and collectively, it is very hard to hear Zionism disparaged. But meanwhile, for those who in its name have been uprooted and dismissed and disenfranchised and dehumanized and–yes– murdered, it's been pretty much a net loss.

The life cycle of the Zionist dream–from nobly-intentioned experiment, at least in the eyes of many, to widely discredited and reviled ideological punching bag–offers valuable lessons. We will not harvest these lessons, however, unless we can consider the subject dispassionately, which is not easy.

Clearly, due to the iron law of unintended consequences, big dreams often provoke big problems. When you push against the prevailing current of destiny in an attempt to channel the flow of

278

the river in a different direction, the ride is unlikely to be smooth. But as your plan proceeds and you sail along, if you see innocent people drowning left and right in the wake of your craft, you have a responsibility there. Your sentiment that they should not have been in that place at that time, in the path of your project, will earn little support from disinterested third parties.

Humanity's next big quest, maybe, is the quest for "cradle to cradle" dreams: because if a cherished dream generates trouble for others—toxic wastes, so to speak—then the project becomes indefensible and unsustainable.

The eco-axiom of "cradle to cradle" as elaborated by McDonough and Braungart and others, challenges us to aspire to a mode of living, an economy, and an approach to industry that generate nothing to "throw away"—because, of course, there is no such place as "away."

Likewise I would say that a social movement that wants to build something beautiful, yet fails to address those who—it turns out—are paying the price, is literally trying to throw those people "away," whether that was the original intent or not.

But they're still here—on our conscience. There is no "away."

Take a very careful look at your dream, whatever it is. Would it qualify for "cradle to cradle" certification? And if not, what do you propose to do about that?

Toolbox: At this point, I'd suggest looking online to find a video featuring William McDonough or Michael Braungart.[46] Watch the clip and put the link in your toolbox.

---

[46] William McDonough has done a number of excellent 20-minute presentations that can be viewed on the TED web site at www.ted.com/talks

Use your cradle-to-cradle awareness

This is a recap for you, in the spirit of McDonough and Braungart:

It's the paradigm, not the people. The idea of enemies is flawed at its foundation. Join with other people and fix the paradigm, in partnership.

Enemies situations are either a design challenge or a redesign challenge.

The *system* is dysfunctional; seek a new system.

Not sure where to seek it? Me either! Get the best brains from your side, the other side, and outside (especially–young people) and address this challenge.

On this voyage of redesign, create benign niches on the ship for fundamentalist believers, but do not give them control of the bridge! The job simply cannot be addressed in a particularist frame of reference. (A Deb axiom: Pluralism can contain particularity, but particularity cannot contain pluralism.)

The cradle-to-cradle NME model can resolve the paradox that people, in one role, can be "doing a good job" while slowly, at the same time, killing the future on a system level, as McDonough and Braungart point out. As a redesign approaches their ideal paradigm, the less dissonance people experience between their actions and their long-term self-interest / collective sustainability.

Diversity is a cornerstone of the NME paradigm, as it is of McDonough and Braungart's approach. They say: *To each, her niche!* This is how we cooperate instead of competing.

The template is not about top-down coercive "social engineering"–but rather consensual, open, participatory co-redesign.

Toolbox: By now you have figured out that I view the McDonough & *Braungart perspective as an indispensable tool for anyone engaged in promoting the global transition from enemies to partnership. Consider buying their*

book (printed on special environmentally friendly material, of course) for your
toolbox, and meanwhile add a bunch more URLs from their online stuff.

Look out for two common traps

Pursuing worthwhile projects that later turn out to be unsustainable, but are nevertheless hard to abandon, is such a common trap: amazingly common. Dreams can be hard to abandon even when they have become nightmares. This insight makes it easier to stop demonizing folks who have fallen into the trap and don't know how to get out.

Look around. Most countries were founded on bloodshed or by denying the rights of the previous inhabitants or the neighbors. In this pattern, today's star rogue state would soon be replaced by a different one. In each and every case, stopping the injustice is crucial. The wrongs must be redressed and the suffering healed—and ideally as soon as possible; but the transformation of the situation will not be hastened by demonizing the players. Something more productive is required.

Nonetheless, demonizing the players is such an easy response: How evil they seem! How enlightened, we who criticize and judge them! Both the demonization and the self-congratulation are traps.

Toolbox: You could put something humorous in the toolbox to remind you to beware of these traps: a toy mouse trap?

Try contextualizing the context

It's often helpful to put the context itself in context: to step back from the frame, and put another frame around it.

In order to have the capacity to see the context of the context; to put the frame inside a larger frame, again and again; to zoom out (as it were) conceptually and progressively–you must want to. When we see the value in this process, we learn to do it. Often, it's fun.

Another Deb axiom: The quest for context trumps the quest for conquest every time.

Toolbox: Say that last sentence five times, as fast as you can: a fun party trick. Write it on an index card and put it in the toolbox.

Rehabilitate a death industry magnate

Here's a field that has yet to be invented: vocational rehabilitation for weapons manufacturers. You could be in the vanguard!

The makers of death toys are not merely manufacturing weapons. Their underlying business, conducted through lobbying and election campaign contributions and the media, is to manufacture *new enemies* so that armies have someone to fight and politicians can get elected by manipulating our fears of "them" and voting for bigger and bigger military budgets.

Progressive activists are fond of castigating the merchants of death. Meantime, the managers and boards of directors and employees in these industries do not see themselves as part of the problem because the standard enemies paradigm dignifies what they do as a patriotic necessity.

What's the point of shrieking curses at them in demonstrations? When we invent new environmentally valuable things for them to manufacture at a profit, they will go there and do that.

What could really help is to create some serious vocational rehabilitation opportunities for these folks. Hence we need a new interdisciplinary field, drawing on business, health sciences, environmental studies, economics, psychology, and whatever else you like, to figure out how to rehabilitate these men and women. If you are a young person trying to find a worthwhile career, consider this one. Be among the first!

Toolbox: Look at your favorite college's course catalog, where this idea will not appear. Talk to the Dean of Studies or the President of your favorite university!

Find a good slogan

Sometimes a slogan is so inspired, it radiates the power of sublime goodness. Remember this one from earlier in this book?

ALL PEOPLE ARE CHOSEN; ALL LAND IS HOLY

(from a sign held by a participant in a Canadian protest demonstration, seen on a video clip on the Internet somewhere…)

And then there's this one: a great line which may or may not have originated with feminist activist Carol Hansen Gray (she signs her emails with it):

ONLY LOVE PREVAILS

Toolbox: Find a good NME slogan that inspires you. Make it into a button or a bracelet or a sticker, for the toolbox. Don't forget to tell everyone what it means. And don't forget the original, either: No More Enemies!

Watch out for the unintended consequences

I think activists for justice for Palestinians spend way too much energy dissing Zionism.

You can't separate people from a dysfunctional dream by bashing the dream or even the dreamers. What they need is a new, more inclusive dream with a broader horizon. Do you have one you can invite them to share?

I think of the Zionist project as a vast outdoor drama or pageant that lasted over a hundred years and is now crashing, having taken hundreds of thousands or even millions of people down with it already. It could be entitled: From Herzl to Hurtful: the unintended consequences of the intended consequences of the Zionist Experiment.

Deb's Law of the Morph Dynamics of Consequences says: The farther away you get from your point of departure and the shakier your original premise and the less proactive you are about periodically auditing your project's impact on other stakeholders, the more your intended consequences are likely to morph into unintended consequences.

Tikkun olam (repairing the world) begins at home. Where do we Jews and/or Israelis find ourselves now, due to the unintended consequences of the group, the movement, the project of which we are (or are viewed as) a part?

What damage has my own team done? That's where my tikkun has to begin. Right there.

How about your team, or your project?

Toolbox: Reader's choice.

Take seven steps toward the new orientation

1. Strive to lead from love (this gets progressively easier).
2. Choose a worthy and sustainable goal (dream) and then conduct yourself so as to be worthy of it.
3. Whatever and whoever you hate–hurry and forgive them! Start by resolving to hate them less today than yesterday, because it's a process. But the quicker you make progress, the better–because when you hate, it's your own life force that you're wasting, as well as theirs.

   If someone you ordinarily respect–a teacher, a religious leader, a writer or artist or entertainer–encourages you, in the name of whatever principle, however sacred, to hate someone or some group–take responsibility for stepping off that path to rethink where you are going under that person's leadership, and why. The holy sages and prophets throughout the ages almost invariably counseled love, not hate; instructions to hate came from disciples who recorded and, perhaps, unintentionally distorted the original holy teachings. So… why go there?
4. Pick great role models and emulate them, but meantime, be open to new teachers who may appear unexpectedly (hint: sometimes, it's someone you loathe…).
5. Expand your team: include your adversaries. This will geometrically enhance the robustness of your program.
6. Take small but bold steps toward your dream or goal, and never ever betray it. (If you find that it is betraying *you*, do an audit.)
7. Treat every answer as a new question, and beware the cozy consensus.

Toolbox: If it will help you, copy this list for the toolbox. Share it with your project team.

Be a NME early adopter

Someone once said that, in a democracy, the most important office is that of…. Citizen!

It's true! Ultimately, the citizens–collectively–are the boss. Cumbersome though democratic governance may be, it's a pretty good system if the citizens are engaged. If the citizens are not engaged, some other force or group will step into the vacuum.

So if you're lucky enough to live in a country with some form of democratic government, however faulty in practice, get involved. Democracy is not a spectator sport, as Liz Coleman, President of Bennington College, said: "There is no such thing as a viable democracy made up of experts, zealots, politicians, and spectators."[47]

All that's required is one brave person to speak out and light the spark of a new idea, a new engagement; then a few more people will gather together around the spark of the idea and create a nucleus to help shape the vision; and then you begin networking…

You could be the early adopter who brings NME to your community, or your country.

Toolbox: a button or a sticker that says: NME EARLY ADOPTER.

---

[47] "Liz Coleman's call to reinvent liberal arts education," TED 2009, filmed Feb. 2009, posted June 2009, at:
http://www.ted.com/talks/liz_coleman_s_call_to_reinvent_liberal_arts_education.html

See through the corporate mask to the people

Some years ago, the *Utne Reader* (a kind of countercultural *Reader's Digest* that began in print and later went online) devoted an entire issue to the question of corporations and their power. Even back then, the consensus seemed to be that it was very nearly too late, if not actually too late, to slow or reverse the trend whereby multinational corporations were outstripping national governments in power.

At the simplest level, the problem of corporate power came about because governments created a new legal entity with the privileges of an individual person but without the responsibilities. They called it a corporation—which simply means an embodiment, an entity. It can engage in commerce and make money, but if it violates laws, it can't be put in jail because it's not actually a person (although sometimes its personnel can be put in jail). If it acts psychotic, endangering itself and others, it can't be hospitalized for an obligatory period of psychiatric observation or rehab.

Today, global corporations seem to run the world, and ordinary people feel powerless and insignificant in comparison.

The thing we seem to have forgotten is that corporations, while not actually people, are made up of people. The people who run them and who work in them and who are paid dividends when they make a profit are, in the end, just people. If we find a way to connect with these people and forge partnerships with them as people, we can find a way to bring some balance back to the functioning of these very large organizations, so that they become functional in pursuit of a healthy, sustainable society rather than an obstacle to healthy sustainability.

There is no point in making "the corporations" or "globalization" or even "the military-industrial complex" our designated enemy. All those entities are made up of people, and we need to find ways of building common cause with those people—from the company board chairman to the chef in the executive dining room, from the janitor in the basement to the CEO and COO in the top-floor corner offices.

They are people and we are people. There has to be a way, so let's look for it.

In fact there are movements these days that engage with corporate management and directors in quest of greater corporate social responsibility. I don't know if that is the whole answer, but it's a good start.

The part that's been utterly neglected is the disconnect that somehow lets us forget that a corporation is a *pretend* entity: Without the people who run it, work in it, and direct it, it would no longer exist. True, corporate personnel can be hired and fired and the corporation will endure. But once we internalize the concept "Refuse to be enemies: demand partnership!" we will find applications to address corporations, too.

There is just that little matter of figuring out how to go about it.

Toolbox: If you get any good ideas on this subject, write 'em down and put 'em in the toolbox. And spread the word.

Become a keyboard alchemist for NME

Writing–your writing–is an excellent realm for the practice of positive net energy transformation in the NME mode.

The passions that fuel your writing–anger and outrage and frustration and despair, as well as joy and hope and generosity and love–are the breathing-in end of the equation. The breathing-out end depends on how you transform all that energy inwardly as you send it back out into the world as prose or poetry, lyric or prayer. If you do your job well, everything you are writing can go out into the world with a loving intention, and can help to transform everyone who reads it.

I am not suggesting a moratorium on satire or critical prose. Even satire, even trenchantly critical texts, can be loving in their intention. The crucial factor is subtle: What is driving the writer? Look on the Internet: There is critical prose that comes from love, and critical prose that comes from hate. Once you start to notice, you can easily tell the difference.

When you write from outrage about social injustice or individual suffering, what is driving you most strongly? Is it hatred of the oppressor, or concern for the oppressed? Fury at an unjust law and the people or groups who support it, or the joyful determination to work with like-minded allies to see that the law is changed? Your reader, even if unconsciously, can feel the difference. Writing that comes mainly from fear, anger or hate will tend to evoke more of the same and hence to be, in the long run, self-defeating.

Toolbox: Put a symbolic blue pencil in there. (Before computers, editors traditionally used a blue pencil to make corrections to a typed draft text.)

Make a Hooray-Hooray stick

Here's a simple exercise: Find a plain stick (like a barbecue skewer, or a ruler) and two inexpensive objects you can attach to either end (for example: tiny dolls; miniature paper cups; small stuffed animals; a pair of coasters you don't need).

Label one of these objects US and label the other THEM.

Attach the US and THEM icons to either end of the stick with glue, string, wire, pipe cleaners, or whatever works.

Voilà! A Hooray-Hooray stick: Hooray for us AND hooray for them, too.

How you use it is up to you, but I would suggest that, whenever you are tempted to indulge in that warm fuzzy feeling of wallowing around in your pride in "us" by comparison with the deficiencies and defects so conspicuous in some other group of "them"–that you haul out this toy and spend some quality time with it. Leave it on your desk for a few days, maybe.

And if you need to use it to make a point to your kids, your parents, or your roommate, you can leave it on the kitchen counter for a while.

Toolbox: When your HOORAY-HOORAY object is not in use, store it in the toolbox.

Look in the mirror

Although our world is unquestionably troubled and confused, there is also a lot of good news around, but you can easily miss it. You have to know how and where to look for it. And you have to believe it's there to be found. This outlook is part of the NME orientation.

Good news is about knowing where to find it, and then looking.

You can begin by looking in a mirror. The good news begins there... with you. (So does the bad news.) Heads up! This is the first thing you were going to put in your toolbox: a small hand mirror. If you don't have one yet, please just buy an inexpensive one in a pharmacy. (Or if you have a teenager at home, maybe they have an extra one. Mine always did.)

As we imagine our world, so it evolves–one implication of which is that, as more of us increasingly look for good news, good news will tend to proliferate. (Similarly: The more we look for enemies, the more they proliferate; that is the other side of that coin.) This does not mean that bad stuff will magically disappear because we want it to; it means that at least some portion of reality, at least some of the time, is driven by self-fulfilling prophecy, by expectations, especially collective expectations. And to that same extent, we have a window of opportunity.

You may feel that you already knew this, and perhaps just needed to be reminded. That's probably true, at least for many people. If the holographic model of reality (the idea that any one bit of the whole, contains the whole) has any validity, and I believe that it does–then all of us already know, on some level, what each one of us knows. The insights I find inside myself are also inside you, and vice versa, waiting for us to remember that they are there, dust them off, and put them to work. If Gandhi knew that our only real enemies are in our own hearts and that we should be fighting all our battles there, without bloodshed—then you and I know it, too.

Toolbox: Look in the little mirror once in a while and see if some new insights appear there, when you look yourself squarely in the eye.

Beware the dark attractions

Oct 1, 2010
Email to a local community list-serve in north-central Israel, from a recent
arrival in the area:
My son would really like to see and climb on tanks. (He's 5.)
Are there any places nearby where we could go to view and climb on
tanks?
Thanks.
-Ted (not his real name)

Fortunately or unfortunately for this dad, there are plenty of places in his area in Israel where kids can see, and climb on, tanks. Many local schools take young children to army bases on Israel's Independence Day in the spring, and the kids climb all over the tanks while teachers and conscript soldiers look on proudly. Meanwhile, an entire nonprofit organization (New Profile) exists to counter the very deep-rooted trend to militarism in Israeli education, which starts in preschool.[48]

My country of birth, the USA, has also had a longstanding fascination with lethal weapons. And the USA is by no means alone.

What to do about the urge, evidently shared by nearly all little boys and quite a few little girls, to play with large, lethal combat vehicles? For kids, this seems like a lot of fun. The mayhem in cartoons and video games is not processed in a child's awareness as actual death. The characters often come back to life, right on the screen. Kids like the mayhem and have little or no perception of real consequences.

What's a parent to do?

Well... I don't know. But while living in Connecticut once upon a time, as we did for a couple of years, my young son was

---

[48] I am not qualified to comment in this vein on what goes on in Palestine; that is someone else's challenge.

happy with large flatbed car carriers and bright-painted bulldozers. He loved the local train station and could watch the traffic on the rails for hours. He didn't seem to need tanks, maybe because tanks weren't part of the everyday reality in Connecticut the way they are in Israel/Palestine. Of course, American kids easily develop a fascination with handguns and rifles, which are a part of American culture.

When Harry Potter first came on the scene, a lot of the fascinating technology of the future imagined by author J.K. Rowling was intriguing without necessarily being violent or lethal: paintings whose subjects came and went in the frame; Quidditch broomsticks that flew; entire train platforms and shopping streets that appeared only to the initiated; animals that talked; and so forth.

As time went on, the technologies in successive Harry Potter sequels grew darker, along with the plots. Was that necessary–whether artistically or commercially? I wonder.

What is it about our era that encourages this momentum?

How might we deflect or reverse it?

For a talented young engineer, is there anything less magical in, for example, designing light-sensitive roofing materials that would absorb the warmth of sunlight in the winter and reflect the sun's rays in the summer, as compared to designing WMD that could wipe out entire nations?

Is the challenge of self-mastery–in Aikido, for example: the martial art with no offensive mode–is that challenge really less intriguing for young people than the challenge of overpowering others by force for one's own enrichment or ego satisfaction?

In a post-enemies world, we will have to know a lot more about the dark attraction of conquest as opposed to the rosier attractions of partnership. We know that it would never work just to prohibit the dark games because, once they are forbidden, they would only become more seductive. We need more knowledge of what does work.

Dark attractions deconstructed: a field in which one could really make a valuable contribution.

Toolbox: Reader's choice.

Memorize the twelve words

A useful exercise, always, is to reduce an idea to a dozen words. So here they are, for NME:

The idea of enemies is obsolete; the paradigm replacing it is partnership.

When you hear someone discoursing in an enemies-driven way, be wary! The enemies-driven perspective is almost always counterproductive in the long run.

We are most of us living in a halfway house, a kind of rehab situation, for recovering enemies-paradigm addicts. A person has a hard time realizing how addicted they are until they get off the drug. Suddenly, the world looks very different, and maybe that's a little scary. But it affords more hope, too.

Toolbox: Add an index card with the twelve words. You can reorganize the wording, if you like: create a new, improved version.

Help a clergyperson today

Not only do we often find both holy war and compassionate caring in a single religion; these two poles may also be found at different times in a single cleric. A clergyperson can be a holy warrior for God at some stage, but after mellowing, perhaps, can become someone who stresses compassion and reconciliation.

When you meet a cleric stuck in the holy war mentality, maybe you could attempt to be really brave and try to help him or her get past that place to where they can discover compassionate partnership with "them"–however different "their" religious beliefs.

Clerics traditionally provide us with guidance. Sometimes, though, it may need to be the other way around.

Toolbox: Put an appropriate item with religious significance or associations in the toolbox.

Decommission just one *enemies* relationship today

An *enemies* relationship and its interactions capture positive human energy and degrade it into (at best) a useless state.

When you refuse to wear the enemies hat with someone, you avoid an enemies interaction and help reorient both of you away from an enemies relationship.

In fact, you can add to the world's reserves of available positive human energy by decommissioning enemies relationships whenever possible.

(In Jewish tradition, there is a saying: Who is a hero? He who turns his enemy into his friend.)

Keep refusing to wear the enemies hat until they get the message. At that point, you have decommissioned an enemies relationship and transformed an enemy into a potential partner.

Congratulations!

Toolbox: Pin "NME" on an old baseball hat.

Give something back

There is a certain painful irony in doing "peace work" as a paid professional: You are literally making a living from the flawed situation you have committed yourself to help repair. In the course of that work, you are subsisting, in a sense, from the suffering and imprisonment and maiming and death of people caught up in conflict–civilians, soldiers, bereaved families, bombing victims, refugees.

During the time I have been living in Jerusalem, these last months, I have walked often past the Shalit family's protest camp in front of the Prime Minister's residence, where a bleak wind buffets the banner-size pictures of their son Gilad, now (2010) in his fifth year of confinement by Hamas. My route to and from the greengrocer's on *Gaza Road* (which bisects an upscale neighborhood of Jewish West Jerusalem; how ironic is that?) takes me past Paris Square, where Jerusalem Women in Black hold their End the Occupation vigil every Friday for an hour, in silence. About four in ten male Palestinians have done time in Israeli detention centers and prisons; the Occupation has interned or detained an estimated 650,000 Palestinians since 1967[49], including an estimated 10,000 women[50]. At this writing, Israel holds approximately 7,000 Palestinian prisoners. Approximately 34 of these are women[51]. All of those being held today are in prisons inside Israel proper where their families cannot easily visit them: a glaring violation of applicable international law.

---

[49] Addameer Prisoners' Support and Human Rights Organization, retrieved at:
http://www.addameer.org/detention/background.html
[50] The Alternative Information Center Palestine/Israel, retrieved at:
http://www.alternativenews.org/english/index.php/topics/news/2723-palestinian-women-in-israeli-prisons-
[51] Women's Organization for Political Prisoners, retrieved at:
http://www.wofpp.org/english/february10.html

Sometimes I stop for a break at the Restobar bistro just across the street from the pictures of the captive Gilad Shalit—on the site of what used to be the Moment Café, which was obliterated in a suicide bombing on March 9, 2002. In my head are various lines from the latest court transcript I am translating into English for the family of Rachel Corrie, who are seeking civil damages of $1 and a verdict from the Haifa District Court that the State of Israel and its Ministry of Defense and its army had some culpability in the death of their idealistic young daughter under the treads of a D9R bulldozer—almost exactly a year after the Moment Café bombing, on March 16, 2003 in a military "buffer zone" in southern Gaza. Ironically, this is a translating job which is well paid by Israeli standards.

In the meantime, in this same period, I am busy raising money for the medical expenses of a Gaza teenager named Yousif, the nephew of my good friend Maha, because no one covers the costs of his immune system medications and he will die unless friends around the world ante up the money, year after year, until a bone marrow transplant eventually stabilizes his condition (a procedure not without risks, and which the hospital keeps postponing, for what they say are valid medical reasons). Every time this child comes to Israel for medical care, he and his aunt need "permits" to get out of Gaza. This boy and his family have long since become accustomed to the Orwellian world of "permits"; how sad is that? I feel good using some of my earnings from the Rachel Corrie trial translations to put gas in my car when I go back and forth to the hospital to visit with Maha and Yousif and to drive them back to Gaza afterwards.

The intertwined fates of these families buffet me as I walk along. I feel them like the breath of a ghostly wind from some other sphere of reality where there is no blame, only sorrow—the Shalits, the Corries, Yousif's family, and all the families who lost someone in the bombing of the Moment Café and in the IDF incursions into residential neighborhoods in the occupied territories, and all the other wars and bombings. Among them is the

Netanyahu family, who lost their son Yonatan in the Entebbe rescue episode all those years ago—irrevocably damaging the psyche of, among many others, his brother Bibi, the current tenant of the Prime Minister's residence across the street from Restobar, behind the Gilad Shalit banners. They are all bound together in sorrow with all the other families of the imprisoned, the beaten, the traumatized, and the despairing, on all sides of this mess.

It seems to me that I owe something back, considering that I'm supporting myself as a professional who is working for peace-and-justice causes. I believe that the most important thing that I owe is this: I must try to (as they say) work myself out of a job. I must do my best to bring about a world in which peace activists will be unemployed. Including me.

Okay. I'm working on it. NME is my contribution. It's what I owe back.

We all owe something back. What do you owe?

Toolbox: Put your IOU in the toolbox.

Remind yourself: They are not obstacles

If you are a campaigner for social justice, think of the work you are doing not as a battle, but as a game or a journey.

From a No More Enemies perspective, if you view the people or the organizations around you as obstacles (and this explicitly includes the ones who disagree with you), then you haven't got it yet.

What could you put in your toolbox as a reminder that people are not obstacles but teachers, or co-learners, or traveling companions, or future partners? You decide.

Toolbox: Reader's choice.

After you follow the money, lead the money!

Look around.

Someone is making lots and lots of money from war and mayhem.

These folks rarely change direction because we sermonize at them. I believe, however, that they could be moved to more constructive pursuits by the allure of challenge and, of course, by money. Instead of "following the money" to find the culprits and stopping there, we could move on to "lead the money" toward the post-enemies paradigm.

We need not just one, but dozens of great ideas for products that are challenging and remunerative and that could tempt the missile makers, the tank makers, the bomb makers, the prison profiteers, the drug profiteers, the strongmen and the mercenaries and all those guys. They don't need our condemnation; it does nothing to dissuade them. They need alternatives. They need offers they can't refuse.

Get busy, people! Ideas! Ideas! Ideas!

Imagine, design, or engineer some environmentally useful and sound products to improve people's wellbeing, things that are nonpolluting and have a huge potential market. Help get the tax laws rewritten to make them highly attractive to produce. Then watch the entrepreneurs of death switch to building those things!

Ideas! Ideas! Ideas!

Toolbox: Schedule a brainstorming session with a few friends and a few beers (or, if you are a practicing Muslim, a few cartons of ice cream) to generate some ideas that could lead these guys to pursue a more benign kind of profit.

Consult your body: honor your opposite

Our bodies have much to teach us about *enemies* and about moving beyond *enemies*.

In our body, we have mechanisms to warm us up and to cool us down; to burn food as energy and to store it for later; to move materials around or put them in storage or in the trash; to build up chemical compounds and to break them down; to raise our blood pressure and to lower it; to send and receive various kinds of messages and to block them. Evidently, some of the functional systems in our bodies once existed independently, i.e., not in a human body, and joined the team somewhere along the line, many eons ago. Some (like mitochondria) even retain their own DNA.

All these counter-posed interest groups had to learn to coexist, for the general good, to support a dynamic, coherent, sustainable stability. We call it our body, but it's also a great metaphor for the post-enemies paradigm.

Your opposite is what makes your existence possible! Honor her/him!

Toolbox: What could you put in there that would illustrate this principle, or help you be more aware of it in your work? You decide.

Be like trees

Humans have a unique transformational skill that is still only vaguely recognized, not widely acknowledged, and too rarely utilized. We have the ability to inhale or absorb negative experiences, and then (instead of breathing the negativity back out again) to breathe out love... and love is the ultimate power that sustains the world.

Probably everyone has this transformative power to some extent, at least potentially. Some people are especially gifted with it, but everyone has it and can cultivate it.

As trees have evolved to inhale carbon dioxide and exhale oxygen to give us life; as green plants have evolved to transmute water and sunlight and soil nutrients into energy for the food chain–humanity is evolving an ever-greater capacity to experience hatred and fear and abuse and suffering and transmute those experiences inwardly into loving energy to give back to the world. This ability is foundational: a pillar of the spiritual food chain that sustains our existence. And the more of us who become adept at it, transforming ourselves in the process, the greener and more sustainable our world will become... on the material plane, and beyond it.

Our everyday experiences are all raw material for this alchemy of love.

Theoretically, as we practice this transformational ability and do what we can to model it for others to use, we are greening the spiritual world. As we practice, the practice itself spreads and we all learn to do it more efficiently. We are growing the spiritual rain forests of the future every time we process received anger into compassion, envy into understanding, injury into forgiveness.

That is the theory: Be like trees. In practice, we can all be looking for ways to take this basic idea and apply it as best we can, in our family life and community life, and in the work we do.

Toolbox: Add a twig, or a branch, or a pine cone, or a photo of a tree.

Remember it's all for the children

His wife, he said, has accused him of caring more for the Pales-
tinians–who killed his son–than his own people.

-- Anne Usher on ynetnews.com, "Bereaved father transports
ailing Palestinians to Israeli hospital"–October 10, 2010.[52]

You love them more than you love us! I wonder how many activists
for reconciliation have heard similar sentiments from family
members and friends.

My daughter felt that way for a while–I think she was about
six or seven. "Mom," said my child, "you love the Palestinians
more than you love us."

This was during a period when both my children were small,
and I had been spending a lot of time and energy working with
neighbors and colleagues, Jewish and Arab, to try to establish a
new joint bicultural elementary school in our area. Official intran-
sigence and a lack of funding and maybe our own inadequate
leadership eventually derailed our effort; our group disbanded
without having set up a Jewish-Arab school. Later on, however,
in the same general neighborhood, another group of young parents succeeded and the school they founded is still operating. The
original binational, bilingual Jewish-Arab school in Israel is the
Oasis of Peace Primary School at Neve Shalom~Wahat al Salam,
near Latrun; that school has served as the model for the others.
There are now four more such schools in various parts of the
country. They are affiliated with the Hand in Hand Association
for Bilingual Education in Israel and are located in Jerusalem,

---

[52] Retrieved at
http://www.ynetnews.com/articles/0,7340,L-3963478,00.html

Misgav in the Galilee, Kufr Qar'e in Wadi Ara, and Beersheba in the Negev.

This *"you love them better than you love us"* dynamic, wherein a family member's deep commitment to reconciliation work can evoke negative reactions in the rest of the family, deserves further attention and investigation. What would prompt a family member to feel that way? What drives the one who devotes such a huge amount of time and effort to reconciliation-related work with, or on behalf of, "the other"? My guess would be that people's motivations vary.

For me, part of the urge to make peace and promote reconciliation is maternal–to make a better future for my kids and for every other mother's children; to help make the world a place in which they don't have to feel this sadness, this dissonance–this wounding, despair-inducing "us or them" dilemma. Our world should not have to be "us or them." Using our creativity, using all the tools that modern science and technology have given us, and working together, we can find a way to move beyond "us or them."

Vow to make your contribution to this process, as a gift to our children: all our children–those who are with us, those who are no longer with us, those not yet born. All our children.

Toolbox: Add a photo of a child you love.

Don't forget Hooray-Hooray

Social justice activists are at very high risk for a variation of the hooray-for-us-and-down-with-them error.

Generally, an activist's social conscience is highly developed, and she or he would never dream of thinking "Down with them!" based on ethnicity, tribal affiliation, skin color, religion, nationality, gender, sexual orientation, etc.

Too often, however, social activists tend to vilify people on *ideological* grounds. This is worse than sub-optimal; it's fatal. It not only closes the door on a productive mutual discourse; it contributes to a cheapening of the public conversation about vital issues. It helps poison the intellectual spring from which all must drink.

Lately, more and more people seem to be waking up to this risk and attempting to build bridges across the ideological chasm that has functioned to divide them. Though still a minority, some people are starting to realize that, liberal or conservative, leftist or right-winger, we all share the same dreams for our children. We all are stakeholders in the same future.

Toolbox: Take your Hooray-for-us-and-Hooray-for-them toy out of the toolbox and spend some more quality time with it.

311

Let's stop kicking ourselves

Imagine passing someone on the street, someone who is evidently walking along on the way to somewhere–school, home, work, the movies, whatever.

Imagine that you see that person doing something strange; every couple of steps, they kick their right foot with their left foot. A couple of steps later, they kick their left foot with their right.

The kicks are obviously painful; they reel, they hesitate, and sometimes they stumble sideways, or even fall backwards.

What kind of progress are they going to make toward their objective? If and when they ever reach their destination, what kind of shape will they be in? How well will they function? How happy and productive could they go on to be?

This is a metaphor for the body politic, polarized between a confrontational, belligerent right wing and a belligerent, confrontational left wing. A society divided against itself in this manner is going nowhere very productive. In recent years, as the level of shrillness and viciousness on talk radio has intensified and the meanness of TV commentary reached new lows, some people have begun to observe that this trend, while winning ratings, is taking us in the wrong direction. We need to be reaching out for nonpartisan, mutually respectful public debate if we want to fix what's wrong in our community, our society and the world.

People with political views unlike my own are not my enemy. They are in this world as a course correction for my own inclination to lean too far over in one direction. I need to treat them well and courteously so that they can be my "loyal opposition" (and preferably they will treat me the same way).

If we don't learn this lesson pretty soon, we are effectively smashing our own compass in the middle of the wilderness in bad weather and trusting to blind luck to show us the way back to safety and a shelter from the storm. Who would willingly do that?

Toolbox: Add any object with a left wing and a right wing, or two feet, etc.

Reach out across the great interdisciplinary void

Modern Western scholarship is divided into hundreds of fields and many hundreds of specialties and subspecialties whose experts delve into ever more detailed areas hitherto uncharted. This is great for vacuuming up new information, but there are two problems with the trend. First, despite a lot of good reporting by journalists who know how to translate abstruse material into everyday language so we can grok it, too little information gets out to the public. What does get out may take a long time to catch people's attention and to be understood. And second, almost the only experts who can understand someone else's field (even a closely related field) are those who by some fluke happened to study more than one area–say, a biochemist who is also knowledgeable about radiology, or a physicist who happens to know something about zoology.

Learning pursued in this fragmented manner has given us fragmented understanding: a lot is understood about a lot of narrowly defined things, in great depth, like intense dots on a screen, yet rarely does anyone attempt to connect the dots to see what the big picture is trying to tell us. Encouragingly, interdisciplinary or multidisciplinary study seems to be gaining ground in recent years, but scholars who specialize in more than one discipline are too often treated badly by the academic tenure system: A university department chairperson is reluctant to go to bat for someone who spends part of their time serving some other department's agenda. Remedies for this problem will be found, but meantime a lot of potentially fruitful syntheses drawing on multiple disciplines fail to get started or to progress.

I call on thinkers in diverse fields–this means you!–to come together more productively with your colleagues (and even with your adversaries) in diverse disciplines, to explore new synergies that only you can build, together, for the general good. Let's start

314

connecting the dots more systematically using bold new partnerships.

Toolbox: Hmmmm. What kind of object conveys that?

Find your angle on NME

You can approach NME from diverse perspectives. Find one that resonates for you and let it shape, or frame, your NME consciousness for a while. Explore ways of using it as a doorway into NME, where the creative tension between opposing forces is a mode of cooperation rather than conquest. How about:

- Management (participatory; all stakeholders; long-term sustainability).
- Ecology (nothing wasted; no one wasted; wellbeing is interdependent).
- Biology (harmonious systems of symbiosis).
- Linguistics (lexicons of partnership; neural pathways to NME).
- Media (partnership-oriented media strategies and their implications).
- Religion (self-mastery; inward learning; humility; respect for other faiths).
- Sports (being in the zone, as a sense of oneness and wholeness with creation).
- Dance (balance, symmetry, grace, movement, connectedness, aliveness).
- Visual arts (letting form emerge as wholly itself onto a blank canvas or from a block of wood or stone: a form of deep listening).
- Music (teasing patterns from the web of sound all around us; dissonance as the foil for harmony; silence as the partner of sound).

Toolbox: Reader's choice.

Forgive someone

What do most people do when they are seeking to repair the world or some particular part of it, large or small?

Mostly they focus on a specific social or political or environmental evil: poverty, hunger, abuse, pollution, drunk driving. Or they may focus on a specific disadvantaged population: single moms, kids in jail, addicts, war vets, or a single ethnic or religious group. Or perhaps they choose a broad phenomenon: desertification, or global climate change, or slavery and human trafficking. Those are all good causes and deserve our engagement.

Meantime, the NME rant aims more broadly to focus on the underlying idea of enemies and how obsolete that idea has become. As masses of people worldwide grasp this concept and adopt it, most of the potential solutions to a great many specific ills will automatically get a huge boost.

If the obverse of enemies is partnership, the secret to getting there is forgiveness. The enemies dynamic is persistent because enemies are like dominoes: the first one falls on the next in line, who falls on the next in line, and on and on.

Forgiveness stops the process here, now: It was done to *me*, but here it stops. If I cannot forgive, I will behave as if I can—and later, maybe, I will be able to mean it. In any case, no more dominoes will be falling in my sector. That's over now.

Forgive someone every day, and you will move us all closer to a world of No More Enemies.

Toolbox: a toy domino. Note that forgiving other people is also great for your health; it floods your body's systems with beneficial enzymes and whatnot. Try it and see.

Retire the label

Don't label anyone your enemy.

To label someone an enemy is to take a human being with all their potential contribution not yet made, and recycle them as garbage.

Don't go there.

Toolbox: Two labels from any product, big enough to write on with a marking pen. On one label, write PARTNER. On the other label, write FUTURE PARTNER. That covers everyone!

Reality check: use reversal

The reason reversal works so well as a reality check is that most people tend to project what bothers them about themselves out onto other people. If you are excessively irritated by people who nag, you probably wish you were less of a nag yourself; if arrogance or absentmindedness makes your blood boil, it may be that you have a tendency to act arrogantly or to be absentminded yourself, but wish you didn't.

This tendency to project is such a basic psychological mechanism that mentioning it seems almost redundant; yet people somehow manage to be unaware of the dynamic just when the awareness could be most useful: when dealing with problematic adversaries.

Sometime around the 1980s, the internationally accepted 1949 armistice line dividing Israel/Palestine into Israeli and Palestinian segments (the Green Line) began to be increasingly ignored by Israeli institutions and the general public, in favor of the "Greater Israel" fantasy (winner take all). Sometime in the late 1990s, I saw a letter to the editor of *Haaretz* by an Israeli Jew who said: How can we believe that the Palestinians really want peace and don't want to seize the entire country and destroy Israel completely? When you look at their maps from the Jordan River to the Mediterranean, it says only "Palestine."

So I wrote a letter to the editor, too, pointing out that when you looked at *Israel's* latest maps from the river to the sea, they said only "Israel"–so what are the Palestinians supposed to think regarding what Israelis really want?

American Byron Katie, who does therapeutic interventions in front of mass audiences, uses a reversal technique very effectively. You can see her doing it on her YouTube clips.

319

Bottom line: Use reversal a lot as a reality check. Just take the situation or the circumstances and invert them. See how things look from there and consider the implications.

Tool box: Reader's choice.

The basic reset: check it out

The new default orientation–No More Enemies–is the first step in disarming angry, disempowered adversaries, by inviting them into the circle: not as an empty gesture, but as a way to rewrite the shared script.

Restoring agency restores honor. Inviting others to take responsibility tends to evoke it. Game-changing moves invite game-changing responses.

This is both the frame and the flavor of the NME orientation.

*Tool box: OK, let's see… Print **NME** on something and frame it. Make a button: NME–the basic reset, or: NME–the new default mode. Make one for the toolbox and another one to wear.*

Trust the process

We have the power if we trust the process. We cannot "make things happen" just by visualizing good outcomes. But we can promote the decisions, dynamics, and developments that promote the constructive actions that lead to good outcomes–first by visualizing the good outcomes, and then by trusting the process.

A lot of process has to do with expectations and in that sense is self-fulfilling.

Affirmation techniques are not meant to replace the hard work that fixes problems. Affirmation is a way to align our energies (even energies we're not aware of having) to tread a more direct and smoother path to the goal.

Moreover, the universal affirmation caveat (after Shakti Gawain and many others: *May this be for the good of All Our Relations,* etc.) helps in two major ways: (1) it avoids conflating our own wishes automatically with the greater good, and (2) it leaves the door open to adjusting our aims if/when we see that we can make them more congruent with the general good.

The ideal is a balance between fidelity to the goal and flexibility to let it evolve along with us.

Toolbox: From a comic strip in the newspaper (or downloaded), cut out a likely character and give them a dialogue balloon that says: Trust the process. (Or: Reader's choice.)

Partner with all fellow stakeholders

In the No More Enemies era, the best and most necessary partner that can help me resolve a problem I have with "them" is... them.

Management experts have been teaching for almost half a century now that the most durable–these days, we would say the most sustainable–outcomes of decision-making happen when the decision-making process is broadly participatory and inclusive.

When all the relevant stakeholders have a real share in analyzing a problem and crafting its solution, they all have a stake in making that solution work. When stakeholders are excluded, they are psychologically primed to be indifferent (in the best case) or even actively opposed (in the worst case) to the successful implementation of the solution. Top-down authoritarian decision-making is not a paradigm for resolving conflicts but rather for creating and perpetuating problems.

Toolbox: A garden stake (as in, stakeholders)?

Consider the patriot paradox

Patriots shout their love of country, yet when they dialogue with peace activists who also love their country, many committed patriots seem to be filled with hatred. Hate comes from fear; what are they afraid of? I think that, for many good people who love their country, the idea of letting go of its accustomed enemies, as enemies, is a very upsetting and even frightening idea. This peculiar paradox should give us pause.

Yes, by envisioning a reality in which enemies are no longer necessary or useful, we can help bring the new paradigm more strongly into being. But meanwhile, we have to have patience for people who have trouble letting go of the old paradigm. Change can be frightening.

Thoughts have agency (and so does patience!).

Imagining a world beyond enemies moves it closer, or moves us closer to it.

And the obverse is also true: Our reluctance to let go of the idea of enemies forces the old enemies-driven reality to linger on, long past the time it was due to be relinquished. What is patriotic about that?

Toolbox: Find an apt quote, or a lyric, or a poem: Breaking up is hard to do; You have to be carefully taught; Ain't gonna study war no more...

Work smarter, when you can

Advocates of cooperation and nonviolence sometimes get discouraged, contemplating the simple fact that a prodigious amount of work is often required to move each person's heart and mind away from believing in the use of power against others and toward the power of believing in others as partners.

Sometimes we can work smarter. Sometimes a single song, or poem, or film, or book, or blog post will move thousands of people at once to a new understanding.

It remains equally true that changing a single heart and mind can require an approach that is tailor-made for each person: If you want to win them over, you may have to push the exact button that will move that particular person. The same fulcrum will not move every mass; the same formula will not open every locked door.

When working on the individual level, it is helpful if you can offer a flexible tool that each person can use in their own particular way, thus enabling them to self-tailor the process to their own unique needs.

The "curious questioner" mode (see the discussion below, on Artsbridge) is very effective in creating a process that helps someone find their own way to change.

Toolbox: A button to push. Or a block and tackle for heavy moving. Or an anthology of poetry (for many magic doorways).

Find your bridge (I): Madaa Silwan

In its own words:

> *Madaa Silwan was established in 2007 by the Palestinian residents of Wadi Hilwah neighborhood in Silwan. The word 'madaa' means horizon.*
> *Our mission is to build a strong, knowledgeable and involved Arab community in Silwan, and to provide educational and recreational activities and courses mainly for children and teenagers.*[53]

Just outside the walls of Jerusalem's old city in an area occupied militarily by Israel, the Palestinian village of Silwan is seeking to expand its survival horizon beyond the man-made disaster that threatens to obliterate it. The community is organizing, using nonviolent techniques pioneered by Gandhi and King, in a struggle to avoid mass displacement. This is the Palestinian peace movement at its most grassroots level. Not enough people know about Madaa. Read on.

Part of the Silwan area is also known, in Hebrew, as the City of David (after the biblical David). Silwan is a Palestinian community. The community as it is today is being incrementally expunged—erased—in a well-funded and politically well-connected effort to build a glorious new Jewish community in place of an existing, densely populated, disadvantaged and neglected Palestinian community. Just to be clear: People are being gradually forced out through intimidation, harassment, confiscation of property, condemnation of buildings, and the looming threat of worse to

---

[53] The Madaa home page is at http://www.madaasilwan.org/
Learn more about Silwan's archeology and its potential for shared co-development, and see what partnership-oriented archeologists are saying, in cooperation with Silwan residents, at the Emek Shaveh web site at http://www.alt-arch.org/

come; they are not being hustled onto buses en masse and driven over the border. (Apart from the gentrification aspect, the technical term for attempting to replace Population A with Population B is "ethnic cleansing.")

The City of David project is a good example of a superficially attractive dream that destroys because it is not inclusive. The Silwan / City of David area has a lot of development potential, sitting as it does on top of some world-class archeological ruins. However, if you go to the very attractive and sophisticated City of David web site operated by the organization (called Elad) pushing this makeover campaign, no mention whatever is made of Palestinians. A web surfer, or a tourist or visitor on the ground, would never guess that there is a dark shadow of deceit and violence hanging over the delightful future portrayed in these promotional materials, which are available in five languages.[54] Clearly, no expense has been spared. But, unless something is added to the City of David web site after this book is published, you will look in vain there for any reference to the area's 55,000 Palestinian Arab residents (plus, at this point, some 300 new Jewish settlers). This omission is highly misleading, bordering on fraudulent.

Meantime, there is no "away" place to which Silwan's Palestinian residents will agree to be discarded. They will not willingly be recycled as waste. Every person of conscience must stand with them until they are admitted into full partnership in their own future.

In a No More Enemies world, this cruel makeover process could never have gotten started in the first place. To rehabilitate a historic neighborhood like Silwan/City of David and to grow its

---

[54] You can see a very slick treatment in Spanish, French, Russian, English, or Hebrew (no Arabic, of course!): http://www.cityofdavid.org.il/index.html

archeology-based tourism, the first people you'd want to engage ought to be the residents.[55]

The contrast could not be more stark: Silwan's Madaa community center has an ethnically and religiously diverse local and international staff, mostly volunteer, including Israeli Jews. It runs on a shoestring budget and is modest and transparent. The City of David project is the antithesis. In this David and Goliath confrontation over the future of a slum community in a hot zone of inter-ethnic friction, the Goliath figure is named (City of) David and the David figure is a soft-spoken Palestinian social worker named Jawad Siyam, founder of Madaa.

Toolbox: A recording of Bob Dylan's "The Times They Are A-Changin'" with these memorable lines: The order is rapidly fadin' / And the first one now / Will later be last / For the times they are a-changin'. (In the NME world, ideally, we will all be treated as "first." That's what partnership means.)

---

[55] For an in-depth report on Silwan from Ir Amim, which advocates for a shared Jerusalem for all its stakeholders: http://www.ir-amim.org.il/eng/?CategoryID=269 and for a scholarly article on sharing the historical legacy of the area: "Toward an Inclusive Archeology in Jerusalem: The Case of Silwan/City of David," Raphael Greenberg, *Public Archaeology*, Vol. 8 No. 1, February, 2009, pp.35–50, which may be viewed in pdf online, at:
http://www.ingentaconnect.com/content/maney/pua/2009/00000008/00000001/art00004#expand/collapse

Find your bridge (II): Artsbridge

We who participate in the work of nonviolent conflict resolution and transformation say we want to talk with one another, to dialogue; but when we open our mouths, it sometimes happens that we push one another away instead of drawing together.

Meantime a lot of research has been done on dialogue tools and this wisdom is slowly percolating around the globe, acquiring more and more multicultural sensitivity as it goes. If you aspire to be part of that movement, it is useful to look into these programs and get some training. Most of my experience has been with attempts to share Western models with nonwestern or mixed groups of participants. At the same time, as anyone can see, concepts from Eastern religions and philosophies—yoga, mindfulness training, and so forth—with or without their original religious dimensions, are becoming integral parts of programs originating or employed in the West and between West and East.

Fusion, model-sharing, and cross-cultural co-evolution seem to be producing new hybrids that are deeply transformative. Artsbridge is one model that has fused dialogue, role-play, and art very powerfully and effectively.

Artsbridge conducted a seminar early in 2010 at the Pluralistic Spiritual Center at Wahat al Salam~Neve Shalom, near Jerusalem. Based in Swampscott, Massachusetts, USA, Artsbridge is a youth leadership training program that uses the arts, as its name suggests, as an integral and enriching component of the dialogue process. The model comes from the world of expressive therapy, art and drama, voice and movement—all the nonverbal ways of interacting and communicating and healing. Verbal interactions alternate with time for participants to do art work addressing a specific theme, which is then shared in a guided process with other participants.

Along with integrating art activities into a dialogue model, the approach also expands a paired dialogue into a triad. The triad consists of a *curious questioner*, a responder, and at least one witness/reflector. The magic phrase in this method is "I am curious about…" which the curious questioner uses—in a wholly non-judgmental way—to help evoke self-discovery and self-disclosure on the part of the responder. In practicing this method and in observing others doing so, I saw that it can be powerfully transformative, and the training for using it is fairly simple. Letting the speaker's agenda drive the interaction, and refraining from judgment about what is said, the curious questioner is rewarded with new insights while facilitating new insights for the speaker and the observer. The latter can then provide feedback and enrich these insights.

The Artsbridge model is designed to take advantage of newer research suggesting that trauma is not processed cognitively and verbally by the brain in the same way that other experience is processed, nor is it stored in the same way or in the same place in the brain. Hence, to gain access to the trauma later in order to heal it, work that utilizes the arts can succeed where a wholly verbal approach may not.

Artsbridge creates a safe space for shared self-revelation while staying with the language of empathy, curiosity, and compassion. You can learn this approach so well that your response to another participant's infuriating statements can be, instead of barely contained rage, a calm question: *I am curious as to how you came to hold that view; could you tell me about that?* —Does that calm reaction sound implausible to you? Perhaps it has to be experienced to be believed. [56] Highly recommended!

Other researchers have examined the kinds of statements that tend to "switch off" people's civilized forebrain functioning, where dialogue can take place, and reroute their neural processing

---

[56] The Artsbridge Institute in Swampscott, Massachusetts, USA is online at: http://artsbridgeinstitute.org/

to the primitive brain stem where the options are limited to "fight or flight"–thus instantly shutting off the dialogue, both neurologically and in practice, in the room, in real time. While good intentions are great as the point of departure, training in how to dia-dialogue effectively is obviously very helpful. The language of judgment-of-others shuts down valuable openings to new understanding, while the language of empathic curiosity, combined with movement and verbal interaction and visual art, expands them.

Artsbridge was founded and is led by Debbie Nathan and the workshop I attended was co-facilitated by Evan Longin.

Toolbox: Any small object from nature, or of human production, that has for you a deep emotional significance that you could explain someday to someone else.

Find your bridge (III): Compassionate Listening

Compassionate Listening is a very basic but powerful technique that allows participants to acquire attentive, empathic, compassionate listening skills that create a safe space to let a dialogue partner open up and speak freely and candidly. These skills come more naturally to some people than to others, and need to be fine-tuned in culturally sensitive ways; but anyone can learn them. The Compassionate Listening movement bases itself to begin with on the writings of the late Gene Knudson Hoffman, an American Quaker woman. There is ample information about Hoffman and the technique in online and print media sources. Some years ago, I took some training in this mode from Mideast Citizen Diplomacy (now The Compassionate Listening Project), based in the Seattle, Washington (USA) area. It was an illuminating experience. [57]

The Compassionate Listening Project was founded and is led by Leah Green.

Toolbox: A large sea shell that lets you hear magical ocean sounds, once you learn how to listen.

Find your bridge (IV): Identities in Dialogue

By way of contrast, the award-winning "Identities in Dialogue" model developed jointly by Palestinians and Jews at the School for Peace at Wahat al Salam / Neve Shalom takes a very different approach. It places the conflict between Jews and Palestinians (or other groups in conflict), including the politics of that conflict, at the center of the interaction. It challenges the participants, as members of groups in conflict with each other, to voice their most brutally offensive (to the other side) thoughts and feelings and to make space for the other side to do likewise. SFP (School for Peace) staff have also facilitated encounters in other countries. The method is not warm and cozy and is not, perhaps, for everyone, but it is widely respected for its honesty and grit. In Israel, Palestinian participants particularly seem to find it refreshing, in contrast to more "nice-nice" methods drawn from the social psychology toolbox developed in the West.

The School for Peace approach incorporates a critical lexicon that analyzes interactions between groups in conflict in terms of racism, post-colonialism, institutionalized oppression, internalization of oppression, reconstructing identity to make space for the other or to eject the internalized oppressor, and so forth. For young people particularly, this lexicon can be attractive because it offers a scholarly frame for their rage and confusion and frustration. In short-term (3-day) workshops for teens, however, the method can send them home frustrated, and sometimes despairing: They are newly united in their mutual understanding of the deep roots of the conflict and nevertheless have made friends with "the other," but they go back to their separate everyday environments without reliable tools to help create change or even to defend their new orientation from criticism at home. The professionals working with this model are acutely aware of this downside to short-term programs. The deficiency can be addressed with long-term follow-up, but that is costly, and funding for follow-up has always been very hard to come by. The year-long dialogue program conducted by the SFP in cooperation with leading Israeli universities, on the other hand, affords ample time for follow-through and the results reflect that.[58]

More recently, SFP programs for adult professionals (mental health professionals, doctors and nurses, lawyers, and young politicians, among others) have expanded their emphasis to incorporate an extended, shared action component aiming to equip participants as change agents at home, at work, and in their communities. These programs incorporate structured, long-term follow-up and joint action components and they have proven extremely fruitful.

Some years ago, I translated into English the SFP's handbook on their method, *Israeli and Palestinian Identities in Dialogue: the School for Peace Approach* (ed. R. Halabi, Rutgers University Press, 2004). This brief volume offers a wealth of hard-earned insights into many of the complexities of facilitating groups in conflict, including the use of bi-national and uni-national sessions (the latter, an SFP innovation); facilitating in pairs; and facilitating using more than one language in the same room.[59]

My own impression over many years is that practitioners of the School for Peace method are at very high risk of burnout, perhaps because the intense and often toxic emotional content that emerges in the workshops tends to accumulate over time until it overloads the capacity of the facilitators to be cleansed of it between seminars. For professionals anywhere who opt to utilize or adapt the SFP model, incorporation of a regular mechanism to help flush out the toxicity to which they are exposed in this work could provide tremendous added value to this model.

---

[58] See "Who is More Humane? An Ethnographic Account of Power Struggles in Jewish-Palestinian Dialogue Encounters," Nava Sonnenschein and Zvi Bekerman, *Peace and Conflict Studies*, 17:2, Fall 2010.

[59] More information on the School for Peace is online at: http://nswas.org/rubrique138.html

Toolbox: Add a small green plant! Read text from **Israeli and Palestinian Identities in Dialogue** *at www.books.google.com; buy it from the SFP or at online bookstores.*

Find your bridge (V): Community-based dialogue

You can acquire some very practical tools to initiate a constructive intergroup "living room dialogue" in your own neighborhood or community, starting from scratch: Just ask Libby and Len Traubman, a San Francisco couple who must be among the world's most committed and experienced practitioners of ongoing home-based intercommunal dialogue. They began decades ago with American-Soviet citizen-to-citizen diplomacy, later got into Jewish-Palestinian dialogue, and lately are sharing their approach internationally. On request, they send out a kit that, over many years now, has seeded a dialogue process in hundreds of communities across the USA and beyond (as far as Africa). They offer DVDs about successful dialogue projects that inspire new groups to begin a dialogue and to persevere. The Traubmans also maintain an exhaustive online archive with a wealth of useful material facilitating and advocating for positive co-transformation and communication all over the world. [60]

In December 2010, the Traubmans circulated by email a presentation on a new internal Jewish community initiative in the United States called the Year of Civil Discourse Initiative[61]. The program uses a template designed by Rachel Eryn Kalish that does away with polarized old political labels like liberal/conservative, left/right, etc. It offers a different lexicon to describe Jewish voices: *Guardians, Modernists* and *Prophets*, and presents each as having both positive and negative attributes. The goal is to "elevate the level of discourse in the Jewish community when discussing Israel" for "people from across the political

---

[60] The Traubmans blog at: http://traubman.igc.org/global.htm
[61] This is a joint project of the Jewish Community Relations Council and the San Francisco-based Jewish Community Federation, in partnership with the Board of Rabbis of Northern California; retrieved at
http://www.jcrc.org/ycd.htm

spectrum." As this and similar initiatives gather momentum, within and between various ethnic and religious communities, the NME network will benefit.

Toolbox: Put the Traubmans' email address in there, from their web site, and write to them.

Find your bridge (VI): Groups that build and protest together

And then there are the groups that dialogue together via joint direct action: rebuilding destroyed homes, replanting uprooted trees, resurfacing ruined roads, and demonstrating against discrimination and displacement. These groups are like a Habitat for Humanity in a combat zone: peace-building through joint "sweat equity" while the shooting is still going on.

In Israel and Palestine, Rabbis for Human Rights[62] and the Israel Committee Against House Demolitions[63] are two prominent ones. In Palestine in the West Bank, the grassroots action committees in villages like Bil'in, Na'lin, and Walaja are leading the transition from a failed strategy of violent armed resistance to an investment in nonviolent grassroots activism among Palestinian civilians living under military occupation. All these groups have local leadership with participation by Palestinians, Israelis, and international volunteers.

Jeff Halper of ICAHD famously said once that the difference between a Zionist and a post-Zionist is witnessing your first home demolition. (I wish it were that simple.) Rabbi Arik Ascherman, director of RHR, has probably helped with his own hands to rebuild enough demolished Palestinian homes to get a realtor's license. In Bil'in, a heavy price is exacted from the local leadership: the late Bassem Ibrahim Abu-Rahma gave his life in 2009, and Abdullah Abu Rahma, coordinator of the Bil'in Popular Committee Against the Wall, was jailed on trumped-up charges. On December 31, 2010, Bassem's sister Jawaher Abu Rahma, 36, died after inhaling tear gas used by IDF troops to disperse the

---

[62] Rabbis for Human Rights (Israel) is online at:
http://www.rhr.org.il/index.php?language=en
[63] Israeli Committee Against House Demolitions: http://www.icahd.org/

weekly protest in Bil'in[64]. Their colleagues in other villages are similarly harassed and jailed. Violent night-time incursions by the Israeli occupation forces are routine. Even the occasional death, however, does not kill the movement, which is led by all its participants: ordinary citizens. I believe that this resilience is boosted by the cross-border cooperation. It is a pure No More Enemies paradigm, seeking equal justice and freedom for all, using cooperative nonviolent means.

I would like to paraphrase Hillel, the famous Jewish sage who, in the first century BC, when asked to define the Torah while standing on one foot, said: "That which is hateful to you, do not do to your fellow. That is the whole Torah; the rest is the explanation; go and learn."[65]

To transform an "enemies" relationship into a partnership, the first step is to develop your capacity to hear the other's hopes and fears, from his or her own mouth, until you can feel them as empathically as you would want your own hopes and fears to be felt. That is the gist. There are a lot of tools out there. Go learn some!

Toolbox: Reader's choice.

---

[64]"Tear Gas Kills a Palestinian Protestor" by Isabel Kershner, *The New York Times - International Herald Tribune,* January 1, 2011, retrieved at http://www.nytimes.com/2011/01/02/world/middleeast/02mideast.html?_r=1&scp=1&sq=Bil'in&st=cse
The IDF disputed the facts of her death: "IDF: No proof Palestinian woman died from tear gas at protest" by Anshel Pfeffer, *Haaretz,* January 3, 2011, retrieved at http://www.haaretz.com/news/diplomacy-defense/idf-no-proof-palestinian-woman-died-from-tear-gas-at-protest-1.335043 The needless suffering continues.
[65] Retrieved at: http://en.wikipedia.org/wiki/Hillel_the_Elder

Be a NME futurist

We need some visionary and assertive No More Enemies futurists.

Futurists–the folks who try to rationally imagine and describe what the future could look like–seem mostly to be very captive to the enemies paradigm. Nearly all the futurist books I see in bookshops talk about the future wars; the future allies who will wage them and against which future enemies they will do battle; the future economies that will support these wars; and so on and so forth.

Yuck!

The shift toward a global NME consciousness calls for futurists who can envision a No-More-Enemies-oriented future. Get these super-depressing, enemies-mentality-infected, win-lose, dominance-oriented, dog-eat-dog futurists out of our heads and let's spend our energies on more harmonious visions.

Deep visioning is the cornerstone of all progress. We imagine it, and then we make it happen. We've had far too many books telling us about the next war and what it will look like.

We need a creative literature of futurism that starts from here: Good-bye war, and good riddance!

Toolbox: Find a depressing and gloomy article about the future and save it. One evening when you want to have fun with friends, get everyone to help rewrite the article the way it would read in a NME world. Think way outside the box and enjoy the ride.

Join God's little repertory company

When you look at historical dramas, we all seem to be part of God's little repertory company, and we keep changing roles: OK now, this time around, YOU over here, you be the good guy, and YOU over there, you be the bad guy. --But I don't WANT to be the bad guy! –Well, tough luck, that's your role for now. –Etc.

If a group of people can be villains in one story and then, twenty or thirty or forty years later the contemporary representatives of that same group are suddenly the heroes or anyhow allies with their ex-enemies in another story–and still carrying that same "group identity" as in the previous movie–then it's not the PEOPLE. It's the story. It's the paradigm.

The 1940s Japanese were, from the American standpoint, the bad guys; a few decades later, the Japanese were a close trading partner for Americans, a leader in industry, etc., etc., etc.: same Japanese; different story. (All of that was, of course, from the American standpoint; from the Japanese standpoint, were they not good guys all along?) So these identities and roles are fluid; they move around.

The social psychology studies of individual and group identity from the late 20th century talk about identity as deep-seated and rigid and resistant to change. I think that's only true from certain standpoints. For example, a person may never relinquish a core identity but can nevertheless expand their sense of self to embrace a broader and more all-inclusive identity. The original identity is not rejected or shed, but subsumed (often painlessly) in the larger, newer, more inclusive identity. Jews who become Buddhists, for example, often remain, in their own view, Jews ("Bujus"). Hence the emergent post-modern idea of identity stresses fluidity and flexibility, permitting all kinds of new hybrid identities to evolve.

341

In Israel/Palestine, a creative new shared identity that would permit Israelis and Palestinians to embrace it equally, without having to renounce, reject, or repudiate their former identity, could go far to shaping a new shared reality. Imagine Sarah and Hagar reborn together on this earth, embracing *all their children* and declaring that *all their children* are loved and wanted; experiencing themselves as *one big family* and creating a new shared identity: children of Sarah and Hagar, awladna / yaldeinu ("our children" in Arabic and Hebrew). Some of these children would be Jewish and some Muslim and some Christian, some Israelis and some Palestinians, and so forth, but some would also be blue-eyed and others brown-eyed. So what? Mothers love their blue-eyed and their brown-eyed children, both.

Many people today are reaching across old boundaries in search of new shared identities. Be a part of that!

Toolbox: Get the script of any play you would enjoy. Pick one that features a vivid inter-group conflict. Have everyone in the group read the same role until you all get very accustomed to your characters. Then switch roles and have everyone play a character from the other group. Evaluate the experience together. How does this generalize to a national or international level?

You can help: Toward a unified theory of NME

What you are offered in this book is a "good enough" theory of NME.[66] Perfecting it is a shared task.

A while back, I became obsessed with the idea of formulating the definitive statement of the theory of No More Enemies. I would lie awake at night thinking, looking for the ultimate framework on which I could hang the elaboration of the idea–something elegant and vivid and memorable and, well, perfect.

Things that are already out there (like, say, Buddhism, for instance) have already covered much of this ground rather well. My burning, passionate desire to midwife a new formulation that would add something relevant to our times, in an up-to-the-minute idiom that speaks to the shared realities of our new millennium, produced some good riffs. I wondered how to go further.

Suddenly I had an epiphany: The definitive all-inclusive perfect theory of NME is not in my power to give as a gift. Enhancing the theory and practice of NME is up to everyone reading this. You can start a conversation. You can become an emissary of NME. You can exchange ideas with others and debate whatever is evoked for you by my presentation. Together, we will evolve the ultimate unified theory of No More Enemies.

Stay tuned!

Toolbox: a photo of Albert Einstein or Lise Meitner, Helen Edwards or Niels Bohr or C.S. Wu, David Bohm or Helen Quinn or Lisa Randall, or some other physicist you admire. "Unified theory" is a term from physics.

---

[66] After English psychiatrist and pediatrician Donald Winnicott's notion of the "good enough" mother.

Reinvent your myths

Fidelity to historical myths has led to lots of people being put in jail or shut up in reservations or shot dead or conscripted against their will into armies, and all sorts of grim mischief like that. This can easily happen because myths do not always stretch and bend along with the flow of reality. If this applies to some beloved myth of your own, then reinvent it.

We humans are not merely consumers of myth; we are also makers of myth.

Stand up and take responsibility for your inner myth-maker. Put it to work in NME mode. See what happens.

Toolbox: Reader's choice.

Ponder this question

If something is *postcolonial*, what is it "pre-"?

Thinking always takes place in some kind of context, conscious or subconscious, within certain mental boundaries, implicit or explicit. Having a clearly delineated playing field is useful because we can't think about everything all at once. On the other hand, it is really useful periodically to examine the field and the boundaries, because those delineations are also a statement. Just beyond the edge of that landscape may lie a new and profound understanding, based partly on an acute look at what we have tended to include and what exclude, and why.

In an academic sense or setting, there are doubtless clear differences between the notions signified by the terms "cross-disciplinary," "multi-disciplinary," "interdisciplinary," and so forth. For our purposes here, the main thing is to transcend the assumed boundaries. How you do it, and what else you include as raw material for your thinking–all of that is significant, of course. But the main thing is the act of intending to expand the boundaries in the first place. After that, many things become possible.

I found a site called "Colonial and Postcolonial Literary Dialogues" online.[67] The home page says that the site is meant to be "a resource for students, scholars, and teachers of postcolonial and multicultural approaches to British and world literature." It offers "rich dialogues between colonial and postcolonial perspectives… analysis, links, and resources for colonial and postcolonial literature, history, and theory… [with] links to other postcolonial studies resources on the web." And so forth. The site identifies itself as a "non-profit site created by students and faculty at Western Michigan University."

---

[67] The site is at: http://www.wmich.edu/dialogues/sitepages/home.html

I thought, wow, what a great idea. And then I thought: If something is postcolonial... what is it "pre-"? Where is it going? Where could it take us?

When I found this site, it was because I was surfing around for information about Lame Deer, having discovered a mysterious note to myself on a scrap of paper, in my handwriting, that said: *Lame Deer: text.* I had no memory of when I had made the note, or why. The Western Michigan University postcolonial site provided a clear idea of who Lame Deer was: a Sioux Indian born around 1900, a Lakota holy man, whose autobiography (with Richard Erdoes) tells us a lot about the Sioux nation and culture, about colonialism in America and its painful history, and about Lame Deer's own life and thinking.

Look around! We are surrounded by possibilities. Train a light on ordinary things and realize that they carry more meaning than the obvious.

If something is postcolonial, what is it *pre-*? Maybe "pre-NME."

Toolbox: Reader's choice.

When dreams collide, think bigger

None of us is fated to be satisfied with small dreams. We all have the sacred right to dream big... as big as we like.

But what happens if we discover that our dream is somehow hurting someone else, someone we had no intention of hurting? Shall we go ahead and try to live our dream at the expense of someone else's suffering? Or shall we resolve to redesign our dream, perhaps expand its boundaries somehow, in some creative way, broadening its embrace so that it no longer is toxic to others? Possibly these other people will help us to do that, if we ask.

If you see someone busy with a dream that is also, by chance or by design, someone else's worst nightmare, you will rarely succeed in separating the dreamer from that socially dysfunctional or morally questionable dream by force. Trashing someone's treasured dream will only increase its power and impact. Denouncing someone's dream usually makes them more loyal to it, not less.

If you want to transform that situation, you can offer them a broader and more inclusive dream: one they can embrace without having to actively disavow the one they cherish already. Instead of demanding that they abandon their dream, you can give them an appealing way to grow bigger than their dream; to look past it to new horizons. They need not repudiate the old dream, or denounce it. Don't demand that! Just inspire them, and watch their feet: they'll start walking toward this new source of inspiration.

Offer them a dream that is more inclusive. Beyond freedom and security for their own group, for example, you could assist them in creating a vision of freedom and security for their own group and for their neighbors, too. Free and secure neighbors increase our own freedom and security a hundredfold.

People have been known to voluntarily embrace new dreams that require, relative to their previous dream, a complete reversal

347

of direction. But if you were to try *forcing them* to make that change of direction, they would resist you.

On the dream level, carrots work better; sticks, not so well. Rather than bludgeoning people, we are better advised to try enticing them or, better yet, inspiring them.

Toolbox: Figure out what kind of natural setting would be conducive to dreaming new dreams, for you: by a lake or a river or by the ocean; in a field or under a tree or in the mountains; or in a big armchair by the window or by the hearth. Find a photograph of such a place in a print or online magazine or gallery, and save it. Put a copy in your toolbox. Go there, mentally, when you want to dream new dreams. Maybe you will meet some of "them" there; especially if you have invited them to join you.

Forget spiritual

Forget "spiritual" if that's not your thing. Look at moving beyond the enemies paradigm as an *operational* template, a structural concept.

Stop thinking of it as a moral problem, if you like, and think of it as a *design* problem.

Toolbox: McDonough and Braungart's **Cradle to Cradle**. *Or find someone who says it better, for you.*

Ask me why I chose this title

You will have noticed that a lot of this book is about the tremendous power of positive visualization, affirmation, expectation, and so forth: not as a replacement for a passionately committed work plan for constructive social change, not as something omnipotent, but as excellent fuel for the engine of that change. When using affirmation to promote change, we generally refrain from even mentioning the bad stuff we want to grow past. Instead, we invoke the good that we are working toward, phrasing the affirmation as if the envisioned good outcome were already here, or at least in process.

In that light, why have I chosen a title with the word "enemies" in it? Isn't "enemies" the precise thing whose power we are trying to drain away? Doesn't using that word in the title give the negative word itself more power?

What about a positive title, stressing the kinds of relationship modalities that "enemies" is going to be replaced by? (Partnership; relationship; connectedness; oneness; synergy; sisterhood and fellowship.)

I thought about this issue a long time. I felt glued to the title "No More Enemies" but, on strategic grounds, it seemed to contradict my own advice. This bothered me... until suddenly I realized how useful the phrase "no more enemies" is for us, right here and now, in this historical moment, in the present state of affairs in our world.

We are not going to segue instantaneously from a world of enemies to a world of loving relationships with our adversaries. Our world today is full of highly elaborated ideas of enemies, and full of angry adversaries armed with both lethal rage and lethal weapons, aimed at one another (with "the other" being seen as the *enemy*). Moreover the very notion of "enemies" is continually sold to us: in the news media, in history textbooks, in video games, in television and Internet and films and who knows what-all.

Growing ourselves beyond this conceptually lethal worldview may require an extended process, in the human scale of things (although in geologic or cosmic time, in God's time, if you will, it could happen in the blink of an eye). In our ordinary daily reality, the enemies paradigm—however obsolete is has already become—is unlikely to disappear overnight. The process could happen more suddenly and much quicker than we think, but probably not overnight.

By the time you finish reading this book, however, if I did my job right, you will never again hear the word "enemies" without automatically also hearing the words: "no more!" We want our minds to be permanently imprinted with the refrain, NO MORE ENEMIES… as a signal of what can be, of what we are aiming for, of what we believe is attainable, of what we are dedicating our efforts to. From now on, when you hear the word "enemies," your mind ought to respond every time: "–no more!"

And you'll be ready to pass it on to others, and expand the circle exponentially.

No more enemies! Enemies no more!!

Toolbox: Translate the slogan "No more enemies!" into another language. How does it sound? Does it need tweaking? It might.

To shift reality, shift your focus

The basic approach used in mediation has a NME flavor. In mediation, the participants move early in the process from a focus on their antagonistic *positions* toward a focus on identifying their possible underlying common *interests*. This reorientation mirrors the shift away from a world of enemies and war toward something more beautiful.

The dynamic that emerges is almost magical. Mediation does not challenge your opening position. It simply suggests that you shift your angle of focus. It puts all positions on hold temporarily while examining, first, each party's own stated interests and then the areas, often unexpectedly rich, of overlapping interests between the sides. In that previously undiscovered and unexamined commonality lie worlds of as-yet unimagined new possibilities.

Sometimes mediation cannot be used or it fails to produce an agreement. Abused and abuser, for example, cannot always transcend their history. Sometimes the weaker or the injured party can't bear even to be in the same room as the other party. No single approach works all the time.

There is a whole literature on this, in many languages and with contributions from many different cultures and societies. We can't begin to cover it all here. For our purposes, it is sufficient that we keep reminding ourselves that today there is a whole science, or art, or craft, of ADR (alternative dispute resolution) at our disposal: some of it new, and some that has been around awhile. These good alternative tools and options deserve to be matched, by us, with renewed courage and renewed faith.

Toolbox: Read something about mediation, restorative justice, and other ADR methods.

352

Find the third (or fourth or fifth) way

So-called intractable problems may not be.

For example: Let's say that everyone wants to have children but there's not enough room on the planet. This is a scenario we could be facing next week.

OK. If we all want children AND we all want to limit the population, we can reach for innovative new family paradigms. (In some places, it's already happening.) We could, for instance, create clusters of friends or cousins to parent one or two children. All would share the lived experience of raising a child, while reducing the number of offspring. Eureka! It does not have to be the case that *either* you *or* I get to have a child while the other doesn't. (Only one woman can physically give birth to the child, of course.)

Perhaps not every apparent either-or dilemma will produce, even on exhaustive examination, an imaginative third, fourth, or fifth way to a good resolution.

At the same time, in no case will we find one if we don't look.

Toolbox: a magnifying glass—to remind us to look.

Work from a NME main menu

You can create for yourself a personalized NME main menu. For example:

- Accept no more enemies!
- Transform adversaries into partners.
- Alchemize fear and hate into love.
- Instead of challenging a skeptic, just inquire curiously.
- Think 10,000 years ahead, but start now.

The sub-menus are up to you and your own circles of shared NME activity.

The sub-menus could cover things like: Which adversaries are you going to attempt to transform into partners this week? How? Who else (friends; colleagues; members of Congress; members of an international association) are you going to involve in this effort? Using what timetable? Starting when?

While you are working in your chosen direction, consider the interactivity of our software and our hardware. The hard wiring in our minds and the thoughts we are thinking are, quite possibly, interactive to some extent over the long haul.

And don't forget the probable, or at least potential, interactivity of *our* interactivity and *other people's* interactivity. There are energy fields we have not yet discovered. Our own progression toward NME has great potential for interaction with other people's progression toward NME. In a few years or decades, all this could dramatically change "human nature" so that what inevitably occurred in prior generations would no longer be inevitable or even likely.

We can only find out by trying, but–based on both new science and old spiritual traditions–we already can have some confidence that we are moving in a productive and fruitful direction.

354

Toolbox: Make a list for yourself of your NME tasks. Include names of people you'd like to collaborate with. Include time frames and target dates. Put the list in your toolbox. Take it out often and review it. When you can cross things off—celebrate!

How big is your paradigm shift?

Paradigm shifts, at least in the popular meaning of the term, come in many flavors and they also have orders of magnitude.

Why limit yourself to facilitating a minor one, when you could be facilitating a major one—like No More Enemies?

Go for it!

Toolbox: Read up on the history of the notion of "paradigm shifts" and put your notes in the toolbox.

Look for pioneering partnership combos

A story[68] by Gina Kolata in *The New York Times* of August 12, 2010 reported on something really different:

In 2003, a group of scientists and executives from the National Institutes of Health, the Food and Drug Administration, the drug and medical-imaging industries, universities and nonprofit groups joined in a project that experts say had no precedent: a collaborative effort to find the biological markers that show the progression of Alzheimer's disease in the human brain.

This consortium, ADNI, for Alzheimer's Disease Neuroimaging Initiative, made tremendous progress in researching Alzheimer's, progress that would not have been possible otherwise, and a similar project has been proposed to address Parkinson's disease. Whodathunkit?!

There are several fascinating innovations that were made possible due to this novel model of cooperation: Competition (among pharmaceutical companies, for instance) was replaced by cooperation. All the data would be open to anyone in the world. Everyone's findings would be made public immediately. No one would own the data, although the drug companies would conceivably profit from the project later on. The scientists involved agreed to voluntarily collaborate, despite longstanding career norms that dictated otherwise. The consortium came together as the result of "a casual conversation in a car" on the way to an airport. The collaboration permitted a very different research approach to be employed. And although there had been diverse productive research studies underway, a common set of data became possible only when the ADNI began. Moreover, over $70

---

[68] "Sharing of Data Leads to Progress on Alzheimer's" by Gina Kolata, *The New York Times-International Herald Tribune*, August 12, 2010; retrieved at http://www.nytimes.com/2010/08/13/health/research/13alzheimer.html

million in funding was raised from a combination of government, private sector, and nonprofit organizations in the first phase of the project.

A telling comment quoted in the *Times* article has relevance for NME:

> *"Companies were caught in a prisoner's dilemma," said Dr. Jason Karlawish, an Alzheimer's researcher at the University of Pennsylvania. "They all wanted to move the field forward, but no one wanted to take the risks of doing it."*

Preparing the way for this cooperation was a complex and even in some ways a frightening undertaking, but it proved to be possible, after all.

The same is true of reorienting ourselves away from the enemies mentality and moving individually and collectively toward a world with No More Enemies. Everyone is afraid, and there are risks, but it can be done. And the rewards that await us are enormous.

Toolbox: Look up "the prisoner's dilemma" and think about its relevance to NME. Put your notes in the toolbox.

Create your template for a No More Enemies workshop

Here is a simple generic template for creating a workshop around the theme of No More Enemies. There are so many different approaches to group and inter-group work today, incorporating fields from art to yoga; I am not suggesting here a specific kind of workshop, but just noting some conceptual highlights that could be included. Check out the template below and then go create your own workshop!

The purpose, in brief: Cultivating a perspective in which the entire world is a vast collection of potential partners and partnerships, and the concept of "enemies" is no longer useful.

Principles:

Adopt the core idea: The idea of enemies is obsolete. Shared sustainability requires a partnership orientation.

Go for the basic reset: The new default orientation of "no more enemies" is the first step in disarming angry, disempowered adversaries, by inviting them into the circle and re-empowering them as partners.

Humanize the other: Enemies are faceless and monolithic and inhuman, symbolized by some fearful icon; partners are diverse and many-faceted and human, and best appreciated one at a time (or a few at a time) and in person. Explore some of the myriad available ways to establish real human contact with "them," whether electronically, face-to-face, or both. Rehearse these ways, plan how to apply them, and role-play them in the workshop. Organize, together, to broaden the impact beyond the confines of the workshop itself.

Play with the evolving paradigm: Moving to liberate people's deep potential (individual and societal) can be even more powerful than the paradigm that focuses on securing people their civil and human rights. ("Rights" paradigms are about the human community making sure that everyone has what they are entitled to; liberating people's potential is about broadening the opportunities for people to contribute and to give of themselves to the human community.) We can recast Maslow's hierarchy of needs. We can use "cradle to cradle" (McDonough & Braungart); Barry Commoner's axioms (ecology); Gaia theory (James Lovelock) and serial endosymbiosis (Lynn Margulis); and other related ideas to help construct a new scientific basis for a different human perspective.

Ask different questions: We can teach ourselves to ask better questions. If we keep asking bad (enemies-paradigm-driven) questions, we will keep getting bad answers.

Discover the magic: Get to know your magic inner filtration system: negative energy in, constructive energy out! Each of us has a magical filtering system inside, which can be switched on to vacuum up negative inputs and give back good energy to the world. Many people are still unaware that we all have this gift, or tool, or ability, or whatever it is called. Use the workshop to get in touch with the magic filter and practice using it. (Be like trees.)

Do periodic reality checks: You can use reversal: the seeker's best friend. Or use some other dynamic reality check that works for you.

Pitfalls in moving toward NME:

- Uncertainty and risk (so there's no risk now?).
- Appearing ridiculous (always a possibility).

- Social ostracism (painful, but leads to great new networks).
- Becoming a target of rage (no fear!).
- Falling short of the goal (so what?).

Payoffs:

- Deep fulfillment.
- A bequest worth leaving our children.
- Inaugurating a new era in human history.

Toolbox: Now create your own workshop template. Get some more people to help shape it. Then find some group to try it out with you. Then broaden the circle.

View NME as a game of reversal

Everyone from Confucius to Jesus to Bob Dylan taught that today's elites are tomorrow's homeless, and vice versa. If it hasn't happened by tomorrow, give it another fifty or a hundred years.

Reversal is part of life. The iconic yin-yang symbol, a circle halved by a wavy line, with a black dot in the white half and a white dot in the black half, is meant to symbolize this fact. When some phenomenon reaches its own limit, it turns around and marches back again; every trend contains the seed of its own demise.

Again, examining things using the notion of reversal can be very useful. Byron Katie, the contemporary self-help guru mentioned earlier, who travels around the world giving her very stimulating presentation entitled "The Work," uses the principle to good effect.[69] In her four-stage process whereby counselees examine issues in their own lives, there is a step that uses reversal explicitly. In one scenario, a woman complains that her husband does not respect her because he does not really pay attention to what she has to say. Byron Katie asks her to consider that perhaps *she* does not really pay attention to *her husband's* talk and that *she* is not respecting *him*.

Whether or not this kind of process produces an earth-shattering revelation in every case, most of the time it will be an enlightening exercise.

The No More Enemies reorientation process can be thought of, overall, as an exercise in reversal. Take a good look at your enemies because they are your partners-to-be. They are the ones you need if you really want to fix what is broken. And take a good look at your current partners. If they keep telling you to destroy your enemy, protect yourself from your enemy, stay apart from your enemy, etc., then those partners are not behaving like

---

[69] Byron Katie's web site is at: http://www.thework.com/index.php

362

partners at all. In fact, they are standing between you and the new partners you need in order to find the solution you seek. Where the new bridge to change should be rising, they are standing in the way and making sure that it can't get built. To convert them from pseudo-partners to real partners may take some work.

Toolbox: Find a good image of the yin-yang circle. Make a plan to convert a pseudo-partner into a real partner.

Practice zooming out

The signs are everywhere that the underlying paradigm is on the cusp of shifting toward partnership.

Lift up your head a minute and look around. Pick any discipline or field. The signs are everywhere–but you have to get above the plane of your usual perspective to notice.

Toolbox: Google the word "cooperation" plus your field of interest: e.g., "cooperation in science." Among the items that came up on that one was: http://www.cooperationscience.com/blog.php Bingo! Try the same exercise with other likely combinations and see what surfaces. Create some group games using this approach.

Re-envision patriotism in a NME mode

Patriotism in our world today is often used less to honor one's own country and more to pump up the hate and fear that citizens of one nation are supposed to feel for the citizens of some other nation. One might almost say that patriotism is cynically manipulated to *create* enemies.

This is a particularly nasty variant of "Hooray for us, down with them."

In a NME world, patriotism will have a very different feeling. People will be proud of their country and proud of its cooperation with others; it won't be necessary to dominate or outperform other countries in order to feel proud of one's own.

There is a lot of research out there about the outcomes of activity based on cooperation as compared with the outcomes of activity based on competition. A landmark book from the 1980s, Alfie Kohn's *No Contest: the Case Against Competition* gives an overview. Newer research suggests that, in fields from education to business to law enforcement, cooperation is making a significant comeback.

For people who are competition-addicted, there is always a safe playground: Compete against yourself instead of seeking adversaries to beat. Challenge others to cooperate. When governments adopt this policy, the world will be a more beautiful and much safer place.

It is not wussy to compete against yourself. When you lose, you can always demand a rematch. When you win—likewise.

Toolbox: Read some of the published studies on the negative side effects of competition, especially on children, and look at some of the alternative educational systems already developed that rely on, and build, cooperation.

Don't tell me we can't do without 'em

When I talk to people about the idea of No More Enemies, often someone will say: "But we can't do without enemies!" (*Why not?*) Or: "But of course there will always be enemies!" (*Why?*)

Recently I was sitting in the kitchen at the house of some old friends in Jerusalem, talking about nothing in particular with their youngest son, now 25. While perhaps more open in his worldview than many other Israeli Jewish youngsters, he is not any kind of full-time political or social change activist. When I mentioned that I was writing a book, he asked what it was about and I said, *about the notion that the idea of "enemies" is obsolete.* He said: *Well, obviously.*

This was encouraging.

Toolbox: Decide to kick your enemies addiction. Update the list of enemies you made a while ago, or create a new one. Work on your plan to convert them into partners. You might need a team; recruit one. You might need a framework; find one. As your project progresses, share what you are learning as widely as you can. Pick a date when you will have transformed at last half of those enemies into partners: on that date, you'll be halfway to enemies-free! Plan a party. Put all your notes in the toolbox as you go along.

Try a metaphor upgrade

Good metaphors from the *enemies* era may need an overhaul to work well for us in the NME era.

How we decide to conceptualize something always has a strong impact on our subsequent experience. It is not the only factor, but it is an important factor.

So much thinking is pre-set in militaristic, enemies-oriented tracks. It tends to skew our thoughts in enemies-oriented directions.

There are metaphors and sayings I have long admired that suddenly, when subjected to a No More Enemies litmus test, seem inadequate. For example:

> *The outcome of the battle is decided in the minds of the participants before the first blow is struck.*

That was always one of my favorites. Reassessing it in a NME mode, however, I see that it frames our experience within an enemies paradigm: battles, blows, victory and defeat, winner and loser.

The same idea—about how our will, our faith, our determination and our vision can shape what happens—could be reworded in terms of mutual empowerment and partnership. Let's say: Adversaries oriented to partnership can transform a looming confrontation into an emergent joint project. Or how about: The nature and quality of the journey is decided in the minds of the participants and of the wanna-be-participants and the should-be-participants, individually and collectively, again and again and again, with each new step taken... according to a powerful vision informed by compassion, humility, respect, and love.

Hahaha! Well... that definitely needs work! It could never be as good a sound bite as the original, but meantime it is completely partnership oriented. Some compromise is in order here.

Toolbox: Find a traditional saying or metaphor that appeals to you, and rephrase it in a (concise!) version that is user-friendly for the No More Enemies era. Or do the same thing in a group, as a game.

Take the leap

These are among the qualities of soul that help us make that leap of identification, that leap of empathy and understanding, toward someone who has been labeled our enemy:

> humility empathy flexibility listening adaptability humor courtesy respect curiosity tolerance-for-ambiguity openness-to-risk creativity generosity resilience perseverance love optimism dreaming compassion adventurousness courage imagination reflection vision

You can add some of your own.

All of these qualities are like stones in the river: you can use them to cross to the other side. The order in which they are helpful to you, need not match the order in which they appear here. Just hop to the next one that is there waiting for you in your own life, and then hop to the next and the next.

Toolbox: A flat stone. It doesn't have to be big enough to stand on, just big enough to remind you what it symbolizes for you.

Tell them you won't wear that hat

People might get angry when you articulate a point of view grounded in the NME paradigm.

It's not surprising that people don't know how to digest the vision of a reality without enemies. The idea can be terribly threatening at first, because it disrupts all the known landmarks of one's mental map: something like an Escher painting. People get queasy. But with patience and perseverance, the idea can become fascinating.

I sent around an email notice of a fundraising event I was running, to raise money for medicines for Yousif, a sick child in Gaza whose aunt is a good friend of mine. I sent it to an email bulletin board serving Anglo-Israelis in my area. Within a day I got an email reply from one of the recipients on that list (quoted below verbatim):

> *How about raising funds for your own people? How about letting your Arab pals take care of their own from their brotherly oil fueled unlimited coffers?*
>
> *When will you smell the coffee and wake up?*

We had some back and forth as I tried to reason with him. He just got madder and madder.

Finally I sent him an email that said, among other things: "You are trying to make me your enemy. I won't go there. I won't wear that hat."

After that, he didn't write back. I don't know if it's because he had retired from the field in disgust, or whether I'd actually given him something useful and new to think about: *You want to make me your enemy. I won't wear that hat.*

I will say the same thing to anyone who wants me to be their enemy. I will say it (given the time!) to a raging militiaman or soldier in any combat zone who comes at me with a weapon and wants to kill me. If I have time, I will tell him: *You can kill me and then* [as Gandhi would have said] *you will have my dead body, but you will not have my cooperation. I will not address you as my enemy even if that's the last decision I get to make on this earth.*

I will not collaborate in perpetuating the *enemies* paradigm into this new millennium. I will not agree to be anyone's enemy. I will not wear that hat.

Toolbox: Practice the mantra until it feels natural to say it with a smile: "I think you are trying to make me your enemy. I will not wear that hat!" — You never know when you might get a good opportunity to use it. I hope it won't be in a battle zone.

End the day with one less enemy today

If you have been working on decommissioning an enemies relationship and have found a way to transform that person, that relationship, then at the end of the day there is one less enemy in the world.

That is the Rumpelstiltskin factor. Go for it.

With focused effort, the state of enmity can be converted to one of mutual learning, and often partnership. And in the process, the enemy is transformed (along with you). Now they are no longer an enemy, but something else: certainly, a co-learner; sometimes, a comrade; with luck, a partner; and more often than one might think–a friend.

The enemies paradigm is on the way out, and you are a very important part of the process.

After you've done this transformation once and recycled an enemy into a partner, you can do it again. And again. These transformations may not get any easier, but you get better at doing them. Guaranteed.

Toolbox: Compose a short bedtime prayer along the lines of: I am thankful for once more having done my best to end my day with one less enemy.

There are no enemies, Dave

Humorist Dave Barry wrote once that, someday in the future, long after the world has mostly destroyed itself with a nuclear war or been destroyed by a comet or whatever, and the only thing left on earth is cockroaches–the cockroaches in the Middle East will still be killing each other.

It's a great line, Dave–but this time you're wrong, and I can prove it.

I'm a nice Jewish girl from New York (somewhat aged now: 63 next birthday) and I've lived with Palestinian and Muslim and Arab families in Israel/Palestine for long periods of time: in the same town, in the same neighborhood, on the same street, and even sometimes in the same house. What I discovered is that we're all one family.

I submit to you that, if I can do it, anyone can do it.

"Enemies" is a construct–an idea made up by folks to describe their own behavior, dating back beyond the mists of prehistory, and passed along down the generations ever since: to us.

We can, however, be the last generation to live in a world of enemies, if we so choose. Now is the time to take this construct and reconstruct it–now, when we've learned beyond any shadow of a doubt that the most powerful shaper of reality is the human imagination. The mystics have told us so for millennia, and now Western science is finding out how right they were.

So, dear reader, here is the task:

Imagine that the notion of enemies is becoming obsolete; imagine it tirelessly. Refuse to be deflected. Recruit friends and family and neighbors and colleagues to imagine it with you. Recruit your representatives in government to join you. Much sooner than we might think (because social networking is now exponentially increasing all around the globe), the notion of enemies will become obsolete. Absolutely guaranteed.

Now's the time—and I aspire to help create a certain sense of urgency so that we can collapse the time frame. Let's bridge our way to a world of partnership soon enough to save all the children already born from the ravages of a world full of enemies.

No more enemies! Enemies no more!

Toolbox: The whole world is your toolbox. Reader's choice.

Afterword: On being the fulcrum

Maybe we all need to dedicate ourselves to something bigger than our own self-interest. When we do, more often than not, we thrive. When we don't, too often we lose our joy. When we are working for some cause larger than just our own private welfare, the universe seems to get behind us and push.

In our time, people everywhere are rediscovering the appeal of a grand creative vision—not for selfish or sectarian ends, but in service to all of humanity. Perhaps this trend is a response to the daunting challenges all around us.

Embracing the paradigm of No More Enemies can be a part of that trend to serve a grand vision for the general welfare.

Recorded human history, insofar as we know, goes back about ten thousand years. Picture some teacher in some classroom somewhere, another ten thousand years from now, saying to her students:

Recorded human history goes back about 20,000 years that we know of. The first 10,000 years were characterized by gross belligerence, essentially biologically programmed, but buttressed by many powerful cultural extensions.

Around ten thousand years ago, the patterns underwent a shift: as if a light bulb had lit for all of humanity. In retrospect, it seems a very sharp, almost instantaneous development—although of course, at the time, it was not. These things don't happen overnight. But evidently, within a relatively short period of time in human terms, almost in a single instant of historical time, the previously evolved paradigm of enemies was scrapped in favor of partnership and co-evolution. From that time on, with a few inevitable regressions here and there, perhaps, human activity overall began reflecting a very different sort of pattern. The outcomes were quite splendid.

377

Think about it: Some group of people at some period of history has to be the fulcrum of this change. Why not us? We need not be intimidated by the idea of being the fulcrum. On the contrary: What an adventure!

Why not be bold enough to look ahead; to energetically and creatively envision an evolving new reality as it could be, a thousand days or ten thousand years hence; to take the first steps toward this transformation? Who is to stop us?!

That's the way to get the basic paradigm shift going.

If we succeed, our era will be admired forever by those who come after us.

And if we fail—well, we can't fail, really. Actively envisioning a better world is its own reward.

No More Enemies!

Thanks

To Sam and Mike, for everything; Maha and the boys, for opening your hearts; Mitzi, for being Mitzi; all my sisters and daughters and nieces, brothers and sons and nephews, biological and spiritual; various Reiches, Joshuas, Philos, Freers, Immermans, and good friends old and new (you know who you are), for patience, encouragement and solidarity; my friends in Wadi Ara and the Jerusalem hills who made this book possible by generously sharing with me your lives, homes, hopes and aspirations over the years; my friends at Wahat al Salam ~ Neve Shalom and the Friends of NS~WAS worldwide, for that special sense of community; Libby and Len, for being on the planet; Davida, for early encouragement; the late Gail Weinstein, for comradely inspiration; the late Rabbi Bruce M. Cohen, for opening the first door; Zel Lurie, for his vote of confidence; Beit Barkai and Beit Yahel, where the welcome is always warm; everyone at the Parallel States Project at the Center for Middle East Studies at Lund University, for daring to be provocative in a big way; all the activists working to make a better world who get up every morning and do it again, no matter the cost; Joanie and Doug and several others, for reading the manuscript and giving me feedback; Leora, for a place to live; Lee Ann, for Kindle assistance; Eleanor and Ginny, chief midwives, and Cherie, official travel agent; Donna, for library considerations; Sivan, for sage and pithy words of advice at a crucial stage; and Jonathan ("obviously"!). I hope the people I inadvertently left out will forgive me. And, one more time: thanks to Amos and Maya, because I couldn't have done it without you.

Acknowledgments

The Ursula K. Le Guin epigraphs are all from her *Tales from Earthsea*, as follows: The epigraphs for the Introduction, Part II, and Part IV are excerpted from "The Finder" by Ursula K. Le Guin, copyright (c) 2001 by the Inter-Vivos Trust for the Le Guin Children; first appeared in *Tales from Earthsea*. The epigraph for Part I is excerpted from "Introduction to *Tales from Earthsea*" by Ursula K. Le Guin, copyright (c) 2001 by the Inter-Vivos Trust for the Le Guin Children. The epigraph for Part III is excerpted from "Dragonfly" by Ursula K. Le Guin, copyright (c) 1997 by the Inter-Vivos Trust for the Le Guin Children; first appeared in *Legends*; from *Tales from Earthsea*.

"My enemy completes me," the epigraph for the last chapter in Part I, is from *The Gnostic Gospels* by Elaine Pagels (New York: Random House, 1979).

The quote from Thich Nhat Hanh in the epigraph to Part II is from his *The Heart of the Buddha's Teaching* (New York: Broadway Books, 1999, p.204).

About the Author

Born in Manhattan and educated at Barnard College, writer and translator Deb Reich first lived in Israel / Palestine in 1966-67 and relocated there in 1981. Apart from a few interludes abroad, she has lived there ever since. She was married to an Israeli and raised two children in Karkur, a small town near the Mediterranean coast.

The quest for a way to "work smarter" toward reconciliation between the groups in conflict in that land, or any land, has been her lifelong preoccupation.

No More Enemies is the result.

40150209R00236

Made in the USA
Middletown, DE
23 March 2019